The Negotiations on Mutual and Balanced Force Reductions

Pergamon Titles of Related Interest

THE 17 VOLUME UNITAR-CEESTEM NIEO LIBRARY
Dolman GLOBAL PLANNING AND RESOURCE MANAGEMENT
Haq DIALOGUE FOR A NEW ORDER
Menon BRIDGES ACROSS THE SOUTH: Technical Cooperation
Among Developing Countries

Related Journals*

GOVERNMENT PUBLICATIONS REVIEW
PROBLEMS OF CONTROL AND INFORMATION THEORY
SOCIO-ECONOMIC PLANNING SCIENCES
WORLD DEVELOPMENT
*Specimen copies available upon request.

PERGAMON
POLICY
STUDIES

The Negotiations on Mutual and Balanced Force Reductions
The Search for Arms Control in Central Europe

John G. Keliher

Published in cooperation with
The National Defense University

Pergamon Press
NEW YORK • OXFORD • TORONTO • SYDNEY • PARIS • FRANKFURT

Pergamon Press Offices:

U.S.A.   Pergamon Press Inc., Maxwell House, Fairview Park,
                             Elmsford, New York 10523, U.S.A.

U.K.   Pergamon Press Ltd., Headington Hill Hall,
                             Oxford OX3 OBW, England

CANADA   Pergamon of Canada, Ltd., Suite 104, 150 Consumers Road,
                             Willowdale, Ontario M2J 1P9, Canada

AUSTRALIA   Pergamon Press (Aust.) Pty. Ltd., P.O. Box 544,
                             Potts Point, NSW 2011, Australia

FRANCE   Pergamon Press SARL, 24 rue des Ecoles,
                             75240 Paris, Cedex 05, France

FEDERAL REPUBLIC   Pergamon Press GmbH, Hammerweg 6, Postfach 1305,
OF GERMANY   6242 Kronberg/Taunus, Federal Republic of Germany

Library of Congress Cataloging in Publication Data

Keliher, John G   1932-
   The negotiations on mutual and balanced force
reductions.

   (Pergamon policy studies on international
politics)
     Bibliography: p.
   Includes index.
   1. Arms control. 2. Disarmament. 3. Europe—
Defenses. I. Title. II. Series.
JX1974.K43   327.1'74'094   80-16473
ISBN 0-08-025964-2

Opinions, conclusions, and recommendations
expressed or implied within are solely
those of the author, and do not necessarily
represent the official views of The National
Defense University, the Department of Defense,
or any other Government agency. This work
has been cleared for open publication, and
there are no limitations or restrictions
upon its distribution.

Printed in the United States of America

TO MY FAMILY

Nancy

Craig, Kathleen, Lisa

Contents

Preface

The negotiations on Mutual and Balanced Force Reductions (MBFR) have been in session since October 1973. Convened to reduce and limit East/West standing armies in Central Europe, the talks have languished both in their own difficulties and in the shadow of the Strategic Arms Limitation Talks (SALT); and, of late, progress has been further stalled as a result of the Soviet invasion of Afghanistan.

Almost every American has some knowledge of the SALT negotiations, yet when it comes to MBFR, few even know that it exists, much less what the negotiations are all about. This is unfortunate, because MBFR has the potential to have a considerable impact on the security of the United States and the Western world.

The idea of reducing the large standing armies facing each other in Central Europe is not a new one. Since the end of World War II, both East and West have forwarded proposals on the subject ranging from nuclear free zones to general disarmament. However, it was not until the apparent inevitability of large unilateral US troop withdrawals from Europe that the East and West permitted arms control in Central Europe to reach the stage of actual negotiations.

Although the negotiations are held in closed sessions, much has been said through official pronouncements and reports in the world press concerning the various aspects and objectives of the East and West in MBFR. The Western press and - because of a Soviet desire to have their positions known - even the Eastern press, have reported a considerable amount of factual information on MBFR. That the press of the Soviet Union and of Eastern Europe is rigidly controlled by the state is advantageous in this regard; statements about MBFR reflect the official positions of the Communist leadership on the negotiations. Because MBFR directly concerns Western Europe and especially the Federal Republic of Germany, considerable information, especially detailed aspects of Eastern proposals, has also been thoroughly reported and analyzed by the West European press and defense writers.

Unfortunately for the individual who desires more than an overview of these negotiations, the task is formidable, because the information which can give one such an in-depth understanding, while available, is widely scattered. My purpose in undertaking this writing was to draw together the previously disclosed facts on MBFR in order to present in as coherent detail and as complete a fashion as possible the story of these negotiations.

Extensive quotations have been used throughout to give the reader a firsthand feel for the issues as they are enunciated by the principal participants themselves. In addition, reduction proposals are analyzed in detail to demonstrate the impact that the proposals would have on the Central European standing armies. Discussions of current key problems facing the negotiators are also presented, along with possible future courses the negotiations might follow.

I wish to acknowledge the splendid work of the men and women of the Foreign Broadcast Information Service who over the years have diligently followed the MBFR negotiations. They have furnished comprehensive, timely, and accurate translations of official and unofficial statements made in the foreign press concerning all aspects of the negotiations. Without their outstanding service, it would have been virtually impossible for this work to have been as thorough in presenting the multitude of details and viewpoints that make up these complicated negotiations.

The expert administrative support given this effort by the staff of the National Defense University Research Directorate is also gratefully acknowledged.

1 Arms Control and the German Problem: 1945-1968

THE IMPORTANCE OF GERMANY IN SOVIET POLICY

Marx believed the Communist revolution would begin in Germany. At the beginning of the twentieth century it was the most advanced capitalist industrial state and therefore, according to Marxist theory, should have been the most vulnerable to a socialist transformation. The fact that the "revolution" actually occurred in Russia did not displace the special position Germany held in Communist ideology. In fact, the Bolsheviks staked their grand strategy for world revolution on coupling backward Russia to advanced Germany to create the first socialist structure capable of survival in a hostile capitalist world.

The attitude of the Soviet Union toward foreign relations has been and continues to be deeply influenced by considerations of Germany. Lenin, following Marx's tenets, believed that the Russian revolution, while welcomed, was potentially of less importance than a revolution occurring in highly industrialized Germany, as envisioned by Marx. Therefore, it is not surprising that Germany was one of the main concerns of early Soviet foreign policy.

Lenin enunciated the basic tenets of Soviet foreign policy in a speech to the Moscow Communist Party leadership on 26 November 1920. He advanced two major premises which have become and continue to be the foundations of Soviet foreign policy from Lenin's time to the present day. The first was the assumption that for the foreseeable future the socialist nations would be weaker than the capitalist nations, and therefore, in order to preserve a base for the revolution and to exploit opportunities to advance it, the Soviets would have to function within the existing international order as spelled out by Lenin's successors (e.g., peaceful coexistence, detente, etc.). (1) The second premise was that the Soviets would need to follow a strategy of promoting conflict between the non-Communist states in order to

1

dissipate their energies and make them vulnerable to Communist exploitation. Lenin saw four areas of antagonisms and contradictions existing within the capitalist world of which the Soviets could take advantage. One was the potential conflict between the United States and Japan, and another was the possibility of establishing Communist control over colonial areas.

Of interest to the theme of this study are the remaining two major sets of contradictions for possible exploitation. Lenin identified the latent tensions between the United States and its Allies as a situation which, if exploited, would significantly weaken the non-Communist world and provide opportunities for Communist expansion. The final contradiction identified by Lenin was the obvious hostility existing between the Allied victors and the vanquished Germans. As Lenin put it in his speech, "Germany is one of the most powerful and advanced of capitalist countries. She cannot tolerate the Versailles Treaty, and Germany is obliged to seek an ally against world imperialism for although she is herself imperialistic, she has been suppressed." (2)

Thus, Soviet Russia began assiduously to cultivate a relationship with defeated Germany. Lenin, and later Stalin, came to the conclusion that it was in Germany that the greatest opportunity existed for intra-capitalist conflicts from which the Soviets could gain. Stalin called Germany the "mine under Europe" in recognition of the deep hostilities which existed between the Allies and the Germans, hostilities which if properly exploited would lead to a general European war which would provide the Soviet Union with opportunities for political and territorial expansion. (3)

A good case can be made that Soviet support of German circumvention of the Versailles Treaty, support of the Nazis, and the German-Soviet nonaggression pact all were clearly aimed at drawing Germany away from the West and setting in motion the intracapitalist war envisioned by Lenin. (4) While the Soviets did not envision being drawn into the war, a war in which they were subsequently nearly destroyed, they did manage to have the good fortune to emerge from it as a world power with greatly expanded political and territorial control in Eastern Europe, including a portion of Germany itself. Since the end of World War II the Soviets have never been content with having only a part of Germany under their domination and have sought to obtain as much control as possible over West Germany.

The following brief history of the period 1945-1968 will of necessity focus on arms control measures and other diplomatic maneuvers of that period which relate to the problems encountered in MBFR. It will also help serve to demonstrate later that there is a relationship between these early proposals and MBFR; that MBFR is really nothing new and, like early arms control proposals, is rooted in the problem of German sovereignty.

COLD WAR AND THE REBIRTH OF GERMANY:
1945-1953

Never had the Soviet Union come so close to winning control of Germany as it did in World War II. Next to China and the United States, Germany ranks as the Soviet Union's most important foreign policy concern. During the first decade after the close of World War II, the Soviet Union's foreign policy in Central Europe was keyed on West Germany. The Soviets' primary objective was to keep West Germany out of the Allied camp. The possibility of reunification of the German nation was held up before the German people as the reward for refusing to join the West. The reunification would be, however, at the price of a Soviet-dominated neutralized Germany. Almost every Soviet diplomatic initiative and arms control proposal made during this period can be directly attributed to moves made by the Allies to bring West Germany into the Western camp as an active political, economic, and military participant.

In 1947 the Allies decided to make the West Germans more economically independent and to give them a greater amount of political responsibility. (5) Stalin chose a show of Soviet military strength to block what he rightly foresaw coming, the formation of the West German state. The most obvious and easiest place for such a Soviet show of strength was Berlin. Stalin cut the ground lifelines to that city, figuring that if the West were forced to yield on Berlin, the West Germans would lack sufficient confidence in Western protection to enter into a close relationship with the Allies. (6)

The West, of course, did not yield, but created not only the Federal Republic of Germany in May of 1949, but also the North Atlantic Treaty Organization in April of that year. It also successfully broke the Berlin Blockade through a massive airlift. In response to the creation of the Federal Republic of Germany (FRG), the Soviets set up a counter regime five months later, in October 1949, calling it the German Democratic Republic (GDR). (7)

In the early 1950s Western European leaders were seriously discussing the formation of a European Defense Community and the possibility of integrating West Germany into such an organization. The Soviet reaction, in an attempt to block West Germany from joining in such a venture, was to dangle the dream of reunification before the German people. On 10 March 1952 the Soviets proposed that Germany be united, neutralized, and armed within limits to be determined by a peace conference. (8) The proposal dropped previous Soviet insistence on a disarmed Germany and raised the prospect of unification in return for neutralization and the removal of foreign military bases from German territory. Reflecting their fear of a West Germany in NATO, the Soviets stipulated as part of the price of reunification that the Germans must not join any military alliance directed against the Soviet Union. Furthermore, German armed forces and military production would have to be kept within limits to be established by a peace treaty.

Moreover, "organizations hostile to democracy and the cause of maintaining peace" would also be prohibited according to the proposals. (9)

Such stringent Soviet provisions, combined with the strong desire of the Adenauer government to align the Federal Republic with the West, caused the Soviet overture to be rejected.   This rejection created debate in Western circles as to whether or not an opportunity to reunite Germany had been lost.   Most historians of the period seem to have judged that it was rejected because the Soviet offer was seen simply as a tactical maneuver designed to delay or forestall the ratification of the European Defense Community, rather than a genuine offer to reunify the German nation. Lending credence to the conclusion that the Soviet offer was primarily a tactical ploy was the fact that a program for the "construction of socialism" in East Germany was initiated by the Soviets and adopted in July 1952 right in the middle of the exchange of notes on the Soviet proposal. (10) The Soviets probably feared that the Communist East German regime would be vulnerable in a united Germany which elected its officials freely, and this led Stalin to conclude that the prospective gains in terms of keeping West Germany out of the Western camp were not worth the risk.   Thus the proposal was allowed to die by Stalin over the issue of free elections. (11)

In response to the West's decision to rearm West Germany, the Soviets offered a series of plans for an all-European collective security system, with the apparent hope that the West would give up the idea of rearming West Germany and incorporating it into NATO.

USE OF ARMS CONTROL TO CURB
WEST GERMAN DEVELOPMENT: 1953-1963

At the London Conference held from 28 September to 3 October 1954, the Allies declared their intention to end the occupation of Germany and to invite the Federal Republic of Germany to join the West European Union and NATO. (12) This intention was formally recognized on 23 October 1954 in Paris where the Western nations signed an agreement admitting the Federal Republic of Germany into the West European Union and NATO.   The protocol to the agreement limited West German ground forces to a maximum of twelve divisions and prohibited the manufacturing of nuclear weapons. (13)

As the Paris Agreement was being ratified by Western capitals, the Soviets continued attempts to block its adoption. On 15 January 1955, the Soviet government issued a warning that its ratification would perpetuate the division of Germany. But if the convention was not ratified, the Soviets stated it would be possible to hold all-German free elections before the end of 1955. (14) In February 1955 a conference held in Warsaw held up a carrot-type proposal that all occupation forces withdraw and Germany be reunified as a neutral nation. In the same month, Molotov, in a speech to the Supreme Soviet, used the stick approach to threaten unspecified countermeasures in the event Germany joined NATO and the West European Union. (15)

West European ratification on 24 March 1955 of the Paris Agreement accepting West Germany as a NATO partner caused the Soviets to carry out Molotov's threat by creating the Warsaw Pact on 14 May 1955. Significantly, East Germany was not integrated into the Pact at its inception. Obviously the Soviets wanted to leave open for at least a while longer what little possibility they had of neutralizing Germany, and to convey the message that East German sovereignty was expandable in exchange for a neutralized Germany. (16)

At the Geneva Summit Conference, 17-23 July 1955, the Soviets, having lost the battle to prevent the integration of West Germany into NATO, approached the German problem in a more oblique manner. In his opening remarks, Prime Minister Anthony Eden of the United Kingdom had suggested the possibility of creating a demilitarized area between East and West Germany, coupled with some sort of arms control in the Central European region that embraced Germany and its neighbors. (17) Bulganin, representing the Soviet Union, countered with the following proposal:

Military groupings of some European nations directed against others should be replaced by a system of security based on the joint efforts of all the nations of Europe . . . establishing a collective security system in Europe could be divided into two stages. (18)

The first stage, explained Bulganin, would consist primarily of a freeze on existing force levels. During the second stage NATO and the Warsaw Pact would be disbanded and replaced by an all-European security system. Conventional forces would be reduced and nuclear weapons would be prohibited. He also called for the withdrawal of foreign troops from Europe and "the reestablishment in this respect of the situation which existed prior to the Second World War." (19) The latter suggestion was an obvious hint for the removal of US troops. The Soviets further proposed that the level of armed forces of nations other than the Big Five (US, USSR, United Kingdom, China, and France) would be limited to "between 150,000 and 200,000 men." (20) This was a clear Soviet attempt to set a ceiling on the strength of the West German armed forces which would be considerably lower than the NATO goal of a Bundeswehr with a strength of 500,000.

At the Foreign Ministers' meeting in Geneva, 27 October-16 November 1954, the United States, United Kingdom, and France tabled a proposal on reunification of Germany. Referring to the Eden plan devised that summer at the Geneva Summit meeting, the Allies proposed provisions for the limitation and control of forces and armament in Central Europe which could be implemented after the reunification of Germany by free elections. Articles 3 and 4 of the proposed treaty stated:

3. Limitation of Forces and Armaments

In a zone comprising areas of comparable size and depth and importance on both sides of the line of demarcation between a reunified Germany and the Eastern European countries, levels for armed forces would be specified so as to establish a military balance which would contribute to European security and help to relieve the burden of armaments. There would be appropriate provisions for the maintenance of this balance. In parts of the zone which lie closest to the line of demarcation, there might be special measures relating to the disposition of military forces and installations.

4. Inspection and Control

The parties would provide information on an agreed progressive basis on their armed forces in the zone. There would be agreement on progressive procedures of mutual inspection to verify such data and to warn against any preparation for surprise attack. (21)

The condition to unite Germany by free elections prior to the implementation of arms control measures in Central Europe was unacceptable to the Soviets. They realized that the German people would vote out the Communist regime in East Germany and that a reunited Germany would be basically hostile toward the Soviet Union. Molotov understandably replied to the proposal by saying,

The very proposal of the Three Powers shows that their purpose is to remilitarize not only West Germany but also East Germany and to bring not only West Germany but also all of Germany into the North Atlantic Bloc. . . . The people of the Soviet Union know German militarism too well to contribute to its revival with their own hands. They know that the revival of German militarism is incompatible with the maintenance of the peace and security of the peoples of Europe. (22)

Molotov also rejected the idea of free elections to reunify Germany by claiming it was a concept which "had not yet matured." Free elections, he maintained, "could lead to the violation of the vital interests of the working masses [read Communist Party cadre] of the German Democratic Republic to which one cannot agree." He went on to cite the Paris Agreements as the reason why the Soviets could not agree any longer to the reunification of Germany through free elections. Instead, he proposed the creation of a German Council which could begin to coordinate actions of the GDR and FRG in the fields of politics, economics, and culture. Such a council, Molotov argued, could create conditions for reunification by free election. (23) Not surprisingly, nothing resulted from the Geneva Conference in the way of concrete proposals on arms reduction in Central Europe.

Poland, rather than the Soviet Union, advanced what proved to be the most significant arms control proposal made by the East up to that time, when in 1957 it advanced the Rapacki Plan. The rearmament of West Germany was of no less concern to the Poles than it was to the Russians. Sitting astride the traditional East/West invasion route, the Poles had been carved up between the Germans and the Russians for centuries and both countries had been reluctant to see Poland survive as a free and sovereign nation. The German and Soviet rape of Poland in 1939, coupled with its subsequent partition, gave the Poles every reason to fear yet another war. Poland, firmly under Soviet domination, was forced to cede large areas of its eastern provinces to the Soviets at the end of World War II. In compensation, Poland was given a large area of what had been eastern Germany. The border between East Germany and Poland became the Oder-Neisse River. The East Germans dutifully recognized this new boundary in the Treaty of Goerlitz in 1950. (24) In 1957, however, the West Germans continued to regard the line as provisional because the Potsdam Agreement, which gave Poland the territory up to the Oder-Neisse, declared that the Oder-Neisse line was provisional pending a peace settlement with Germany. (25) Considering that Poland would have the most to lose of any East European nation should another war break out between Germany and the Soviet Union, it was natural that Polish fear of a rearmed Germany would be comparable to that of the Soviet Union.

Poland's approach toward Central European security was basically threefold: (1) to maintain the status quo in Europe; that is, to get Western, chiefly West German, recognition of the Oder-Neisse line as the permanent boundary between the German Democratic Republic and Poland; (2) to secure recognition of the German Democratic Republic as a sovereign nation, and thereby assure the continued division of Germany; and (3) to halt the remilitarization of West Germany and to block any attempts by the Federal Republic to acquire nuclear weapons. The Poles wanted to replace the West's reliance on nuclear weapons to balance the conventional strength of the Warsaw Pact by the creation of a nuclear free zone in Central Europe and to get West Germany to support nonproliferation to block the possibility of West Germany possessing nuclear warheads. (26)

The Rapacki Plan met with a mixed reaction in the West. While the Scandinavian countries and Great Britain believed it had some merit and should be explored further, the United States and the FRG responses were negative. The primary argument advanced against the Rapacki Plan was that it would freeze the existing numerical superiority of the Warsaw Pact in conventional forces. (27)

In answer to the West's objections, Adam Rapacki, the Polish Foreign Minister, stated to the UN General Assembly on 2 October 1957:

The remilitarization of the Federal Republic of Germany and the concentration of arms and troops on its territory contribute to a policy which is very dangerous to the cause of peace in Europe and in the world. . . . Western Germany must not be allowed to become an atomic powder-keg in the middle of Europe. (28)

Concerning the recognition of the Oder-Neisse line, Rapacki remarked, "That frontier is final, irrevocable, and not open for bargaining." (29)

Rapacki closed his relatively short speech with the following proposal:

> In the interest of Poland's security and a relaxation of tension in Europe and after consultation with the other parties of the Warsaw Treaty, the Government of the People's Republic of Poland declares that if the two German states should consent to enforce the prohibition of the production and stockpiling of nuclear weapons in their respective territories, the People's Republic of Poland is prepared simultaneously to institute the same prohibition in its territory. (30)

Czechoslovakia quickly agreed to join Poland and the two Germanies in the denuclearized zone. Early in 1958, in response to Western criticism that his plan was too general, Rapacki presented a more detailed plan. Among the main points were:

> The states included in this zone would undertake the obligation not to manufacture, maintain nor import for their own use or permit the location of nuclear weapons on their territory. The Four Powers (France, Great Britain, United States and USSR) would undertake not to maintain or transfer nuclear weapons in this zone and no nuclear equipment or installation would be established in this zone by other states. (31)

In answer to Western criticism of how such a proposal would be policed, Rapacki proposed in his memorandum that a system would be developed which consisted of "ground as well as aerial control" with "adequate control posts with rights and possibilities of action which would ensure the effectiveness of inspection." (32)

In reply, the United States stated the plan was "too limited in scope to reduce the danger of nuclear war or provide a dependable basis for the security of Europe." More importantly, the reply went on:

> The proposals overlook the central problems of European security because they provide no method for balanced and equitable limitation of military capabilities and would perpetuate the basic cause of tension in Europe by accepting the continuation of the division of Germany. (33)

The United States further charged that the East was seeking unilateral advantages by "endangering the security of West Europe where forces without nuclear weapons would be a great disadvantage to the numerically greater mass of Soviet troops." (34)

Strong Western criticism continued toward the Rapacki Plan. The key argument continued to be that the denying of nuclear weapons to NATO in Central Europe would deprive the Western Allies of the necessary equalizer to the superior numbers of Warsaw Pact conventional forces. Thus, it would upset the existing military balance in the area and seriously weaken the defense of Western Europe.

In reply to these criticisms, Rapacki held a news conference on 4 November 1958 at which he proposed a modification to his plan which would be "the maximum step possible toward taking into account the . . . reservations put forward in connection with the previous proposal." In essence, Rapacki made two key changes. The plan would now be implemented in two stages. In the first stage there would be a ban on production of nuclear weapons within the zone of the two Germanies, Poland, and Czechoslovakia; then Rapacki made a subtle change in his original stage one, which had previously required a ban on all nuclear equipment to those armies which did not yet have them. In deference perhaps to a Soviet desire to have nuclear weapons in the zone, the Poles suggested "the freezing of nuclear armaments in the proposed zone." The second stage would be preceded by talks on the "appropriate reduction of conventional forces." The reductions would be effected simultaneously with the complete denuclearization of the zone. "Appropriate control measures" would also be agreed upon. (35)

The Soviets were basically unhappy with the Rapacki Plan and its twists and turns. They were offended by this display of Polish initiative in the arena of international diplomacy and it was only with considerable difficulty that the Polish Government was able to secure Soviet agreement to proposing the plan formally in February of 1958. The revised plan's second phase, which stressed conventional reductions, was not cleared with the Soviets and was particularly unacceptable to them, given their reliance on a massive Soviet ground force presence in East Germany, Poland, and Czechoslavakia. (36)

The modified Rapacki Plan was allowed to stand until, in February 1964, the Polish leader, Wladyslaw Gomulka, revised Rapacki's proposal, which thereafter was known as the Gomulka Plan. Basically, stage one, proposing a nuclear freeze, remained, but stage two, which had called for the abolition of foreign military bases and the reduction of conventional armaments within the proposed zone, was completely dropped. (37)

The Cuban Missile Crisis, in 1962, showed the Soviets that their policy of confrontation was not achieving a weakening of Western resolve to resist communism, but rather it was strengthening it. The crisis also dramatically pointed out the weakness of the Soviet strategic military power compared to that of the United States. Other factors also made the policy of confrontation obsolete. The Soviets badly needed the technology of the West. They were losing the arms race as well as the standard of living race. If the Soviets were not going to change their system to make their economy more effective by decentralization (and it was obvious they were not), then they had to compensate by importing the technology from the West. A policy of confrontation with the West would not allow this. Furthermore, the growing Sino-Soviet split raised the possibility of eventual war between these two nations. A two-front nuclear war would insure the destruction of the Soviet Union.

ARMS CONTROL AND EARLY DETENTE:
1963-1968

The year 1963 saw the beginning of what was termed East/West "detente." Although marred by the Berlin crisis and the Soviet invasion of Czechoslovakia in 1968, the concept of detente was maintained, albeit at times quite shakily, throughout this period.

Detente is nothing more than the "peaceful coexistence" popularized by Khrushchev. Actually, peaceful coexistence goes back to the time of Lenin when the Bolsheviks realized they were too weak to survive without making compromises and agreements with the capitalist world. Since that time, periods of accommodation have been a hallmark of Soviet foreign policy. An extreme example of such accommodation was the Soviet/Nazi Pact of 1939.

Detente in the present period was initiated by Khrushchev in order to extract the Soviet Union from the predicament Stalin's intransigent policies had brought on following World War II. These policies had caused the Western nations to close ranks and build up their military potential, further isolating the Soviet Union and causing it to fall increasingly behind the West in economic and military strength. (38)

Unwilling to institute economic reform which would require a degree of decentralization of political power, the Soviets opted for receiving economic aid from the West, a decision which, in the words of Richard Pipes, was a "tacit admission of stupendous failure" for the Soviet system. (39) From the military point of view, reinstating detente/peaceful coexistence also had the objective of getting the West to relax its military guard while the Soviets enhanced their military strength. The Soviets themselves have openly admitted that detente is little more than peaceful coexistence. (40)

> The two concepts [detente and peaceful coexistence] are distinguished by the fact that whereas peaceful coexistence is employed to define the desired character of relations among states with different social systems, the relaxation of tension is used to describe the change for the better in the state of relations among them. (41) (Emphasis added)

Alluding to the primary reason for detente, Georgiyev stated that

> the improvement in the international climate resulting from the relaxation of tension has also created a favorable atmosphere for

enlivening economic scientific-technical and cultural cooperation among states. (42)

It was under the then fledgling concept of detente that Gomulka proposed his revised Rapacki Plan in 1964. Late in 1964, Gomulka spoke at the United Nations General Assembly on 14 December in support of a Rapacki/Gomulka Plan for a freeze on nuclear weapons in Central Europe. He concluded his remarks with the following:

> I must stress our strong belief that the time is ripe for examining the problem of European security in its entirety. In our considered opinion, the advisability of convening for this purpose a conference of all-European States with the participation, of course, of both the Soviet Union and the United States, should be closely examined. (43)

The West ignored Gomulka's call. The Rapacki and Gomulka proposals had given a modicum of autonomy to Polish foreign policy. The rejection of them by the West no doubt deepened the Poles' sense of dependence on the Soviet Union. (44)

In January of 1965 the Political Consultative Committee of the Warsaw Pact strongly condemned the plan of NATO to form a multilateral nuclear force. The communique eloquently illustrated the deep fear of the East that West Germany would acquire access to nuclear weapons. The communique stated that the development of such a nuclear force would

> mean a proliferation of nuclear weapons and in particular the presentation of these weapons to the West German militarists. . . . A NATO multilateral nuclear force aims at the consolidation of a separate American-West German bloc within the north Atlantic Alliance. . . . When the FRG became a member of the North Atlantic Pact, it gained an opportunity to create in violation of the Potsdam Agreements . . . an aggressive military force. Access to nuclear weapons would undoubtedly stimulate the desire of the West German revanchant forces to change the situation that came about in Europe after the end of the Second World War and to realize the territorial claims upon the GDR and other states. . . . The Warsaw Treaty states resolutely oppose giving nuclear weapons to the Federal Republic of Germany in any form whatever - directly or indirectly through grouping of states, for its exclusive use or in any form of participation in the use of these weapons. . . . The Federal Republic of Germany is writing off the unification of Germany. (45)

The above statement summarizes the whole range of Eastern fears and objectives toward West Germany, fears and objectives which they have been expressing and pursuing since the end of World War II. The communique dangled the long-standing Eastern offer to support a German peace settlement in exchange for recognition of the existing frontier and pledges "by the two German states not to add nuclear weapons to their armed forces and to carry out measures toward disarmament." (46) But the East was obviously aware that its hope of a neutralized, impotent West Germany was not to be. They had been rebuffed too many times since the early 1950s. A shift in the policies toward Germany and the Central European question essentially began with this communique. While not totally giving up the idea of German neutralization, the Soviets obviously concluded that the recognition of the GDR and the division of Germany into two sovereign nations was, for the foreseeable future, the best solution. Therefore, they began a call for the recognition of the current status in Central Europe by stating within the communique, "for a conference of European states to discuss measures ensuring collective security in Europe." (47)

The initial call for a European Security Conference was the beginning of a general shift in Eastern policy away from a primary emphasis on disarmament and toward a drive for a political conference which would formally recognize the post-World War II boundaries of Eastern Europe.

The East nevertheless continued to press for arms control in Central Europe. For instance, the Bucharest Declaration, issued during the Warsaw Pact Political Consultative Committee meeting of July 1966 in Romania, called for the following measures to develop military detente in Europe: (a) the dismantling of foreign military bases, (b) the withdrawal of all foreign troops to within national frontiers, (c) the creation of denuclearized zones, and (d) the barring of both German states from access to nuclear weapons. These points had all been previously proposed, primarily in the earlier Polish Rapacki and Gomulka disarmament plans. However, new and significant proposals were made to reduce the size of the armies of both East and West Germany, and to set numerical ceilings on these forces. (48) It was obvious that if the Soviets could not get a disarmed Germany, they would settle for whatever restrictions on the Bundeswehr they could get and they would not, if necessary, oppose the placing of reciprocal restrictions on East Germany.

But the primary theme of the Bucharest Declaration was the proposal to have a conference that would settle the German question by recognition of the current borders. Another theme was for Europeans to solve their own problems (for this purpose, the Soviets called themselves Europeans), and, in order to do this, the United States must withdraw its forces from Western Europe. On that subject the conference statement declared:

> The policy promoted by the USA in the post-war years is all the more dangerous for the European peoples as it is increasingly based on the coalition with the militaristic and revanchist forces in West Germany. These forces are directly impelling the USA toward promoting an even more dangerous line on Europe. (49)

The Soviets believed at the time that the best course of action was to separate the West Germans and the Americans. How this would be done was not made totally clear, but one step was the disestablishment of NATO and the Warsaw Pact and replacement of them with a European security organization. With the Americans out of Europe, the Soviets probably reasoned, the West Germans would be unable to resist Eastern pressure to reduce forces and to recognize the Oder-Neisse line. This desire to drive out the Americans was to be modified in the years ahead, but in 1966 the Soviets were pushing the idea of a "Europe for the Europeans" which of course would include the Russians. The Soviets had their satellite states explore and encourage an exchange of views with the West on the prospects for a European security conference. The drive received additional official impetus with a call by the European Communist Party meeting in Karlovy Vary, Czechoslovakia, on 26 April 1967, for "a conference of all-European states on the question of security and peaceful cooperation in Europe." (50) The advocacy of a legitimization of the division of Europe as proposed by the East and the decoupling of Western Europe from the American nuclear umbrella was obviously not acceptable to the West and it received little serious consideration.

While the East was pushing more for a security conference, the West began to get more serious about force reductions. NATO was experiencing problems in 1966-67. Inflation was hitting the West hard, the Vietnam War was creating a strong antimilitary movement in the United States, and Western European countries were beginning to look at the high cost of their armed forces in the age of inflation. Detente encouraged these feelings as the Soviet threat seemed diminished. NATO was beginning to question its future role in European affairs from the standpoint of how much a military as opposed to a political role the alliance should play.

In the United States throughout the spring and summer of 1966 there had been a growing public discussion concerning America's role in NATO. In an exchange between Senator Robert Kennedy and Secretary of Defense McNamara during congressional testimony on 21 June 1966, the senator had asked:

Should the Russians be willing to withdraw at least part of their 20 divisions that presently exist in Germany, would we in turn be willing to lessen our presence in Europe and perhaps make some changes in NATO?

Secretary McNamara replied:

I am sure that our troop deployment and the total military strength of NATO are functions of both political and military actions of the Warsaw Pact, particularly the Soviet Union. So the direct answer is yes. (51)

Other voices could be heard remarking on the possibility of bilateral US-Soviet troop reductions. The Wiesner Committee on Arms Control and Disarmament of the 1966 White House-sponsored Conference on

International Cooperation stated in its report:

> We believe that the United States should encourage an examination
> of the problem of parallel troop reductions in West and East
> Germany by the United States and the Soviet Union. Reductions are
> not to be conceived as tantamount to withdrawal which would
> change the military balance but rather as adjustments equitable for
> both sides which would preserve the balance at less cost and strain
> for each. An exploration in these terms would have to begin with
> the Western allies most concerned but if it is to have an effect it
> must proceed to exchange with the Soviet Union. (52)

The second school of thought on America's role in NATO, led by Senator
Mike Mansfield, held the position that the United States should take
unilateral force reductions.

Senator Mansfield in a Senate speech on 27 July 1966 stated that the
approximately one million US troops and dependents in Western Europe
were totally unwarranted in light of the commitments to Vietnam and
the financial strain that this force placed on the United States. He
called for a "substantial reduction in the number of units stationed in
Western Europe as well as the number of dependents now living there."
Specifically, he called for a return to the United States of all the 75,000
servicemen and dependents leaving France at the request of de Gaulle
and for a 10 percent reduction of US troop strength in Germany and
elsewhere in Western Europe. The reduction would be mandatory, but
how it whould be taken would be left up to the military. (53) On 31
August 1966 the Senator from Montana proffered a resolution which
called for "a substantial reduction of US Forces permanently stationed
in Europe." (54) The resolution did not contain the specifics of his 27
July speech nor was it to be acted upon. Rather, it was to demonstrate
the opinion of a group of Senators led by Mansfield that it was time for
unilateral force cuts.

On 19 January1967 Mansfield presented his resolution again, calling
it an "Expression of Sense of Senate with Respect to Troop Deployment
in Europe." He was supported by 42 senators who cosponsored a call for
"a substantial reduction of US Forces permanently stationed in Europe
which can be made without adversely affecting either our resolve or
ability to meet our commitment under the North Atlantic Treaty." (55)

Senator Joseph Clark strongly criticized the Mansfield resolution,
arguing that any reduction of forces in Europe should be contingent on
the Soviet Union making comparable reductions of the forces in Eastern
Europe. He proposed an amendment, the core of which read:

> Whereas the reduction of United States forces in Western Europe if
> balanced by parallel reductions of Soviet Union forces in Eastern
> Europe, would produce a significant easing of tensions and help to
> promote a peaceful settlement in Europe. . . . It is therefore the
> Sense of the Senate that the Administration explore with its North
> Atlantic Treaty Organization allies and with the Soviet Union the

possibilities for balanced reduction of United States and Soviet troops and weapons in Central Europe. (56)

The issue of unilateral troop withdrawals at this stage was being expressed in resolution format as "Sense of the Senate" expressions. Such resolutions, while not requiring Administration compliance, seemed warnings of stronger Senate measures to come, if the Administration did not take actions on its own initiative to cut force strength in Western Europe.

By 1967 a subtle change could be detected in East/West attitudes toward arms control in Central Europe. The core of the problem was still Germany. Up to that time the Soviets had given high priority to measures that would result in a neutralized Germany not offering a military threat to the East. The East had aimed at a stabilization of the situation in Central Europe only through such means as would contribute to the Soviet objective of a neutralized Germany under Communist domination. Specific arms control measures proposed by the Soviets were designed either to complement the objective of a neutralized Germany or to slow or halt Allied initiatives to rearm and integrate West Germany into the NATO Alliance.

The West, despite being faced by the large Soviet military threat, had seen the question of arms control as a problem secondary to that of an overall European settlement. Such a settlement would have as its main goal the reunification of a Germany free to choose its relationships. If, as the West expected, the Germans chose to remain in NATO, then the Western Powers would have been prepared to adopt various arms control measures to allay Eastern fears of a resurgence of German revanchism.

But in the mid-1960s almost complete reversal of emphasis occurred both in the East and West. The Soviets realized that their long-sought objective of a neutralized Germany under their domination was not to be. Furthermore, Eastern arms control proposals that had been designed to curb the development of the Bundeswehr also proved to be unsuccessful. As a result, the East shifted emphasis from neutralization of Germany to a European recognition of the status quo in Central Europe, i.e., recognition of Soviet hegemony. The Soviets reasoned that an all-European security conference would furnish such recognition.

The West, on the other hand, began to come under new pressures which made arms control per se quite attractive. The escalating American involvement in Vietnam was causing a diminishing and a rethinking of the American role in NATO. It was also raising doubts with congressional members led by Senator Mansfield as to whether the United States could afford to keep such a large force in Europe. Inflation was beginning to eat away at Western defense budgets, creating pressure to cut defense spending. All of these factors led the West to begin considering the use of arms control measures as a means to combat these pressures.

2 The Road to MBFR: 1968-1973

In an attempt to channel the strong currents running against traditional Western views of military security, NATO formed a study group in 1967 under the chairmanship of the Belgian Foreign Minister, Pierre Harmel, to study the "Future Tasks of the Alliance." The study, known unofficially as the "Harmel Report," was approved by the NATO Ministerial Meeting in Brussels on 14 December 1967. (1) Basically, it concluded that the NATO Alliance had two primary functions. The first was "to maintain adequate military strength and political solidarity to deter aggression," and the second, "to pursue the search for progress towards a more stable relationship in which the underlying political issues can be solved." (2) In other words, NATO visualized that it would assume a greater political role in the era of detente. The report recognized that there could not be a stable situation in Europe without a solution to the German question, and observed that "this will be part of a process of active preparation for the time when fruitful discussions of these complex questions may be possible bilaterally or multilaterally between Eastern and Western nations." The report further suggested that until such discussions could be held, "the lack of stability and uncertainty still precludes a balanced reduction of military forces. . . ." (3) Hence, NATO took official recognition of the eventual need of coming to grips with the East on the European security issue.

From the standpoint of arms control measures, it was the thirteenth point in the Harmel Report which was to set in motion what were later to become the negotiations on Mutual and Balanced Force Reductions:

> The Allies are studying disarmament and practical arms control measures, including the possibility of balanced force reductions. These studies will be intensified. Their active pursuit reflects the will of the Allies to work for an effective detente with the East. (4)

MBFR was going to be, for the West, the counter-issue to the East's desire for a European Security Conference. The NATO Ministers drew on their approval of the Harmel Report to issue a declaration on MBFR at their Ministerial Meeting in Reykjavik, Iceland, in June 1968. This Ministerial Declaration officially began the process which eventually led to negotiations on Mutual and Balanced Force Reductions in October of 1973. In Article Four, the Ministers "affirmed the need to assure a <u>balance of forces</u> between NATO and the Pact and the military capability of NATO should not be reduced except as part of a pattern of mutual force reductions balanced in scope and timing." In Article Seven, the Ministers "agreed that it was desirable that a process leading to mutual force reductions should be initiated." To that end they decided to make "all necessary preparations for discussions on this subject with the Soviet Union and other countries of Eastern Europe. . . ." (5)

The Ministers listed the following principles as being essential for such a reduction:

a. Mutual force reductions should be reciprocal and balanced in scope and timing.

b. Mutual reductions should represent a substantial and significant step which will serve to maintain the present degree of security at reduced cost, but should not be such as to risk destabilizing the situation in Europe.

c. Mutual reductions should be consonant with the aim of creating confidence in Europe generally and in the case of each party concerned.

d. To this end, any new arrangements regarding forces should be consistent with the vital security interests of all partners and capable of being carried out effectively. (6)

Thus, the offer was officially made to the East to discuss reduction of the forces facing each other in Central Europe. Now both East and West had proposed formal negotiations on security in Central Europe, but neither side was ready to accept the other's invitation. There began a period in which both sides "talked past" each other, with the East discussing security in the form of recognition of the status quo, and the West, in the form of force reductions. This period was to last through almost four years of East/West dialogue.

Contributing significantly to the delay in getting East/West talks on European security started was the Soviet invasion of Czechoslovakia in August of 1968. The decision to invade was not one that was taken lightly by the Soviets. They knew full well what the reaction of the West would be and the retarding effect it would have on their proposal for a European security conference. It was a dilemma that had occurred before, though not to such a degree, in East Germany in 1953 and in Hungary and Poland in 1956, when the Soviet Army had crushed its Socialist brothers. The plain fact of the matter was that Soviet-style communism could survive in Eastern Europe only through the presence of the Soviet Army.

The Soviets, in view of the lack of Western reactions to Soviet actions in Hungary and elsewhere, could be fairly certain that the West would not physically intervene and would limit its protests to verbal fulminations. Nevertheless, they tried to justify their invasion by characterizing it as a "socialist duty." In a Pravda article of 26 September 1968, the Soviets claimed they had a legal right based on ideology to interfere with military force in the internal affairs of other socialist countries. The "antisocialist forces" in Czechoslovakia were using the right of self-determination to "cover up demands for so-called neutrality and Czechoslovakia's withdrawal from the socialist commonwealth."

This would have led the country "into the jaws of the West German revanchists." The Warsaw Pact armed forces were therefore only fulfilling their "internationalist duty" in properly reacting to the "antisocialist forces" at work in Czechoslovakia. The Soviets took the position that

> in the Marxist conception the norms of law, including the norms governing relations among socialist countries, cannot be interpreted in a narrow formal way, outside the general context of the class struggle in the present day world . . . norms of law are subordinated to the laws of class struggle. (7)

This concept as explained by Pravda clearly laid down a marker to the West - detente notwithstanding - that in a situation in which the Soviets felt their hegemony over Eastern Europe threatened, they would not hesitate to use armed force to preserve the status quo. This policy became known in the West as the "Brezhnev Doctrine."

The West, by keeping out of previous East European revolts, was from a de facto standpoint already adhering to what the Soviets wanted formally recognized in a European security conference: the right of the Soviet Union to do what was necessary to retain hegemony over Eastern Europe.

The invasion had a sobering effect on those in the West who were beginning to think that the cold war era had indeed come to a close. While the invasion did not kill detente, it certainly set back the cause with the practical result that the West did nothing to bring a European security conference any closer to reality.

Nevertheless, only seven months after the implementation of the Brezhnev Doctrine in Czechoslovakia, the Warsaw Pact Political Consultative Committee met in Budapest and issued a communique on 17 March 1969, once again calling for a European security conference. In part, the communique stated that "problems must be solved peacefully through talks and not through the use of force nor the threat of force." (8) This statement was extremely ironic, given the recent invasion of Czechoslovakia, and the fact that the disgraced chairman of the Czech Communist Party, Alexander Dubcek, was a signator of the communique. The communique graphically set the conditions required for a successful security conference: (a) inviolability of the existing frontiers (i.e., recognition of the Oder-Neisse line), (b) recognition of the existence of the German Democratic Republic, (c) renunciation by the Federal Republic of Germany of its claim to represent the entire German people, (d) renunciation of the possession of nuclear weapons by West Germany, and (e) recognition that West Berlin does not belong to West Germany. (9) This was a tough set of demands for the West to accept, and with the Czech invasion fresh on the Western conscience, totally unacceptable.

The communique did not address MBFR, in keeping with the "talk past" method being employed by both East and West concerning their favorite proposals, but it did call for a transition from general statements about peace to concrete detente and disarmament measures.

In the obvious toning down of the language used in referring to West Germany, the communique was also significant. This was due, no doubt, to the considerable change in West German attitudes toward its dealings with the East. There had been a growing West German sentiment away from the rigid policies exemplified by the Hallstein Doctrine, which had threatened any nation which recognized East Germany with a withdrawal of West German recognition. The change in attitude was led by Willy Brandt and his Social Democrats. Brandt's willingness to compromise with the East led to his famous "Ostpolitik" policy. The indication that West Germany was becoming more flexible in its attitude toward the East was encouraging to the Soviets. If Bonn would eventually agree to recognition of the Oder-Neisse line, then much of the Soviet objective in a security conference could be realized. Polemics toward the FRG were therefore inappropriate.

At the same time, the long-simmering Sino-Soviet border dispute broke out in the winter of 1969 in open warfare over possession of islands in the Ussuri River. The threat of a war between the Soviet Union and Communist China was never greater, and the Soviets obviously needed to tranquilize their Western front in case they went to war with China. In a nuclear conflict, the Soviet Union could not stand up to both the West and China and survive. The Soviets were hopeful that the so-called progressive forces in West Europe exemplified by Willy Brandt would insure that a European security conference would be held.

But the Czech invasion has not been forgotten by the West. The NATO Ministerial Meeting in Washington which commemorated the twentieth anniversary of NATO reiterated a "readiness to seek with the other states concerned, specific practical measures for mutual and balanced force reductions." The Ministers noted their displeasure over Czechoslovakia by calling it a "serious setback to hopes for improvement in East/West relations," but they reaffirmed their intention to "continue the search for real progress towards this objective by contacts and to explore all appropriate openings for negotiations." (10) With this latter statement, the Ministers indirectly implied endorsement of the idea of a conference with the East. Subsequently, the dialogue between East and West began to take on a more direct attitude in contrast to the previous proclivity to talk past each other in citing each other's desires. Nevertheless, the Soviets, stained by Czechoslovakia, would have to negotiate seriously, on a quid pro quo basis, in order to have a European security conference. More and more it was becoming very obvious to the East that if it wanted such a conference, the quo for it would have to be negotiations on force reductions as well as some concessions on the Berlin access question.

The Foreign Ministers of the Warsaw Pact countries met in Prague on 31 October 1969. Their communique dealt exclusively with the idea of a security conference. The text was short and to the point and was significantly lacking in any vitriolic propaganda aimed at West Germany. (11) This was doubtlessly a result of the election of Willy Brandt as the new Chancellor of the Federal Republic. Brandt's views on making changes in West Germany's attitude to the East and on some of the issues of long contention, such as recognition of the Oder-Neisse line, caused a switch in the tune of this Warsaw Pact communique, which singled out the following questions to be discussed at such a conference:

a. The creation of security in Europe, renunciation of the use of force, and the threat of force in relations between European states, and,

b. Widening commercial, economic, technical, scientific relations between European states, serving the development of political cooperation, based on the equality of rights. (12)

While not mentioning MBFR, the communique did state that the success of such an all-European conference "would make possible the future examinations of such other problems of European states where solutions would contribute to consolidating peace in Europe." (13)

Despite efforts by the Nixon administration to get MBFR talks going with the Russians, a certain number of Senators, led by Mike Mansfield, were growing restive at the lack of administration initiatives toward reducing US forces in Europe. Fueled by the increasing antiwar/military fever in the United States over Vietnam, Senator Mansfield reintroduced on 1 December 1969 his "Sense of the Senate" resolution (first introduced in 1966) which called for "a substantial reduction of US forces permanently stationed in Europe." (14) He rejected the argument that the time was not right for such reduction and stated:

My understanding is that there is still no agreed NATO proposal for balanced force reductions and it is not planned there will be one until early summer. Even then there is no reason to assume that discussions, much less full negotiations will begin, for there has been no indication, direct or indirect, that the Soviet Union is interested in such discussions. (15)

The message was clear - unless the administration could get the Soviets to agree to talks on troop reductions soon, Mansfield was going to force the administration to make unilateral cuts. Hindsight shows that the growing pressure for a unilateral US withdrawal was being closely watched in Moscow.   Soviet leaders were studying the implication of such an occurrence but were not making any public pronouncements on the subject either in press comments or official communiques.

Soviet and East European Communist leaders met on 4 December 1969.   They issued a communique which briefly mentioned that "extensive international support is being given" to the holding of an all-European conference. It cited the key issues of such a conference as the recognition of East Germany as a sovereign nation, as well as the acceptance of the Oder-Neisse line as the western Polish border. The main thrust of the text of the communique was to take satisfactory note of the changes in West German attitudes as a result of the election of the Social Democrats and Willy Brandt. Especially noted was the signing of the nuclear nonproliferation treaty by West Germany. The communique paid only minor lip service to arms control by stating that it was "necessary to advance along the road to ending the arms race and of general and complete disarmament including nuclear disarma-ment." (16)

The next day, on 5 December 1969, NATO issued its "Declaration on European Security." It was a lengthy 15-point document which was divided into subsections entitled Arms Control and Disarmament; Germany and Berlin; Economic, Technical, and Cultural Exchange; and Perspectives for Negotiations. (17)

The Declaration hit hard at the "Brezhnev Doctrine" by stating that the principle of national independence was the basis for European security, and noted that "past experiences have shown that there is as yet no common interpretation of these principles." It was most noteworthy in its treatment of MBFR. No previous NATO document dealt in such detail with what the West would expect from an MBFR agreement. The Ministers chided the East by citing the previous NATO statement on MBFR negotiations and commented that "up to now their suggestion had led to no result." The Ministers went on to say that despite the lack of an Eastern response, the Allied studies on MBFR would continue "in order to prepare a realistic basis for active exploration at an early date and thereby establish whether it could serve as a starting point for fruitful negotiations." These studies, reported the Ministers, had progressed sufficiently to "permit the establishment of certain criteria which such reductions should meet." The studies indicated, according to the Declaration, that "significant reductions under adequate verification and control would be envisaged under any agreement on mutual and balanced force reductions which should be consistent with the vital security interest of all parties." The Ministers also recommended that further studies should be done on confidence-building measures to accompany any reduction and listed several which had been proposed earlier at the Geneva Foreign Ministers Meeting and the Geneva Surprise Attack Conference:

Such measures could include advance notification of military movements and maneuvers, exchange of observers at military maneuvers and possibly the establishment of observation posts. Examination of the techniques and methods of inspection should also be further developed. (18)

One thing was obvious about this declaration: the West was envisioning much more than just a reduction without any sort of capability to verify and monitor the post-agreement period. It was serving notice to the East that the West wanted MBFR to be a serious military/technical type of negotiations and not just token troop withdrawals under the umbrella of political expediency and detente.

In commenting on the Berlin situation, the Declaration suggested that the "elimination of difficulties created in the past with respect to Berlin, especially with regard to access, would increase the prospects for serious discussions on other concrete issues which continue to divide East and West." Clearly the first step to a conference on European security, as far as the West was concerned, was a demonstration of an Eastern willingness to compromise over West Berlin talks which began on 26 March 1970. (19)

The NATO Ministers, meeting the following year in Rome in May 1970, issued two important documents known collectively as the Rome Declaration. One was a communique which dealt briefly with the whole range of current Europeans problems, but considered mainly the proposed European security conference. (20) The second document was entitled "Mutual Balanced Force Reductions Declaration." In this paper, much of the language of the 5 December 1969 Ministerial Declaration concerning MBFR studies reappeared. New and significant was the NATO view that any MBFR negotiations be focused on Central Europe. The paper listed the following points of the NATO position:

- Mutual force reductions should . . . not operate to the military disadvantage of either side having regard for the differences arising from geographical and other considerations.

- Reductions should be on the basis of reciprocity and phased and balanced as to their scope and timing.

- Reductions should include stationed and indigenous forces and their weapons systems in the area concerned, and,

- There must be adequate verification and controls to ensure the observance of agreements. (21)

From the above, it should have been again quite clear to the East that NATO intended to improve its security through MBFR by pursuing a military/technical arms agreement, as opposed to a purely political agreement enhancing detente.

Within a month, the Warsaw Pact Ministers of Foreign Affairs issued a communique and a memorandum on the conclusion reached in their meeting in Budapest on 22 June 1970. They noted "with satisfaction that during bilateral and multilateral consultations . . . the positions of the interested states grew closer on a number of important questions related to the all-European conference." (22)   The memorandum reiterated many of the points previously cited as a rationale for having an all-European conference. In addition, it gave a good indication that some sort of arms control discussion might be possible by agreeing "to include in the all-European conference the question of creating a body on questions of European security." The communique elaborated on this point:

> . . . a study of the question of reducing foreign armed forces would serve the interest of detente and security in Europe. In order to create in the shortest possible period of time the most favorable conditions for the discussion of appropriate questions at the all-European Conference and in the interests of the productivity of studying the questions concerning the reduction of <u>foreign</u> armed forces, this question could be discussed in the body which it is proposed to set up at the all-European Conference or in another manner acceptable to the interested states. (23)

Several significant points appeared in the NATO and Warsaw Pact statements just described. In the NATO statement, the Allies implied that: (a) the geographical disparity in favor of the Soviet Union would be a factor in MBFR; (b) the term "balanced" might imply that the East would be expected to take greater reductions than the West; (c) reductions would not only be expected in stationed forces or what the Soviets referred to as foreign (United States, British, Canadian, and Russian), but in indigenous forces as well; and (d) reduction would be confined to Central Europe. In the Warsaw Pact Foreign Minister's memorandum, the East reversed its former position of having a European conference solely for Europeans as part of its effort to drive the United States out of Europe. Now, they called for the inclusion of the United States and Canada in the conference - a significant change which hinted at a shift in Soviet policy toward the United States presence in Europe.

Additionally, the East was showing signs of preferring to separate discussions on troop reductions from the political negotiations and hold them as a follow-on to the all-European Conference. The East obviously wanted a greater participation in the political conference in order to secure wide recognition of the post-World War II borders and to secure favorable trading agreements with as many nations as possible, but in the case of military reductions, they preferred a smaller participation. While the West called for both foreign and indigenous reductions, the East continued its long-held position to have reductions in foreign troops only. This was a holdover from the Soviet objective of decoupling the United States from Germany by forcing US troops out of Europe.

Two significant topics proposed by the East for coverage in a European Security Conference was settled prematurely with the FRG in the latter half of 1970 when Willy Brandt, under his policy of "Ostpolitik," concluded two treaties with the East. In one signed with the Soviets on 12 August, the Federal Republic agreed to recognize that the "frontiers of all states in Europe were inviolable including the Oder-Neisse line . . . and the frontier between the Federal Republic of Germany and the German Democratic Republic." (24)

The second treaty, which was signed with Poland on 18 November, simply reaffirmed recognition of the Oder-Neisse line. (25)   While getting West German recognition of the Oder-Neisse line accomplished, one of the main objectives of a European Security Conference, the Soviets still pressed for the conference in order that all European nations, and the United States as well, would recognize the postwar realities of Eastern Europe.   The communique of the Warsaw Pact Summit meeting held in Berlin on 2 December 1970 noted with satisfaction the treaties signed by the Federal Republic. It went on to state, in a rather optimistic tone, that conditions were ripening for the settlement of other problems in Europe. But then, in a direct challenge to the West's drive for a satisfactory Berlin Accord before discussing overall European security, the communique called for a convening of the conference without delay. (26)   Two days later, on 4 December 1970, the NATO Ministers issued a reply in which they reaffirmed that their prerequisite for such a conference continued to be a satisfactory conclusion of the Berlin talks. (27)

The Ministers reiterated their previous statements on MBFR, regretted that the East had not responded specifically, but noted the Eastern bloc's desire for a reduction of foreign forces. The Ministers renewed their invitation to hold exploratory talks on the basis of the Rome Declaration and to

> examine different possibilities in the field of force reductions in the Central Region of Europe including the possible mutual and balanced reduction of both stationed and indigenous forces. (28)

The West was once more committing itself to reductions of indigenous forces while the East still preferred a narrower scope of reductions consisting of only foreign forces, meaning primarily Soviet and US forces.

The broadening of the scope of reductions by the West reflected Allied desires to accommodate budgetary and antimilitary pressures within their own countries somewhat similar to those being forced on the United States.   The enlargement in the scope of negotiations, to include indigenous forces in order to satisfy Allied domestic pressure, would prove to be a double-edged sword once actual negotiations got underway; it presented the Soviets with the unexpected opportunity to try once again to reduce and limit West German forces. The year 1971 opened with little indication that there would be any real movement on MBFR. The Soviets still were refusing to recognize the West's offer to discuss force reductions in Central Europe despite elaborations by the West of what they expected out of MBFR.

Meanwhile, the war in Vietnam dragged on, causing an ever-increasing wave of antiwar/antimilitary feeling in the United States. In Europe, the Seventh US Army was reduced considerably in actual manpower to furnish replacements for Vietnam. Those personnel who were assigned to the Seventh Army remained only a short time, either prior to going to Vietnam, or to fill up the time prior to discharge. In short, the Seventh Army became a shadow of its former self with a low state of readiness and morale. The balance of payments deficit, in part caused by failure of the Allies to assume a share of the cost of maintaining the US Army in Europe, the problems of the Seventh Army, and the fact that detente had made the Soviet threat appear more benign, all led to ever-increasing congressional pressure, fueled by the antiwar sentiment, to reduce sharply the US ground force presence in Europe. Congressional feeling was reaching a point where it was entirely conceivable that Congress would legislate a large unilateral withdrawal of US forces in Europe. The Soviets were well informed on this trend in Congress and were no doubt considering the impact of such a massive unilateral US withdrawal.

In March 1971, the Soviets gave the first indication that they would seriously entertain participation in negotiations on force reductions when they made it an official part of the platform of the 24th Communist Party Congress. In a speech on 30 March, Brezhnev outlined the foreign policy course of the Soviet Union for the next five years. It consisted of several so-called "basic concrete tasks." One of these basic tasks was still the desire to have an all-European conference despite the agreement by West Germany to recognize the existing borders:

> To proceed from the final recognition of the territorial changes that took place in Europe as a result of World War II. To bring about a radical turn towards detente and peace on this continent. To ensure the convocation and success of an all-European conference. (29)

Point four of Brezhnev's speech called for a halt to the arms race, the convocation of a world disarmament conference, reducing military expenditures, reducing the probability of accidental wars, and the dismantling of foreign bases. The last part of point four was significant: "We stand for a reduction of armed forces and armaments in areas where the military confrontation is especially dangerous, above all, in Central Europe." (30) With this, Brezhnev seemed not only to agree with the MBFR concept but, in addition, to the limitation of any force reductions to the Central European region.

The congressional drive led by Senator Mike Mansfield in May 1971 to reduce US forces in Europe reached a critical stage. Mansfield believed he had finally achieved enough Senate backing to pass his resolution. Five days prior to the vote on this proposal, perhaps coincidentally, perhaps deliberately, Brezhnev took the occasion of the 50th Anniversary of the Georgian Republic on 14 May 1971 in Tbilisi to state the following:

In connection with the reaction of the West to the proposals put forward by the [24th Party] Congress, I want to mention one detail. Some of the NATO countries have shown an evident interest and even nervousness over the question of reduction of armed forces and armaments in Central Europe. Their spokesmen ask: What armed forces - foreign or national? What armaments - nuclear or conventional - are to be reduced? Or, perhaps, they ask, the Soviet proposals concern all this taken together? In connection with this, we, too have a question: Don't these curious people resemble a person who tries to judge the flavor of wine by its appearance alone without imbibing it? If anything is not clear to somebody, very well, then we can make it clear. But you have to muster the resolve to try the proposal you are interested in by tasting it. Translated into diplomatic language, this means - to start negotiations. (31)

The "taste of the wine" statement was enthusiastically welcomed by the US Administration officials. They immediately seized the opportunity to attack the Mansfield proposal, claiming it would destroy any chance to get the Soviets to agree to withdrawals under MBFR.
In a television interview just prior to the introduction of the Mansfield amendment vote, Secretary of State William P. Rogers remarked:

If we reduce our force levels in Europe at this time we think it would be a very dangerous situation. We would want to do it in the context of a mutual and balanced force reduction. Why should we in the United States reduce unilaterally and thereby kiss goodbye to any chance that we might have to negotiate successfully to reduce the Soviet presence. And the tension in Europe could be reduced if we could have a mutual and balanced force reduction. (32)

Mansfield was not to be deterred. He chose the Military Selective Service Act as the vehicle on which to tack his resolution on troop withdrawals as an amendment. In his introductory speech he rejected the idea that a unilateral US troop cut would kill any chance of getting Soviet reductions. He argued in part:

Cutting our Seventh Army forces is an equally reasonable way to induce the Soviets to reduce their manpower in the satellites. I suggest such a cut on our part would act as effectively to obtain this end as would any force reductions. Russia would be hard put to explain why it was necessary to retain such large forces to protect the Satellites against a pruned-back NATO. (33)

Mansfield's amendment had become significantly stronger and more specific since it was first introduced as a Sense of the Senate Resolution. It now read:

a. The Congress hereby finds that the number of United States military personnel stationed in Europe can be significantly reduced without endangering the security of Western Europe and that such a reduction would have a favorable effect on this Nation's balance of payment problems and would help avoid recurring international monetary crises involving the value of the dollar abroad. It is therefore the purpose of this section to provide for such a reduction at the earliest practical date.

b. No funds appropriated by Congress may be used after December 31, 1971 for the purpose of supporting or maintaining in Europe any military personnel of the United States in excess of 150,000. (34)

In effect, Mansfield was asking for a 50 percent reduction in US forces in Europe. Such a massive withdrawal would without a doubt seriously destabilize West European security.

A spirited debate followed Mansfield's introduction speech, with ten Senators taking the floor to attack the Mansfield proposal and five to defend it.

Senator Hugh Scott said in part, "I believe this should be part of a bilateral move not a unilateral one. Recent statements by Soviet leaders indicate that there is a very real chance that such a bilateral reduction can be effected." (35)

But it was Senator Clifford P. Hansen who argued most persuasively for the defeat of the Mansfield amendment. Concerning the consequences of a unilateral withdrawal of 150,000 US troops, he stated:

It would leave the Soviet Union in a preponderant military position from which it could more easily impose its will in Western Europe; it would create a fundamental dilemma for West Germany; disarm and accommodate to the policies of the Soviet Union or embark on a vast program of rearmament - perhaps including the development of nuclear weapons to provide for its own defense; and it would demonstrate to friend and foe alike that the United States had determined, in contradiction of the lessons bitterly learned in two world wars, that it no longer considered American security to be indivisible from the security of Europe. (36)

Later in his speech he made direct reference to the recent Soviet hints:

I have no assurance that the recent statements of Mr. Brezhnev, first at the 24th Communist Party Congress, later on last Friday [the Tbilisi speech] means that at last the Soviet Union is prepared to relax the tension that it has imposed on Central Europe. The statements do, however, contain some new elements that move toward our thinking. The Soviet Foreign Minister confirmed to our Ambassador in Moscow early this week that the Soviets are prepared to undertake discussions of mutual and balanced force reductions and are interested in further exchanges on the subject. . . . It would be the greatest folly not to thoroughly explore the meaning of these statements. . . . We must not surrender the one incentive that compels the Soviets toward these negotiations. That incentive is the knowledge that only through reciprocal reductions can the Soviets hope to reduce the size of the military power opposing it across the face of Europe. (37)

Senator Robert Dole, speaking against the amendment, stated in part that "unilateral US troop reductions in Europe would destroy any hope of mutual and balanced force reduction negotiations at a time when such negotiations appear to be a real possibility." (38)

The New York Times of 19 May also attacked the amendment in the hope of influencing the outcome of the vote. In two articles on the subject, the Times called for the defeat of the measure. The paper pointed out that the Soviets had shown a positive response to starting talks on mutual and balanced force reductions and concluded that MFBR would never happen if the Mansfield amendment were passed. (39)

In cosponsoring the amendment, Senator Harold E. Hughes took the line that the Mansfield amendment was responsible for getting the Soviets to commit themselves to MBFR negotiations. He was closer to the truth than most people realized,when he said:

In the few days since Senator Mansfield introduced his amendment we have seen the Soviet Union express new willingness to negotiate mutual force reductions in Europe. If press reports are accurate, the Soviet Union has even modified its long-standing insistence on a European Security Conference and is now willing to conduct separate talks on troop cuts. It is my belief that this new opportunity would not have come about but for the galvanizing effect on the Mansfield amendment. (40)

Senator Ted Kennedy also credited the Mansfield amendment with getting the Soviets to talk about troop reductions. The efforts of Senator Mansfield over the preceding six years were in part, according to Kennedy, "designed to encourage negotiations with the Soviet Union to achieve mutual reductions in NATO and Warsaw Pact forces" and only the effort of Mansfield "has assured a receptive attitude by the Administration to the recent bid by the Soviets for mutual force reductions." (41)

Kennedy's point was a valid one. The threat of a large precipitous unilateral US withdrawal from Western Europe undoubtedly greatly worried the Soviets as well as the West Europeans. Such a withdrawal could create a power vacuum in Central Europe that could galvanize the West Europeans to greater unity in the face of the Soviet threat, and thus conceivably result in the West Germans getting control of nuclear weapons, causing an increase in the strength of the Bundeswehr to compensate for United States withdrawal. While there was no certainty that such a chain of events would occur - indeed the opposite could happen - it was in the Soviets' best interest to lessen the chances of such an occurrence. In any major change of the status quo in Central Europe, the Soviet Union would clearly have a great deal to lose.

While one could credit Mansfield with helping to bring the Soviets and the US Government to the negotiating table, there was equal truth to the statements made by the Senators attacking the amendment when they pointed out (along with the New York Times and the Administration) that if the Mansfield amendment were to be passed and the United States slashed its troop strength in Western Europe by half, the chances of mutual troop reduction talks would be almost nil. Such argumentation obviously was more persuasive. When the time came for a vote, the Mansfield amendment was rejected. Thirty-six Senators voted "yes" but 61 voted "nay." Despite the loss, there was a clear message in the mood of Congress which could not be ignored. The Administration would have to show progress in MBFR if it hoped to continue to hold off unilateral force cuts.

On 18 May 1971, during the course of a state visit to the Soviet Union by Prime Minister Trudeau of Canada, Premier Kosygin made the following remarks at a luncheon given in Trudeau's honor:

> Much attention is now being devoted to the question of reducing armed forces and armaments. Animated discussion on this account concerning in particular the possibility of reducing foreign troops are now underway in certain countries. Our proposals on this question were again set out the other day by Secretary Brezhnev in Tbilisi. If for its part, the West displayed the readiness to really undertake practical steps in this direction, then we will do everything possible for the reaching of an agreement. (42)

Now it was the Soviets who were taking the initiative in military force reductions. Putting them into the platform of the 24th CPSU Conference and calling for the West to reply to Soviet initiatives were clear signals that the Soviet leadership had decided it was in their best interests to enter into MBFR resolutions. (43) Apparently the Soviets' decision to participate was based on the belief that, for the present, keeping the United States in Europe would be in their best interest. Beginning with the call to include the United States in any all-European security conference, the Soviets had reversed their previous policy of getting the United States entirely out of Europe. Unable to prevent a rearmed and formidable West German nation whose armed forces had nuclear delivery means, the Soviets obviously had rethought their previous policy and decided that retention of US forces in Europe, certainly for the near term, was desirable in order to keep the FRG in check. The continual Soviet reiteration of interest in force reductions at the height of the drive in Congress for unilateral US troop cuts in Europe certainly lends credence to this conclusion.

At the North Atlantic Council meeting on the 3rd and 4th of June 1971 in Lisbon, Portugal, the Ministers "welcomed the response of Soviet leaders indicating possible readiness to consider reductions of armed forces and armaments in Central Europe," and expressed their readiness to appoint a representative to participate in East/West exploratory talks on convening MBFR negotiations. The Ministers did not immediately appoint such an individual, or "Explorer" as the position was called, and were not to appoint one until 6 October 1971. (44)

A review of public statements issued in the month of June 1971 from the Soviet leadership clearly expressed Soviet willingness to discuss force reductions. Kirilenko, Kosygin, Podgorny, and Mazurov all cited Brezhnev's Tbilisi speech as the basis from which to begin discussions on force reductions in Central Europe. Brezhnev himself, on 11 June 1971, added that the Soviet Union was willing to discuss reductions of both foreign and national forces, a point the West had been pressing. (45) It was a point that the Soviets were glad to accept, for, instead of just discussing US and possibly some British withdrawals, it gave the Soviets an opening to achieve long-standing goals of reducing and putting ceilings on the Bundeswehr. The insistence by the West on inclusion of indigenous forces in MBFR was no doubt an added inventive for the Soviets to participate.

On 6 October 1971 the North Atlantic Council, acting on instructions of the Ministers laid down in Lisbon in June 1971, appointed the recently resigned NATO Secretary General, Mr. Manlio Brosio, to be the Allied "Explorer" for MBFR. He was instructed to determine in talks with the Russians whether or not a basis for realistic negotiations existed. (46)

During this same time period the last obstacle to the convening of a Conference on Security and Cooperation in Europe (CSCE), as the all-European Security Conference was now being called by the West, had been cleared away with the Four Powers Agreement on Berlin reached on 3 September 1971. (47)

Throughout the fall of 1971 the Soviet leadership issued a continual stream of statements on their readiness to talk force reductions in Central Europe. Yet, despite their readiness, they did not call Mr. Brosio to Moscow. This apparent dichotomy may be explained by the fact the Soviets had earlier indicated that CSCE must be discussed and arranged for prior to any discussion on the convening of a conference on MBFR, and secondly, as the Soviets had earlier pointed out, discussion on MBFR should not be bloc-to-bloc but open to all interested nations. If the Soviets had received a NATO-appointed official, it could have been construed as accepting the bloc-to-bloc concept.

The NATO Ministerial Communique of December 1971 noted the progress that had been made in East/West problem areas such as the Berlin Agreement and affirmed NATO's intention to move ahead in bilateral and multilateral exploratory talks on CSCE. On MBFR, the Ministers "noted with regret that the Soviet Government has so far failed to respond to the Allied initiative" of appointing Mr. Brosio as their spokesman and reaffirmed their belief "that prior explorations of this question are essential in preparation for eventual multilateral negotiations." (48)

On 26 January the Warsaw Pact Political Consultative Committee met in Prague and issued a lengthy communique spelling out the agenda they envisioned for a CSCE conference. They stated their belief "that an all-American conference can be convened in 1972 and regard the statements by a number of West European states to the effect that they adhere to the same view as a factor in favor of this." (49)

On MBFR the East stated, "The examination and determination of ways toward solving this question should not be the prerogative of the existing military alliances in Europe. Appropriate agreement could be reached on the way of conducting talks on this question." (50) It was clear that the East did not see such negotiations being confined to NATO and Warsaw Pact nations. This was partly in keeping with the East's long-standing announced goal of eliminating NATO and the Warsaw Pact alliances. Such a dismemberment of NATO and the Warsaw Pact alliances would have little effect on the Soviet grip on Eastern Europe, as the Soviets could simply maintain individual treaties with East European nations which would give them the same prerogatives and maintain the same military agreements that had existed under the Warsaw Pact treaty. On the other hand, dismemberment of NATO would give the Soviet Union an opportunity to play individual agreements between the Soviet Union and these countries to the advantage of Moscow. By not restricting the resolutions to the two alliances, the East could keep its options open on France which possessed strong nuclear forces but was militarily no longer part of NATO.

In May 1972, President Nixon went to Moscow and signed the SALT I accords. According to press reports, the Soviets had agreed at the signing to start preliminary talks on MBFR in exchange for US approval for the starting of CSCE preliminary talks scheduled for summer of 1972 in Helsinki. The communique issued at the end of Nixon's visit on 29 May made no reference to such linkage, but simply stated in part:

Both sides believe that the goal of ensuring stability and security in Europe would be served by a reciprocal reduction of armed forces and armaments, first of all, in Central Europe. Any agreement on this question should not diminish the security of any of the sides. Appropriate agreement should be reached as soon as practicable between the states concerned on the procedures for negotiations on this subject in a special forum. (51)

On 31 May the NATO Foreign Ministers, upon the conclusion of their meeting in Bonn, issued a communique which included the proposal "that multilateral explorations on mutual and balanced force reductions be undertaken as soon as practical, either before or in parallel with multilateral preparatory talks on a Conference on Security and Cooperation in Europe." (52) Thus, while preparations got underway for CSCE, with NATO's blessing, no such action was forthcoming for MBFR. The East continued to make a general call for such a conference through public pronouncements throughout the summer, but without making any specific commitments.

In September, Henry Kissinger visited Moscow once again, and upon conclusion of his visit, it was announced that the Soviet Union had accepted the Western position that a separate East/West conference on the reductions of military forces in Central Europe should be held the next year at about the same time as broad political talks on CSCE began. (53)

In a note to the East on 15 November 1972 the Allies proposed that exploratory talks on MBFR in Central Europe begin on 31 January 1973 in a place "stilll to be agreed through diplomatic channels." (The Allies had made it known that they preferred Geneva.) The note listed the countries which it was presumed would send representatives to the exploratory talks:

> The Governments of Belgium, Canada, the Federal Republic of Germany, Luxembourg, the Netherlands, the United Kingdom, and the United States are communicating this proposal to the Governments of Czechoslovakia, Poland, Hungary, and the USSR. The Government of the Federal Republic of Germany is communicating this proposal to the Government of the German Democratic Republic also. The Governments of Denmark, Greece, Italy, Norway, and Turkey will confirm their intentions to be represented at the exploratory talks. (54)

The East did not reply to the Allied note for two months. During this period, however, the Soviets continued to give every indication that they supported the concept of mutual force reductions, and they continued to stress the need to keep the talks separate from CSCE. In his speech on the occasion of the 50th Anniversary of the Soviet Union, Brezhnev declared, "The Soviet Union favors serious preparation for and effective conduct of these negotiations." (55)

On the arrival of French President Pompidou at Minsk on 11 January, 1973, Brezhnev implicitly confirmed Soviet partication in the preliminary talks opening at the end of January: These [talks] will start with questions of procedure. The actual questions of the reduction of forces and arms will not arise in concrete terms until somewhat later after the European Conference." (56) Brezhnev was thus making sure that any progress on MBFR was conditional on the successful completion of the CSCE conference. In reply to a statement that France did not intend to attend the MBFR talks, Brezhnev remarked, "We want the negotiations on any reduction of arms to be held outside any concept of blocs and that will be the case. But it is not yet possible to say how things will develop." (57)

Indeed, getting France to agree to participate in the negotiations was one of the primary Soviet objectives of the Pompidou visit. It was obvious from Brezhnev's comment that convincing Pompidou to participate in the MBFR talks would be high on the agenda of topics at this meeting. The Soviets would obviously prefer to have the large French Army, as well as its Air Force, both equipped with nuclear weapons, fall under any future MBFR agreement. But the communique which was issued after the visit on 12 January made no mention of MBFR, except to state that the all-European conference should "not be dependent on any other negotiations," and that it is a "major independent action of European and world politics. (58) Brezhnev had clearly failed in his attempt to get France to join the MBFR talks.

On 19 January 1973, the Warsaw Pact replied to the Allied note of November 1972. They accepted the date of 31 January 1973 for the start of the preliminary talks, but suggested Vienna instead of Geneva as the location. (59) The note pressed for the inclusion in the talks of Bulgaria and Romania at a minimum. At the maximum, it asserted the right of "other" European nations (read "France") to join at that phase or later on in the talks. The note further stated that as the East saw it, the purpose of the preliminary talks was to

> study and solve questions of organization and procedure related to the holding of talks on the reduction of armed forces and arms in Europe, to determine the composition of the participants in these talks, the date and place of holding them, draft proposals concerning the agenda, and the order of holding the talks.

Still keeping the door open for France, the statement added that "the consultations are not to decide beforehand the question of what countries will be partners to the agreement or agreements on the reduction of armed forces and arms." (60)

On 25 January 1973, NATO rejected the Eastern idea that the MBFR talks should be open to all interested states. The Allies made it clear to the East they preferred to limit the proposed negotiations to those countries having troops in Central Europe. They suggested that the participation question could be discussed further at the preliminary talks. Vienna was accepted by the Allies providing arrangements could be completed in time. The East replied that they reserved the right to raise the question of other interested nations, including neutrals, but they would be in Vienna on 31 January for preliminary consultations on the reduction of armed forces and armaments in Europe.

After 2½ years of intensive East/West dialogue, force reductions in Central Europe were to be seriously discussed in face-to-face consultations. The complexity of these negotiations was to prove far greater than any of the participants had imagined as they prepared to leave for Vienna.

3 Preparatory Consultations: January-June 1973

The issue of participation, raised some two months before the preliminary consultations actually began, was carried into the consultations themselves. The East was resisting and clearly expected to continue to resist the Allied concept of participation. By holding out for the idea of all European states participating in the preliminary talks, it left the door open for France, the nation the Soviets wanted most earnestly in the talks. The Eastern press made continual reference to France when discussing arms reduction. Bulgaria, often serving as a spokesman for Soviet ideas during this phase of MBFR preparations, stated in a radio broadcast of 20 January 1973 that if MBFR were limited as proposed by the West, "France which opposes bloc-to-bloc negotiations would not participate." (1)

Radio Belgrade succinctly summed up the rationale behind the Soviet desire to avoid a NATO-Warsaw Pact exclusiveness in the talks. In a broadcast of 19 January 1973 it said:

> Avoiding the rigidly bloc character of the proposed talks, the Soviet Union is making a gesture which enables France to join the negotiations in some way. This is significant in view of the up to now adverse attitude of Paris. It is clear to Moscow that without France's participation there are not many chances for success of the negotiations on the reduction of armed forces in Europe. (2)

Romania, which at that time was playing an exceedingly independent role in foreign policy, had been pushing vigorously for force reductions to be included in the Conference on Security and Cooperation in Europe (CSCE). The Romanians concluded that the restricted membership and the proposed area of reductions confined to Central Europe would effectively prevent any force reductions in the Balkans. Romania was looking for some sort of international agreement that would place at least strong moral restrictions on the use of the Brezhnev Doctrine against Romania. However, a Yugoslavian press report from Belgrade, issued on the day the talks started in Vienna, reported that Bucharest no longer insisted on disarmament talks within CSCE. (3) Obviously bowing to strong Soviet pressure, the Romanians, despite their views and the fact that they were not invited by the Allies, showed up in Vienna. But the warning signs were readily apparent in the Eastern press that the West would be hit hard on the question of participants when the preliminary talks began.

At 4:00 p.m. on Wednesday, the 31st of January 1973, the delegates were welcomed by the Austrian foreign minister (later president), Dr. Rudolph Kirchschlager, in the Hofburg Palace in the heart of Vienna. Nineteen nations were in attendance, two more than the West had invited. The two uninvited but present nations were Romania and Bulgaria. Despite the Soviet protestations about bloc-to-bloc negotiations, their presence insured that the entire Warsaw Pact was present. The NATO nations, with the exception of France and Iceland, were also all present when Portugal unexpectedly sent an observer team to the talks. (4)

The Soviet press stated that the purpose of the preliminary talks was "to settle organization and procedural questions ... namely determination of the composition of the participants, the date and venue of the negotiations and the formulation of proposals regarding the agenda and the procedure of the negotiations." (5)

As the talks were convening, the Eastern press took the opportunity to make numerous pronouncements claiming the credit for initiating the MBFR talks. Several long articles were issued claiming that the Soviets had been trying to get arms reduction talks going since 1946. The Soviets claimed that they had proposed some 14 arms reduction measures since that time, culminating in the 24th CPSU Congress offer to discuss reduction of forces in Central Europe. No credit was given to the West for any effort nor, for that matter, was the previous Soviet refusal to engage in meaningful disarmament proposals discussed. In the Eastern bloc only the Yugoslav press described the real situation, which stated on 30 January in a radio broadcast that the talks came

at the initiative of the NATO member countries or to be more precise it is a supplement to the initiative by the Warsaw Pact countries concerning negotiations on European security. The Socialist countries agreed to the NATO initiative since they were convinced the Western countries were paving the way for the convocation of an all European security conference. (6)

The linkage between the CSCE and MBFR was a subject which neither East nor West discussed openly, although the Eastern press occasionally made vague references that "for successful talks on force reduction the political climate in Europe must be appropriate" and a "successful European security conference is a prerequisite to such an atmosphere." (7)

This was the first indication that as far as the Soviets were concerned, progress in MBFR would depend on how quickly progress could be made in CSCE, with a distinct possibility being that a conclusion would have to be reached in CSCE prior to any significant progress in MBFR. Accordingly, the West expressed fears concerning the seriousness of Soviet participation in MBFR. Were they in it simply because they had no choice? The Soviets very much wanted to have a European security conference. If the only way they could get one was to agree to preliminary talks on MBFR, the West could not be sure of Soviet seriousness for actual MBFR negotiations. Perhaps, some reasoned, the Soviets would simply mark time in MBFR until CSCE was completed and then drop out of MBFR. This led to Allied talk of reverse linkage; that is, requiring the Soviets to show progress in arms reduction in order to have a successful conclusion to CSCE. (8) In sum, the Eastern leaders, despite all their pronouncements concerning the importance of arms reduction, had not yet convinced the West by the start of the preliminary talks that they really wanted MBFR.

The talks no sooner got underway than they became snarled over the question of Hungary's participation. The West wanted Hungary as a direct participant. The East wanted Hungary as a special participant. (9) One only had to look at the map of Central Europe to understand why NATO wanted Hungary as a direct participant. Hungary is located in a pivotal region of Central Europe. Forces stationed in Hungary consist of a Hungarian army of 83,000 and the Soviet Southern Group of Forces with a strength of some 55,000 men organized into two motorized rifle divisions and two tank divisions. (10) This force was the main cause of concern on both sides. Similar to the Central Group of Forces in Czechoslovakia, the Southern Group of Forces was created out of residual Soviet forces which had entered Hungary in 1956 to subdue the Hungarian revolution. The Soviets, not wanting a repetition of such an affair, left this force in place.

From the Western viewpoint, the forces in Hungary are in a geographical location that allows them to strike either in support of a major Warsaw Pact attack across the North German plain or to move south into Yugoslavia and Italy. The threat of most concern to NATO was a thrust through neutral Austria into southern West Germany to protect the left flank of the main attack coming out of East Germany and aimed at the Rhine River. (11) NATO thus believed it was necessary to include the forces in Hungary under an MBFR agreement.

One could argue that the Soviets envisioned other missions for their troops in Hungary. The Soviet troops stationed in Hungary were in themselves not so vital strictly from the standpoint of flank security for the Soviets to fight so hard for their exclusion from MBFR. Rather, their exclusions was probably more for political and hegemonistic reasons. If Hungary were included in the area of reductions, then all Soviet ground forces stationed outside the Soviet Union in Eastern Europe would be subject to MBFR reduction. This would not be true in the case of the United States. United States forces stationed in Italy as well as those in Spain and the British Isles would be exempt. From the standpoint of international prestige, the Soviets could not tolerate this.

An indication of the probable primary mission of Soviet and

Hungarian forces in case of war was given by the Soviet continued insistence that if Hungary became a direct participant, Italy would have to become one also. A tactically realistic Warsaw Pact objective for the forces in Hungary would be to strike into Northern Italy or Trieste to block an Italian reinforcement of Yugoslavia. Probably of equal concern, along with previously mentioned reasons, were the possible actions needed to retain control over Hungary and Romania as well as possible Soviet action concerning Yugoslavia in a post-Tito environment. If Soviet forces in Hungary were constrained from moving out of Hungary and if the Brezhnev Doctrine were then invoked against Romania, MBFR treaty provisions might then have to be broken in order to implement contingency plans. As the only Soviet forces in the Balkan region, the Southern Group of Forces acts as a threat to Yugoslavia and Romania as well as to the Hungarians themselves. (12) Any restrictions or reductions in these forces could result in these forces appearing less threatening and hence encourage a looser attitude among the Balkan nations toward the Soviet Union.

Resisting vigorously any Allied suggestion that Hungary should be a direct participant, the Soviets effectively brought the preliminary talks to a standstill for over three months. Whenever the West would propose Hungary as a direct participant, the East would demand Italy also be made a direct participant. (13) The Hungarian press offered a fairly unbiased account of the problem in a general article on MBFR published 31 October 1973. On the subject of Hungarian participation, the article stated that the issue was important because "it was tantamount to a delineation of the zone of the troop reduction." The article went on to say that the focal point of the dispute was the Hungarian-Italian issue:

> The reason for this was that under a reduction in accordance with the NATO stance much more significant and combat worthy Warsaw Pact forces would have been reduced, while countries of great military potential would have been left out on the other side. Taking the similarity between the strategic positions of Hungary and Italy into considerations, the socialist countries proposed the participation of these two countries with an equal status. The NATO countries and particularly the United States insisted on Italy's exclusion. (14)

The Allies were firmly opposed to bringing Italy in as a direct participant because it would expand the area of reductions and shift the forces away from Central Europe. Furthermore, it would put MBFR into the Mediterranean area and then conceivably into the Balkans. It would also imply caving in to the East's demand that all interested parties should participate in the preliminary talks. As a result, the question of who should participate in MBFR became a complex issue with no easy solution, one which caused both sides to rapidly harden their positions.

On 16 February the Polish press reported that an East/West agreement had been reached that Romania would become a special instead of a direct participant, which, the Polish implied, was a concession to the West. (15) Eastern prestige was also a factor. On 2 March the Polish made the point that Hungary is situated on the southern flank of the Warsaw Pact "and as a flank country should be a special participant because the NATO flank countries are all special participants." (16)

By May 1973 it was obvious that the Soviet Union was not going to give in on the Hungarian question. In what was billed by the Western press as a major concession to the Soviets, the West reluctantly agreed to grant Hungary special participatory status. The continuing congressional pressure during the preliminary talks for unilateral US troop withdrawals no doubt played a contributing part in the West's falling off its position. The Allied negotiators needed to show progress toward achieving Eastern agreement to conduct talks on MBFR in order to keep these congressional pressures at bay. The Soviets, perhaps still lukewarm about such MBFR talks, apparently felt no great need to help the Western negotiators. As one Western newspaper put it:

It is, of course, totally illogical to talk about reducing forces in Central Europe and exclude Soviet and Hungarian forces from the scope of the negotiations. But this is what the Kremlin has finally forced the Western powers to accept in order to move on even to the question of the agenda. (17)

Another Western newspaper stated:

In briefings given to the press yesterday, the West attempted to put on a good face on the concessions it had to make, saying the Hungarian question was not fully resolved and the West reserved the right to bring up the matter again. (18)

A plenary session was held in the main conference room of the International Atomic Energy Agency in Vienna on 14 May 1973 in order to formalize the agreements that had been reached thus far. The administrative difficulties of setting up the plenary were considerable and the election of the Chairman was done at a cocktail party by drawing lots. The British delegate, Mr. J.A. Thomson, was selected by this process. (19)

There were three speakers at the plenary, which lasted less than 20 minutes. The Soviet delegate, Oleg Khlestov, led off with a listing of the nations which were attending the preparatory consultations and then listed those nations which would be "potential participants in possible agreements related to Central Europe." (20) These were Belgium, Canada, Czechoslovakia, the German Democratic Republic, the Federal Republic of Germany, Luxemburg, the Netherlands, Poland, the Soviet Union, the United Kingdom, and the United States. Additions to this list would be agreed upon by consensus of the direct participants and could be "general or for the limited purposes of taking part in a particular decision or decisions relating to this subject." (21) Khlestov listed the remaining states as special participants. They were Bulgaria, Denmark, Greece, Hungary, Italy, Norway, Romania, and Turkey. (22)

In what was described as a face-saving gesture, the Netherlands Representative, Mr. P. Quarles Van Ufford, read a prepared statement on the Hungarian situation. In part he stated:

> The arrangements for the participation of Hungary in these consultations are without prejudice to the nature of Hungary's participation in future negotiations, decisions, or agreed measures or to the security of any party, and that in particular, the question of how and to what extent Hungary will be included in future decisions, agreements, or measures must be examined and decided during the pending neogotiations. (23)

In reply to the Netherlands Representative, the Hungarian Representative, Mr. Endre Ustor, stated:

> As the representatives of Hungary and of other Socialist states have explained during the course of the consultations, Hungary could consider participation in possible decisions, agreements or measures only if the appropriate conditions are fulfilled. (24)

At a press conference after the plenary, Ustor made it clear that "the appropriate conditions" were that Hungary would only become a direct participant if the West agreed to give the same status to Italy. (25)

The plenary also set forth the procedures by which future plenaries would be conducted. In brief they were: all participants would be seated alphabetically according to the English language, chairmanship would rotate, all participants would have the right to speak and circulate papers, the meetings would be open only to the participants, and what was said would be confidential. (26)

Of interest was the continued reference by Khlestov during the plenary to Central Europe as being the focus of the talks, although he did manage to reiterate at the conclusion of the meeting that the possibility of inviting other European states to participate as observers was still open. This was in effect a parting reference to the Soviet desire to include France and possibly other countries in the talks. However, with the need to achieve East/West consensus on all future matters in the talks, it was doubtful (given the Hungarian defeat) that the Allies would agree to opening the talks to other nations in the future. Furthermore the designation of the indigenous Central European countries of Belgium, Luxemburg, the Netherlands, and the Federal Republic of Germany on the West, and the German Democratic Republic, Poland, and Czechoslovakia on the Eastern side, as direct participants effectively delineated the area of reductions to Central Europe and, with the exception of Hungary, it was the area of reductions desired by the West.

Nothing proved easy to settle in Vienna in the spring of 1973. Even the title of the negotiations was a subject of controversy. The West had, since 1968, called the proposed talks "Mutual and Balanced Force Reductions." The word "balanced" had appeared frequently in various arms control proposals since World War II, beginning with the Proposals for general world disarmament at the United Nations in 1946. While the Soviets objected to many things in these earlier proposals, they said nothing in opposition to the word "balanced." However, when the word appeared in the proposed Allied title for the present-day talks, the East made early and vociferous objections. "The question of balanced reductions will doubtless become the biggest obstacle both during the preliminary talks and later in the negotiations," was a perceptive statement made by the Yugoslav press on 6 February 1973. (27)

Sometime prior to the start of the preliminary talks the East had concluded that the Allied use of the term "balanced" in Mutual and Balanced Force Reductions was detrimental to Eastern interests. The Hungarian Press in an English-language broadcast on 3 February 1973 said:

> The Socialist states disapprove of the word "balanced." The American and NATO states have been carrying on a strange mathematical game with this seemingly innocent word. Their idea of a balanced force reduction would be if the East would reduce more armed forces and armaments than the West ... supposedly because there are more Eastern than Western forces stationed in Europe. Moreover, if American forces are withdrawn they must cross an ocean while the forces withdrawn beyond the borders of the Soviet Union would be much closer to their present stations. (28)

The West never actually publicly ascribed these specific meanings to the word "balanced." But these positions were known; namely, that the West was considering a reduction of ground forces only, and in ground forces the East clearly predominated. It was also true that the Soviets could simply redeploy their withdrawn forces back about 1,000 kilometers while the other superpower, the United States, must withdraw their forces some 10,000 kilometers across the Atlantic Ocean. They voiced strong objections to the use of the term in the title of the talks. The East, when referring to MBFR, called it "Mutual Force Reductions" or "Reduction of Forces" or their preferred title, "Reduction of Armed Forces and Armaments in Central Europe." The latter title was the one the Soviet pushed for as the official title of the talks. The Warsaw Pact argued for a much narrower title focused almost exclusively on reductions and eliminating the contentious term "balanced." (29)

In a compromise which came closer to the Soviet position than that of the West, it was agreed that the title of the talks would be "Mutual Reduction of Forces and Armaments and Associated Measures in Central Europe." The phrase "and associated measures" was included to convey the Western insistence that the talks must address matters other than the simple reduction of forces. The West had maintained that talks must also consider verification and confidence-building measures and that measures must be taken to ensure equitable and balanced reductions. (30)

Unlike the Strategic Arms Limitation Talks with their catchy acronym, SALT, the official title of MBFR does not lend itself to a successful acronym. It is interesting to note that the official title is used by neither the West nor the East except in official conference documents. The West and the rest of the non-Communist world still use the term MBFR while the East uses "Reduction of Armed Forces and Armaments in Central Europe."

The preliminary consultations informally adjourned on 23 June 1973 without agreeing on a date for the start of the actual negotiations. Brezhnev was due to meet with Nixon in Washington in late June and wanted to discuss the date at the summit. At Helsinki the East was being hit quite hard by the West, especially on the human rights issue. Brezhnev was anxious to conclude CSCE. The main objectives of CSCE had already been won by the West German recognition of the Oder-Neisse River as the border between the GDR and Poland and it was obvious that the West would agree to recognition of this line under CSCE. Brezhnev may have wanted Nixon to pressure the Allies to get on with CSCE in exchange for Soviet agreement to start MBFR. The joint communique issued at the conclusion of the Nixon-Brezhnev summit showed that Brezhnev achieved only limited success on this point. In exchange for a short statement encouraging a rapid completion of CSCE, Brezhnev agreed to start the actual MBFR negotiations on 30 October 1973 in Vienna. (31)

With the Brezhnev-Nixon agreement on the date for starting the negotiations, the final communique was issued from Vienna on June 28 by the representatives who stayed behind waiting for agreement on the starting date. The final communique was a brief four-paragraph statement, which mentions the agenda problem twice:

> The participants in the consultations had a useful and constructive exchange of views on an agenda for the forthcoming negotiations. They agreed that during the negotiations, mutual reduction of forces and armaments and associated measures in Central Europe will be considered....It was decided that in the course of negotiations, any topic relevant to the subject matter may be introduced for neogotiations by any of those states which will take the necessary decisions (32) without prejudice to the right of all participants to speak and to circulate papers on the subject matter. This exchange of views on an agenda will greatly facilitate the work of the forthcoming negotiations. (33)

With the conclusion of the preliminary consultations, some indications of the Soviet approach to MBFR began to become evident. As far as direct participants were concerned, the Soviets were in agreement with the lineup proposed by the West except for the two notable exceptions of Hungary and France. With France, Brezhnev had been unsuccessful in persuading Pompidou to join the talks. With their satellite, Hungary, they were successful in blocking the West's desire to have that country as a direct participant. The linkage that was established by the East between Hungary and Italy coupled with the West's desire to restrict MBFR to Central Europe effectively precluded the direct participation of Hungary in MBFR. In this regard, the East probably was bluffing about Italy, for it was doubtful, given the Romanian desire to expand MBFR into the Balkans, that the Soviets would want the Italians in MBFR. If the Italians were in, this could justify MBFR expansion into the Balkans as the Romanians wanted. These sets of circumstances effectively deterred expansion of MBFR out of the Central European region.

The Soviets were also successful in defeating the West on the issue of the title of the talks. They specifically opposed the use of the term "balanced." According to the Soviets, the word "balanced" used in the context of Mutual and Balanced Force Reductions implied the concept of asymmetrical reductions which meant that the East must reduce a greater number of troops than the West in order to achieve a balance of forces; that is, parity in the numbers of forces on each side.

Concerning the agenda, the Eastern leaders indicated that they wished to hold MBFR to a simple reduction exercise by their refusal to have anything on the agenda but reductions. In contrast the West wanted items on the agenda such as verification and confidence-building measures that would make MBFR a true military/technical arms control agreement. This difference was most critical because it showed that the East looked upon MBFR as essentially a political/detente enhancing exercise while the West saw it as a military/technical negotiation. It further indicated that the West was going to have a tough time if it wanted meaningful discussions on any subject other than reductions once the actual negotiations began.

The box score on concessions at the preliminary consultations favored the Soviets. Getting the West to back down on the inclusion of Hungary as a direct participant, dropping the key word "balanced" from the title of the talks, and blocking agreement on a formal agenda to include confidence-building measures all portended rough going for the West at the actual negotiations. These concessions also gave evidence that the Soviets were not concerned with MBFR/CSCE linkage and were quite possibly trying to break any such linkage, or at least test Western resolve to tighten the linkage. De facto linkage had been established when Brezhnev and Kissinger had agreed in September 1973 on starting MBFR in exchange for the West's agreeing to CSCE. On the other hand, it simply might have been a manifestation of the typical hard-line approach taken by the Soviets to any negotiation and their natural penchant to push for terms that were as favorable as possible.

One should recognize, however, that the ability of the West to drive a hard bargain in the preliminary talks was considerably handicapped by the consequences of a deadlock or failure. Unilateral US troop cuts were again being pressed vigorously by Senator Mansfield and others during this time period. A complete deadlock or failure of the preliminary negotiations would have resulted in the collapse of the main

Administration argument with Congress against a unilateral US withdrawal from Western Europe. Because of such a possibility, Western concessions, during the preliminary consultations, were constrained within manageable proportions.

The issue of unilateral US troop reductions in Europe had lain smoldering throughout the preliminary talks. Shortly after this initial phase ended, the Administration sent its top spokesman to Congress to speak against such troop cuts. In testifying before the House Foreign Affairs Committee, Deputy Secretary of State Kenneth Rush told the Committee that the Administration unequivocally opposed any unilateral reduction of American forces in Europe. Concerning the MBFR talks, Rush stated:

> We are now poised to begin a series of negotiations that could be among the most portentous of the postwar era. It would be unthinkable to jeopardize these negotiations by unilateral action. Such a step would make almost inconceivable the conduct of reciprocal negotiations. The very likelihood of such a decision would remove the incentive of the Warsaw Pact states to negotiate at all. (34)

Testifying for unilateral force reductions before the Senate Foreign Relations Subcommittee on Arms Control on 25 July was its leading advocate, Senator Mike Mansfield. In a lengthy 33-page statement, Mansfield reiterated his call for a 50 percent reduction of US personnel stationed overseas within three years. Mansfield stated that his position was "based solely on his belief that troops should not be maintained on foreign soil 28 years after a war." (35) Senator Mansfield showed the fact that the US forces in Europe today are not left over from fighting the Nazis. As a matter of record, the strength of US forces in Europe fell to approximately 100,000 in the postwar demobilization and was not increased until the Soviets initiated the Berlin Blockade and the Korean war had begun.

When the Military Procurement Authorization Act was brought before the House for approval on 31 July 1973, advocates of unilateral troop withdrawals made serious efforts to amend the arms bill to force the Administration to take troop cuts. The amendment offered by Representative Otis G. Pike was explicitly aimed at reducing US forces in Europe. Pike would prohibit the stationing of American troops in any foreign country that was spending a smaller percentage of its gross national product on defense than was the United States. (36) With the European allies in NATO spending an average of 3.7 percent of their gross national product on defense compared to the US 7.5 percent, it was obvious that Pike's objective was a complete withdrawal of US forces from Europe. Pike charged in the subsequent discussions that the European allies were not paying a fair share of the cost of defending Western Europe:

They think that we should spend 7.5% of our gross national product for national defense and they can get away with spending 2, 3, or 4% because they know that the taxpayers of America will take care of them. (37)

Pike's amendment was attacked by Representative William J. Randall. Speaking for the Administration, Randall called the proposal "demagogic" and "destructive" and "designed to kill NATO." Concerning MFBR, he said:

> If we at this time on this floor pass any kind of amendment that amounts to a unilateral reduction then how can we expect to have any possible success as we confer on MBFR in October in Vienna? In other words, the Soviets will have what they want before they sit down at the conference table. They may not even show up for the conference. (38)

The House was not willing to vote a troop reduction under Representative Pike's criteria and soundly defeated the measure by a vote of 282 to 130. (39)

Immediately after the defeat of the Pike amendment, Representative Ronald Dellums introduced an amendment proposing a ceiling of 300,000 personnel stationed overseas, which in effect would require the then current all-service force of 600,000 personnel to be reduced by 50 percent. In introducing his amendment, Representative Dellums noted the concessions made at the preliminary consultations:

> Our negotiators are working with what they believe is a gun at their back. They are so afraid that Congress will become impatient and take matters into their own hands, that they are willing to make very real concessions to get quick results as shown by the dropping of the principle of "balance" in what should now be called the mutual force reduction talks. (40)

But then in a reverse argumentation, he stated:

> This bargaining disadvantage can only be overcome if before the talks begin we remove some of the indefensible fat from the NATO structure and give our negotiators a less vulnerable position and breathing space from political pressure. (41)

The majority of the House obviously did not subscribe to this line of reasoning and defeated the amendment 336 to 67.

A further amendment by Representative Thomas P. O'Neill Jr. requiring a cut of 100,000 troops was introduced and quickly attacked by Administration backers led by Republican leader Gerald Ford, who contended that any substantial cut of US forces in Western Europe would destroy NATO. (42) Other opponents again raised the issue of MBFR as the rationale for holding the line on troop cuts, and the amendment was defeated 242 to 163. (43)

Despite the hard-won victory of the Administration in blocking House unilateral force cuts, the storm flags were clearly flying. With the Senate due to take up the Defense Appropriations Act, there was little doubt that Senator Mansfield would make a major effort to force a unilateral reduction of US forces in Europe as a condition for the Act's approval.

The 1973 version of the Mansfield Resolution was expanded to include troops stationed not only in Europe but in other overseas areas as well, in an attempt to gain broader congressional support. The amendment called for a unilateral cut of the 500,000 land-based US personnel by 50 percent phased over a three-year period. The main objective of Mansfield remained, nevertheless, the 300,000 US ground forces stationed in Western Europe. The size of the proposed Mansfield cut would force the Administration not only to withdraw all of the forces still stationed in Southeast Asia (a withdrawal already contemplated), but would make withdrawal of at least 100,000 troops from Europe unavoidable. (44)

Argumentation for early Mansfield amendments cited costs as the pressing rationale for vigorously pushing unilateral force reductions. Figures were quoted as high as $1.7 billion as the loss in foreign exchange. Offsets or burden-sharing arrangements probably reduced the loss to no more than $500-700 million annually. (45) Supporters, therefore, shifted their emphasis instead to budgetary costs and national priorities. Sentiment in 1973 was still strongly antimilitary. Liberal opponents of defense spending claimed the need to reorder national priorities so as to be able to address so-called more pressing domestic needs. There was no occasion for such high defense spending in the era of detente, they argued, ignoring the alleged Brezhnev statement to East European leaders that detente was a tactic intended to lull the West until the Soviets could catch up and surpass the West by the 1980s. (46)

Mansfield and his supporters correctly saw MBFR as designed to block unilateral force cuts. Once MBFR talks began, it would be almost impossible for the Administration to reverse itself and make a unilateral withdrawal. Mansfield argued that unilateral US withdrawals would serve as moral examples to the Soviets, that the Soviets "would be hard put to explain why it was necessary to retain such large forces to protect the satellites against a pruned-back NATO." (47) Why the Soviets would suddenly feel obliged to make significant reductions on the basis of moral pressure was not explained by Senator Mansfield.

The Administration's argument against unilateral troop cuts cited several points: (a) the United States needs credibility in its commitments to Allies, (b) only an adequate defense makes detente possible, and (c) US forces in Europe are essential bargaining chips in the upcoming MBFR talks. The first two arguments had become fairly shopworn and had little impact with troop withdrawal advocates. The third argument would prove to be the most persuasive in turning back Senator Mansfield's previous attempts to force unilateral withdrawals.

The Administration, finding the MBFR rationale so effective, used it time and time again as pressure began building in the Congress over voting unilateral withdrawals. Nixon, Kissinger, Schlesinger, and others like Kenneth Rush repeatedly argued that after years of resisting the idea, the Senate now seemed prepared to give the Russians for free what they seemed ready to pay for. The President addressed this issue in his message to Congress on 10 September, stating, "On the very eve of negotiations, the troop cuts in Europe . . . would destroy our chances of reaching an agreement with the Warsaw Pact countries to reduce troop levels in Europe on a mutual basis." (48) This was the argument by which the Administration again hoped to throw back the Mansfield amendment.

On 25 September 1973 Senators Jackson, Nunn, Brock, and Percy offered a compromise proposal to the much more severe troop cut proposal of Senator Mansfield, which had been tabled earlier but had not yet come up for a vote. Jackson's proposal was offered as an amendment to the Defense Appropriations Authorization Act of 1974. The amendment would require the President to negotiate agreements with the NATO Allies to offset the estimated annual $11.7 billion spent in keeping US forces in Europe. If the Allies failed to help offset the balance-of-payment deficits within 12 months, the United States would reduce its forces in Europe by a percentage equal to the balance-of-payment deficit. (49) For example, if the offset were only 75 percent, then 25 percent of the force level in Europe would be withdrawn; if the shortfall were 10 percent, then 10 percent of the forces would be withdrawn.

In introducing the amendment, Senator Jackson stated:

We offer this bipartisan initiative in the conviction that a strong North Atlantic Alliance is vital to the security of the United States to the successful negotiation of mutual and balanced force reductions in Europe...and as guarantor of a significant, adequate American presence in Europe. (50)

Senator Percy remarked:

I have come to the conclusion that the two critical factors to consider are MBFR and costs. I have felt that significant unilateral US reductions might be considered by the Soviet Union to be an indication of diminishing US interest in European security. ...I don't think, however, that this position detracts from a position in favor of European countries bearing a larger share of the costs of the common defense, thus lifting some of the financial burden from the shoulders of the United States. I think both goals are advantageous, and, in fact, are interrelated. Only if the United States remains economically strong can we hope to negotiate successfully at the MBFR talks. (51)

Significantly, Senator Mansfield supported the Jackson amendment because it was "not at all inconsistent with the efforts to remove substantial US troops from Europe." (52) With Mansfield's support, the Senate approved the amendment by a vote of 84 to 5. (53)

The following day was an historic one in the saga of Mansfield's attempt to secure unilateral US force reductions in Europe. For a brief space of five hours Mansfield savored the fruits of victory. His amendment to an earlier troop reduction amendment of Senator Cranston was unexpectedly passed by the Senate. (54)

While basically still aiming his reduction proposal against Europe, Mansfield had, in an attempt to gain support for his proposal, broadened its scope from Europe to worldwide. He was now asking for a 50 percent reduction in the number of land-based military forces stationed overseas by 30 June 1976, with 25 percent of the total reduction required to be completed by 1 July 1974, and 50 percent by 1 July 1975. (55)

In opposition to the Mansfield amendment, Senators Tower, Thurmond, and Scott warned that if the amendment became law it would kill the MBFR talks. Surprisingly, Senator Kennedy, normally an advocate of troop reductions, spoke out against the Mansfield amendment. Supporting the upcoming MBFR talks, Kennedy stated:

> I strongly believe that we in Congress must give these talks a chance to succeed by not legislating a reduction in US forces deployed abroad, affecting the NATO Alliance, immediately before these talks begin. (56)

Despite the strong Administration pressure to defeat the amendment, it unexpectedly passed, supported by senators who, while long opposing Mansfield's amendment when it was aimed strictly at NATO, found the broader scope of reductions more acceptable. Continuing resentment toward European Allies' failure to share more defense costs and the desire to reduce government defense spending also played key roles in its passage by a vote of 49 to 46. (57)

Immediately after passage of the amendment, the shocked Administration organized a counterattack to reverse the vote. High Administration officials telephoned key senators. Even General Goodpaster, Supreme Allied Commander, Europe, called senators from Belgium. The Administration was eager to kill the amendment in a Senate vote as soon as possible, even though the amendment would have been dropped in a later Senate House Conference, because they saw the vote as a symbolic signal of a changing Senate attitude toward unilateral troop reductions. (58)

In the end, the Administration was successful and won the revote by a margin of 51 to 44. (59) Four senators were persuaded to change their vote by the Administration, and two senators who had been absent from the first vote also voted for the Administration. One of the senators who switched his vote, Senator Aiken, stated that he voted for Mansfield the first time "as an indicator of my feelings toward European countries bearing a little more of the costs." But then he changed, he said, because after throwing a scare into the White House on the first vote, the Senate should withhold precipitous action until MBFR talks were concluded. (60)

The next day, 27 September, Senator Humphrey introduced another troop reduction amendment which called for a reduction of 125,000 personnel stationed overseas to be completed not later than 30 June 1975, with not less than 30,000 of this total withdrawn by 30 June 1974. Senator Humphrey underscored that his amendment was not designed to weaken NATO: "The purpose of this amendment is surely not in any way to weaken our position in upcoming negotiations with the Soviet Union on mutual balanced force reductions." (61) Humphrey envisioned that the reductions would come primarily from the Pacific areas. During extensive debate the total to be reduced was dropped to 110,000 and the amendment was passed by an overwhelming vote of 73 to 14. (62) Many Republican senators joined in supporting the amendment despite President Nixon's warning that any troop reduction measures approved by the Senate would harm the US position at the forthcoming MBFR talks. (63)

Despite the protestations from all concerned that no one wanted to harm the US position at the MBFR talks, and the narrow defeat of the Mansfield amendment in the Senate and the Pike, Dellums, and other proposals in the House, events in the summer/fall of 1973 clearly showed the NATO Allies, and more importantly the East, that the Administration would enter the MBFR negotiations with a congressional gun at its back to show results or face unilateral force cuts. West Europeans, fearing a US sellout, had looked upon such a prospect with alarm. The East, no doubt, would be hoping that it would cause the West to agree quickly to a political type of agreement consisting only of symmetrical reductions; such an agreement would retain the Eastern advantage in active duty manpower in Central Europe.

Looking back over all of the congressional maneuvering, one finds it ironic that neither side, especially the Mansfield camp, recognized that if the Soviets truly wanted the United States out of Europe on the scale advocated by Mansfield, they would not have let even CSCE stand in the way of such an opportunity. It seemed to have passed unnoticed in Congress that the Soviets just might be in MBFR to a large degree because they were fearful of the possible effects of a massive US withdrawal on stability in Central Europe.

4 The Initial Proposals and the Forces in Question

The formal talks on the subject of MBFR began on 30 October 1973 in Vienna, Austria. The first meeting was held in the Kongresshaus (1) on the Margareten Gurtel in Vienna's Fifth District about mid-distance between the heart of Vienna and the famous summer palace of the Hapsburgs, Schonbrunn. The hall itself was "German modern," a cold, cement structure built after World War II and starkly furnished. The delegates sat uncomfortably on folding metal chairs around a green felt-covered doughnut-shaped table with a live potted green plant placed squarely in its middle. (2) Considering the numerous majestic buildings available in Vienna, the delegates couldn't help but wonder what importance the Austrians gave to this 19-nation conference of the most heavily armed countries in the world. The conference was opened with a three-minute welcoming speech by the Austrian foreign minister and later president, Rudolph Kirchschlager. (3)

Following Kirchschlager's brief welcome, the participants, both "direct" and "special," spoke in alphabetical order beginning with Belgium. On the first day those speaking besides Belgium were Bulgaria, Canada, East Germany, the Netherlands, Norway, Luxemburg, Italy, and Romania. (4)

The speeches were short and pro forma with only the Belgian ambassador, Adriaenssen, making any note of the then ongoing high tension between the United States and the Soviet Union over the situation in the Middle East when he spoke of the primary responsibility of the two superpowers in seeking stability and a solution to the problem of force reductions. (5)

Speaking on the second day, October 31, were Turkey, the United Kingdom, the Soviet Union, and the United States. It was incumbent on each of the two superpowers to make the major speech for its side regarding the respective East/West positions concerning the talks. What they said, however, was not expected to be of much surprise, as the basic positions of both East and West had been articulated openly earlier in the fall. The Western position had been used to help defeat

the Mansfield drive in Congress to cut unilaterally US forces in Europe
on the eve of the talks.

The press was reporting that the United States would be prepared to
pull out some 30,000 troops in return for the withdrawal of some 68,000
Soviets; this would be followed with a second stage of additional
reductions, which would consist of reductions of indigenous European
forces down to a common manpower ceiling. The leaking of those
aspects of the Western position angered the Europeans who cautioned
that, while they understood the American problem of unilateral
withdrawals, there would be no agreement if the United States moved
too hastily. Another Western diplomat was quoted as saying, "Salving
the American Congress is still an important element, but it is hard to
see what can reasonably be achieved from some token Soviet withdrawals." (6) Clearly, the Western Europeans were going to be keeping
the same close watch on the Americans in the months to come as they
had done in the preliminary talks.

The Union of Soviet Socialist Republic's ambassador, O.G. Khlestov,
spoke immediately after a short speech by the Turkish ambassador,
Turrel. Khlestov's speech mirrored that of Secretary Brezhnev to the
World Conference of Peace Forces, a Communist-front organization
which had met in Moscow on 26 October 1973. (7) At the conference
Brezhnev said the following about MBFR:

> We hope and believe that the political basis worked out by the
> general European conference and all-sided and peaceful cooperation
> will be complemented and strengthened by measures for military
> relaxation of tension on the continent. It is to this end, as you know,
> that the talks which start in Vienna in five days' time will be
> devoted. These talks are a matter of great importance for Europe
> and for the whole situation in the world.
>
> The Soviet Union is approaching them most seriously and
> responsibly; it approaches them in a constructive and realistic
> manner. Our position is clear and understandable. We consider it
> necessary to agree on the reduction in a defined region of central
> Europe of both foreign and national and air forces of the countries
> participating in the negotiations. From our point of view it is
> important that the future reduction not disturb the existing balance
> of power in central Europe and in the European continent in general.
> If this principle is disturbed, the whole question will become a bone
> of contention and an object of unending disputes.
>
> How soon will it be possible to start the actual reduction of
> armed forces and armaments? This is also something that has to be
> agreed upon in Vienna. The Soviet Union would be ready for
> realistic steps in this area as early as 1973. In the early future it
> might be possible to conclude concrete agreements on this. Such an
> agreement would undoubtedly be a new, big step toward improving
> also the political atmosphere in Europe. It would help confirm on
> this continent an atmosphere of trust, goodwill and peaceful

cooperation. As you know, we have repeatedly said that detente and development of international cooperation cannot be the privilege of any one limited area of the globe. (8)

Speaking for the United States was Representative Ambassador Stanley R. Resor, who had been appointed to the position on 8 October. The head of the US Delegation to the preliminary talks, Mr. Jonathan Dean, of the State Department, was appointed as his deputy. From 1965 to 1971, Mr. Resor had served as Secretary of the Army, but had been in private law practice until his appointment to the MBFR talks. (9)

Ambassador Resor's speech was a major one taking over twenty minutes to give. In the Allied approach expressed by Ambassador Resor, there were significant differences in the approach to MBFR when compared with the Soviet proposal outlined by Brezhnev and Khlestov. He spoke of the great challenge awaiting the delegation in trying to find ways to reduce the large concentration of military power in Central Europe:

> We do not expect these talks to be easy. These negotiations represent a radical new departure in international diplomacy. There has been nothing quite like these before. Both in the subject matter they will address and in their pattern of participation they break new ground. (10)

"Our main tasks will be to achieve a more stable military balance at lower levels of forces with undiminished security for all participants at the talks," (11) added Resor, and then he went on to the heart of the Allied position when he stated that the West saw three disparities which existed in the agreed area of reductions. These were destabilizing to the security of Central Europe. There were disparities "in manpower, the character of the forces, and in geography." (12)   Concerning manpower, Ambassador Resor said:

> ...The countries of the Warsaw Pact have more ground personnel on active duty in central Europe than does NATO. We consider that to narrow and finally eliminate this disparity in manpower through mutual reductions would improve the stability in Central Europe.

> With respect to character of forces, the Warsaw Pact forces maintain a concentration of heavy armor in Central Europe.... It is an objective fact that a marked imbalance in tanks exists in Central Europe.... A substantial reduction in the armored capability of the USSR in Central Europe would...enhance stability in Europe.

> The geographic disparity has this consequence for mutual reduction: any Soviet forces withdrawn from Central Europe into the territory of the Soviet Union could return quickly and easily; US forces withdrawn to the United States would be an ocean away. (13)

The ultimate goal of these negotiations, said Resor, would be "approximate parity in the form of a common ceiling for the ground forces of each side in Central Europe." This goal would be achieved in more than one phase," he continued, "with the first phase consisting of US and Soviet ground force reductions."

The last main point made by Ambassador Resor was that reductions alone would not result in greater stability. Other measures were also needed. "These would include stabilizing measures, verification measures, and noncircumventing provisions." (14)

Thus, with the conference only two days old, the lines were drawn on positions which clearly differed, thus making very plausible the prediction of some of the participants that it would probably be years before any substantial results were achieved. (15) The key differences were: the equal reductions proposal of the Soviets against the asymmetrical reductions of the West; the demand by the East that air forces and nuclear forces in addition to ground forces be reduced; the two-stage negotiations envisioned by the West against the one-stage negotiations, with several reduction phases to follow as proffered by the East; and finally the problem of how to equalize the fact that the Soviets would only withdraw about 1,000 kilometers back to Western Russia, while the US forces would have to be withdrawn some 10,000 kilometers across the Atlantic. (16)

All these problems, plus the West's desire to include "Associated Measures" (open verification, pre-announcement of maneuvers, and other measures which the East looked upon as nothing more than an excuse for spying), would have to be discussed. Ways would have to be found to move East and West together onto some common ground that would be mutually acceptable.

Each side would have to be satisfied that its perception of the concept of undiminished security would not be violated. Everything pointed to a long and arduous road that would require many years of dialogue and much patience if a meaningful treaty was to be hammered out.

The talks were scarcely a week old when the East formally presented a proposal detailing the concept outlined by Secretary General Brezhnev at the World Conference of Peace Forces and by the speech of Soviet Ambassador Khlestov on 31 October. On 8 November, the anniversary of the Bolshevik takeover of Russia in 1917, the second plenary of the talks was held at the Kongresshaus. The delegations had barely settled themselves uncomfortably on their steel folding chairs when Ambassador Khlestov asked for the floor and presented the Eastern proposal. (17)

It was not long before the Western press got wind of the Soviet proposal, but details were slow in leaking out because of the promise on both sides to keep the talks confidential. On 16 November 1973 the Baltimore Sun's correspondent, Gene Oishi, reported from Bonn that the Soviet proposal "was in line with a policy speech given by Leonid I. Brezhnev, Soviet Community Party Chief in Moscow, on October 26, and was an 'elaboration' of the Brezhnev guidelines." (18) Oishi went on to report that "the Soviet plan calls for each side reducing its forces by 5 percent and by another 15 percent in 1977." (19) A report by Richard Homan of the Washington Post on 18 November revealed that details of the Soviet proposal had been deliberately leaked by the Soviets to the Western press. (20)

The most specific report of the Soviet proposal to come out in the days shortly after 8 November was a Reuters story of 19 November which added the information that the three-stage proposal would encompass nuclear and air force units as well as ground forces. The report went on to add that "Russia, speaking for the main Warsaw Pact nations, wants the cuts to be proportional according to the size of national and stationed forces in Central Europe." (21) The Reuters dispatch revealed the significant Soviet position that the indigenous forces selected for reduction must be demobilized while the forces of the United States, United Kingdom, Canada, and the Soviet Union that were selected for reduction would simply withdraw. (22) The Reuters report added that the reduction would be taken by units rather than by thinning out of existing units, and that these units would be expected to withdraw with all their weapons and equipment. (23) In the Eastern press there was no mention of the proposal until 2 December when Pravda, accusing the West of leaking the plan, outlined it essentially as the Western press had previously reported. (24)

Caught by surprise at the Eastern proposal, the West hurriedly advanced its own proposal two weeks later on 22 November. Reuters reported that the Western plan was in two phases. The first phase was a cut in Soviet and US manpower followed by a second phase of indigenous manpower cuts down to a common ceiling of 700,000 ground force personnel on each side. (25) Based on Western estimates of the size of Warsaw Pact ground forces, this would mean the East would be taking considerably more reductions than the West. It was also reported that the West had presented an estimate of NATO and Warsaw Pact ground force manpower and main battle tanks assigned to active units. According to the Western count, NATO had 777,000 active duty ground force personnel in the agreed area of reduction facing 925,000 active duty Warsaw Pact ground force soldiers; of these 193,000 were American and 460,000 were Russian, respectively. NATO was out-numbered in main battle tanks in active units: 6,000 NATO tanks versus 15,500 for the Warsaw Pact. (26)

Once Ambassador Resor had presented the Western proposal on 23 November, the Eastern press began to be increasingly critical of the Western two-phase approach while at the same time extolling the virtues of the Eastern approach. The Tass-attributed report in Pravda of 2 December observed that in the West's two-stage plan the first stage called for a reduction of US and Soviet ground troops only, but the content of the second stage had not been revealed. (27) This remark was obviously related to Soviet concern about the fact there were no clear-cut guarantees that the Bundeswehr would be reduced under the West's plan. In this article and others in the same time frame, the East concentrated criticism on the sparseness of details on the Western second-phase reduction.

Once the contents of the Soviet reduction proposal became known, Moscow's treatment of the proposal went from acknowledgement of the details to specific comparisons of the Soviet plan with that of the West. In a Radio Moscow broadcast of 5 December 1973, Vladimir Komlev stated:

> The Western states' plan aims primarily at restricting the reduction in the armed forces to ground troops alone and at extending it in the first stage only to the armies of the Soviet Union and the United States. In this connection the Soviet Union is supposed to withdraw nearly two and one-half times more troops than the United States from the area in which the armed forces will be reduced. This by itself imposes the conclusion that the Western states want to gain substantial one-sided military advantages at the expense of the Socialist states. This conclusion is even more obvious in the light of Western proposals that the reduction of the troops of the other Western European states should be postponed indefinitely. According to these proposals, NATO's most numerous armed forces, including the West German Bundeswehr which has 500,000 men would not be reduced. As is well known the armed forces of the FRG account for nearly 50 percent of NATO's troops in Central Europe. (28)

This would be the first of many indications over the years of the Eastern desire to see the Bundeswehr reduced and limited.

The most detailed description of the Eastern proposal to that time was made public by the Soviets on 14 December 1973 in Novoye Vremya and is quoted here in its entirety to allow for an appreciation of the amount of detail of the Eastern proposal the Soviets were willing to reveal in the open press.

> The socialist countries propose that the reduction of armed forces and armaments in Central Europe take place in three stages. In the first stage, during 1975, the United States, Britain, Canada, the FRG, Belgium, Luxembourg and the Netherlands will reduce their troops by 20,000 men along with the corresponding arms and combat equipment. A similar reduction will be carried out at the same time by the USSR, the GDR, Poland and the CSSR.

> Of course, to a certain extent this would be a symbolic step. But it would be of important political and practical significance since it would clearly show the readiness of all the above states to embark on a real reduction of their armed forces and armaments in Central Europe and would promote the strengthening of natural trust. The implementation of such a reduction would also make it possible to gain certain experience and would prepare good ground for the implementation of bigger reductions in subsequent stages.

In the second stage, during 1976, it is proposed to reduce the armed forces and armaments of each of the states party to the agreement by five percent, and in the third stage, in 1977, by another ten percent.

As far as the procedures of the reduction of foreign and national armed forces and armaments is concerned, it is proposed in particular that it be effected on the basis of the approximate homogeneity and uniformity of the units being reduced by means of the withdrawal or disbandment of entire tank and motorized infantry formations (divisions and brigades) and units (regiments and battalions), units of combat aviation (regiments, wings and squadrons), artillery, missile and antiaircraft missile units and support units (regiments and battalions) as well as units and subunits equipped with nuclear weapons.

The view is that the foreign troops subject to reduction be withdrawn to within the bounds of national borders together with all the armaments and combat equipment. Warehousing of armaments and combat equipment of the withdrawing foreign troops in the region of reduction is not allowed.

The units and formations of national troops being reduced should be disbanded with the simultaneous demobilization of personnel. The armaments and combat equipment of the troops being reduced are to be excluded from the combat strength of national armed forces.

The Soviet Union and the other socialist countries attach important significance to the absolute fulfillment by all sides of the pledges made by them. They proceed from the premise that control over the fulfillment of a future agreement can be fully insured with the aid of national facilities. It could also be provided for that the states party to the agreement officially inform each other of the start and completion of practical measures to reduce their own armed forces and armaments in Europe.

In addition to this, each party to the agreement could have an established right to ask about the implementation of bilateral or multilateral consultation between the interested sides and if need be demand that consultation be held between all the states party to the agreement for the purposes of insuring the implementation of the agreement.

It goes without saying that the states party to an agreement of the reduction of armed forces and armaments in Central Europe should not make any international pledges which contradict the provisions of such an agreement. (29)

The publication of the complete Eastern proposal indicated the East was more concerned with conducting a propaganda campaign to capture world opinion than to adhere to the agreed procedure that proposals and discussions be kept within the negotiating forum.

The article cited the "fairness" of the Eastern proposal when compared to the Western proposal, the latter being designed, according to the East, to exempt the FRG from reductions and to upset the existing correlation of forces in Central Europe. (30)

The two proposals, both Eastern and Western, were so far apart in their approach to the problem of arms control in Central Europe that it was quite apparent to the negotiators that no agreement could be obtained unless both sides could resolve the great differences between the two positions. The West saw the current active duty force ratio as destabilizing and wanted to change it, the East saw it as favorable to them and thus it was stabilizing and to be preserved. Thus, both sides began a process that continues today - the search for common ground.

THE FORCES IN QUESTION

No study of MBFR would be complete without a discussion of the balance of forces in Central Europe. In this case the discussion will be brief and will not undertake an analysis of the balance. Such an effort would be beyond the scope of this study, and as Eastern and Western statements have shown, there is no consensus on the balance. (31)

It is important to recognize that there is no such thing as the balance of forces in Central Europe. In fact, there are several balances depending upon what time frames, geographical areas, and subject forces are included. Most individuals, when referring to the balance, are in actuality referring to the capabilities of both sides to wage war. Most analyses of the balance are also done from this perspective and are primarily concerned with the abilities of the two sides to mobilize and fight a war in Central Europe.

While the active duty forces in the proposed area of MBFR reductions would be included in such analyses, many other factors are also included which are not in MBFR; for example, other military organizations such as navies, border guards, reserves, forces located outside the proposed area of reductions that would be injected during times of crises as well as the mobilization capability, logistics capability, etc., of the two alliances. From the viewpoint of the MBFR negotiations, the wartime balance is not the main concern. Rather, it is the balance between East and West peacetime active duty ground force strengths within the proposed area of reductions.

This difference tends to cause confusion when MBFR objectives are discussed in the context of their impact on the balance. The East insists that there is a balance of forces in Central Europe and continually cites prominent Western defense officials who seem to agree. On the other hand, the Western position in MBFR contends that there is a serious asymmetry of the balance in favor of the Warsaw Pact. Who is right? Both views are largely correct, if one realizes there is a difference between the balance for fighting a war in Central

Europe and the balance in active duty peacetime ground manpower stationed in the Benelux, FRG, GDR, Poland, and Czechoslovakia.

While most Western leaders deem the wartime balance adequate, this does not mean that it is a balance comfortably in NATO's favor. Indeed, it is not, and while it is generally agreed that NATO forces are strong enough to deter a Warsaw Pact attack, the force improvement program undertaken by the Soviets in Eastern Europe since the start of MBFR has caused the West to question whether such an attack could be defeated, hence, the Carter administration's efforts to strengthen NATO, both with additional US troops and equipment, as well as proposing the NATO Long Term Defense Program (LTDP) in May 1977.

The LTDP is designed to improve NATO's conventional forces, especially their capability to respond to an attack by standing Warsaw Pact forces after very little warning. (32) It is also recognition of the fact that, as a result of the massive Warsaw Pact force improvement program, the days of the clear-cut balance between better Western weaponry manned by high-caliber soldiers and backed up by a massive nuclear superiority opposing a numerically superior but technically inferior Warsaw Pact, are gone. A black and white situation has turned to grey as the technological gap closes with the introduction of newer, more sophisticated Soviet equipment.   There is definite cause to question the future of the balance, as the Soviets match Western forces in strike aircraft and clearly surpass them in ground-based air defense systems; there is also cause to question the future of the balance when the Soviets introduce a new mobile medium intermediate ballistic missile targeted against Western Europe; finally, there is cause for concern when the Soviet divisions and their East German counterparts increase their combat power and staying power to such a degree that, except for manpower, they approach the equal of US or FRG divisions. The deliberate and conscious effort by the East to close the technology gap is a clear sign that the Soviets are out to move the military balance in Central Europe more in their favor.

This is not to say the Soviets are attempting to tip the balance to the extent of believing they could successfully invade Western Europe. The military strength and the political will of Western Europe and the United States would have to deteriorate to a degree currently unimaginable before the Soviets would feel the risk of invasion was at an acceptable level.   As long as NATO maintains a military strength sufficient to deny Eastern chances for success in such a conflict, one could say that there is sufficient military balance in Central Europe to deter war.

The overall judgment of Western analysts is that the balance is such that any military aggression on the part of the East remains unattractive. The consequences for the Warsaw Pact of launching such an attack are incalculable.   If the Soviet Union decided to attack Western Europe, the Kremlin leaders would need to have an almost 100 percent assurance of success. If for any reason the attack bogged down into a stalemate or turned against the Soviets, the weakness of the relationship between the Soviet Union and its satellites would start the unraveling of the Soviet hold over Eastern Europe, an unraveling which could continue all the way back to Moscow. This is recognized by the Soviets, hence their caution on precipitating a situation in which an East/West conflict in Central Europe could start.

Manifestly then, Soviet objectives in the use of military forces in Central Europe are primarily for ends short of war and, while it is reasonably safe to assume that the strength of the West will remain sufficient to deter an actual invasion, the question then becomes: Will the strength of the West remain sufficient to give confidence to the parliaments and peoples of Western Europe to stand up to the political and ideological pressures placed on Western Europe by the Soviets, or will they feel, as a consequence of military weakness, the need to grant economic and political concessions to the East? The Soviets openly admit that detente is nothing more than peaceful coexistence, and peaceful coexistence is nothing more than conducting war against capitalism without resort to shooting. By building up its active forces strength on the borders of Western Europe, the Soviets accomplish two important objectives: first, they maintain their hegemony over the Eastern Europeans and maintain the division of Germany; and secondly, they create the image of a massive Communist force poised to unleash thousands of tanks, aircraft, nuclear weapons, and millions of men against the West should the West choose not to cooperate in maintaining the political status quo and supplying the East with the technology and products its own system is incapable of producing. The key factor for the Soviets in this strategy is the necessity of maintaining their peacetime ground force numerical superiority in Central Europe.

This is where MBFR can be helpful to the West by seeking improved early warning in the event of a crisis situation and a more benign posture for Warsaw Pact active forces through reduction to equality and residual limitations. But it must be kept in mind that MBFR is primarily not an attempt to change the wartime balance of forces. It can not do this because the MBFR charter only allows it to address active duty manpower and equipment in a peacetime configuration and environment.

The West, through a large-scale reduction of Eastern active duty forces, wants to (a) increase the tactical warning time for NATO in the event of a Warsaw Pact attack and (b) reduce the power projection capability of the standing Warsaw Pact armies to intimidate the West. On the other hand, the Eastern powers (i.e., the Soviets) are quite content with the existing ratio of active forces because they realize it is favorable to them and thus they wish the ratio to remain unchanged.

The facts are clear that the East holds a marked superiority to ground manpower, and this superiority is primarily due to the large number of Soviet ground forces stationed in the German Democratic Republic, Poland, and Czechoslovakia. A comparison of stationed versus indigenous ground force strengths of the West and East illustrates this effect:

Stationed Ground Forces		Indigenous Ground Forces	
West	East (i.e., Soviet)	West	East
254,000	475,000	477,000	487,000

As the table shows, NATO and Pact indigenous force strengths are nearly equal. Thus, the preponderance of Soviet forces is clearly the causative factor for the large disparity of ground manpower in the proposed area of reductions.

Ironically, the ground forces today would be close to parity if the Soviets had not chosen to leave a large force in Czechoslovakia after the 1968 invasion. A Soviet Group of Forces of some five divisions and 70,000 men was not withdrawn with the rest of the invaders after Soviet authority had been restored. (33)

That was the last major increase in Soviet strength in Eastern Europe. This is not to say that there have not been gradual increases in manpower in the area since that time, partly due to more sophisticated Western perceptions of Soviet military power and to internal reorganizations in Soviet military power and to internal reorganizations in Soviet tank and motorized divisions. (34) With the intense force improvement that has been going on within the Warsaw Pact, chiefly with enlargement of Soviet and East German divisions, expansion of tank units, and introduction of more sophisticated air defense and artillery equipment, an increase in strength of that magnitude would be considered quite minimal.

The Soviets frequently claim, somewhat mystically, that the existing correlation of forces has been historically developed over the years since World War II and has kept the peace since that time, and that "there must not be an alteration of the correlation of forces that has historically taken shape in Central Europe, because any attempt to alter it in favor of one of the sides would undermine the very basis of the talks." (35) The Soviets have been absolutely adamant in MBFR that the current correlation of forces, i.e., balance, in Central Europe must remain unchanged, and they vigorously attack the West's call for asymmetrical reductions as a device to upset the force ratio in favor of the West.

Brezhnev's speech to the World Conference of Peace Forces on 26 October 1973 was prophetic when he warned:

> ...it is very important that future reductions not disturb the existing balance of power in Central Europe and on the European continent in general. If this principle is disturbed the whole question will become a bone of contention and an object of unending dispute.... (36)

It was not only the West which realized that the East had superiority in manpower and tanks in Central Europe but their own Socialist brothers as well. In 1973 the following statement appeared in the Albanian press when it was still reflecting the Chinese viewpoint: (37)

> The Soviet social imperialists availing themselves of the actual superiority in men and materials want the troop and armament reductions in Central Europe to be carried out in equal percentage and equal quantity. In this way they would ensure a superior military position in Central Europe. (38)

In sum, it should be kept in mind that the question of the balance of forces and the MBFR negotiations are not synonomous - that MBFR only addresses certain segments, albeit critical ones, of what makes up the wartime balance of forces in Central Europe. Rather, it is the peacetime balance of active duty forces which is of concern to MBFR. Western spokesmen are not talking out of both sides of their mouths when they claim there is a rough balance of forces in Central Europe, while at the same time citing the large asymmetry existing in favor of the Warsaw Pact in active duty ground manpower.

5 Analysis of the Reduction Proposals

In order to analyze the Eastern and Western proposals, a data base is required. But there is yet no agreed East/West data base for MBFR. In fact, the problem of data has been the single most controversial aspect of the whole negotiation. Subsequently in this study the causes, controversies, and possible solutions to the data problem will be discussed. Nevertheless, some of the main points need to be sketched out at this time in order to explain the data used in the following analysis.

In essence, the East does not accept the Western estimates of Eastern forces, and the West does not accept Eastern force strengths tabled in Vienna. There appears to be no argument on the strengths of Western forces. Some of the numbers tabled in Vienna have been made public, and some can be deduced while others cannot. This creates gaps which, for purposes of analysis, must be filled by unofficial data on the forces in question.

The following analysis will use a combination of both official and unofficial data. Whenever possible, official figures advanced in Vienna by both East and West will be used. However, not all of the relevant data have been made public. Consequently, when additional data are required, other sources such as the International Institute for Strategic Studies' estimates of the forces in Central Europe will be used.

EASTERN PROPOSAL OF 1973 (1)

The original Eastern proposal tabled on 8 November 1973 was described in detail in the 14 December 1973 Novoye Vremya, as quoted in chapter 4 (page 54). It is briefly reviewed here to serve as a starting point.

The East proposed that the negotiations take place in one phase; that is, all necessary agreements concerning who would reduce and how much would be concluded before the first reduction took place. Then reductions would take place in three stages.

The original Eastern proposal called for the reduction of 20,000 ground and air personnel by all direct participants in 1975. That is, every direct participant would agree to contribute some personnel to make up the 20,000 total on each side.

The second stage, to have been conducted in 1976, was to see a further 5 percent reduction in the ground and air manpower of all direct participants, to be followed by a third stage in 1977 of another 10 percent. Altogether, the East called for symmetrical equal percentage reductions of approximately 17 percent to be taken in units of like type, e.g., infantry units of like size, tank regiments and battalions, aviation units such as wings or squadrons, artillery units, and support units, as well as units equipped with nuclear weapons. Stationed forces would be withdrawn and (in a direct slap at the US policy of storing in Germany equipment for units based in the United States) the withdrawing units would be forbidden to leave their equipment behind. Of even greater significance was the demand that all indigenous forces tabbed for reduction be totally demobilized and their equipment put in storage.

In March of 1975, the East modified its position on the proposed first stage in order, as the Soviet press stated, to "take the Western position into account." (2) At that time the Soviets proposed that Stage I be split into two equal six-month periods. The first six months would see a reduction of 10,000 Soviet and US personnel each, along with their arms and equipment. In the second six months, a reduction of 5,000 Polish and West German ground and air personnel would take place, along with an additional 5,000 personnel made up of units contributed by the Netherlands, Belgium, Luxemburg, Canada, and the United Kingdom on the West, and 5,000 personnel from the GDR and Czechoslovakia. (3)

No data were advanced by the East in support of their proposal because the Soviet Union had always been extremely reluctant to release information on Soviet armed forces, especially strength or order of battle figures. Lack of data also lent credibility to the thesis that the East viewed the reductions as essentially a political exercise designed to enhance detente and maintain the status quo in the "correlation of forces" which favored the East. (4)

On the other hand, it did not require a detailed computation to recognize that a 17 percent across-the-board percentage, when applied to reductions, would create (because of its relatively short time span of three years) considerable turmoil and even destabilization. This flew in the face of the announced Soviet goal of maintaining the status quo and led the West to question the intention of the East to carry out all three stages of its proposal.

West	Total Strengths (5)	East
777,000	Ground	925,000
193,000	Air	200,000
970,000	Total	1,125,000

Applying the 17 percent reduction ratio to the above totals yields the amount of reduction each alliance would have had to make under the 1973 Eastern proposal using Western data.

	Stage I	Stage II [6] (5%)	Stage III (10%)	Total
NATO [7]	20,000	48,500	97,000	165,500
Pact [8]	20,000	56,250	112,500	188,750

Thus, remaining ground and air forces after reduction (rounded) would be:

NATO	805,000	Warsaw Pact	936,000

To demonstrate the impact of the proposal on individual direct participants, and because only a few national strengths have been publicly released, it was necessary to supplement official figures with data from the Military Balance (9) to arrive at the following base strengths:

NATO DIRECT PARTICIPANTS AND FRANCE

	Ground	Air	Total
US	193,000	35,000	228,000
UK	58,000	9,000	67,000
CAN	3,000	2,000	5,000
BEL	62,000	19,000	81,000
NETH	75,000	21,000	96,000
FRG	341,000	117,000	458,000
FRANCE	60,000	0	60,000

WARSAW PACT DIRECT PARTICIPANTS

	Ground	Air	Total
USSR	475,000	60,000	535,000
GDR	105,000	36,000	141,000
POL	220,000	62,000	282,000
CZECH	135,000	46,000	181,000

Applying the reduction percentage to each nation's forces demonstrates the impact of the 1973 proposal on each direct participant.

NATO REDUCTIONS*

	Stage I	Stage II	Stage III	Total
US	10,000	11,400	22,800	44,200
UK	1,350	3,350	6,700	11,400
CAN	100	250	500	850
BEL	1,650	4,050	8,100	13,800
NETH	1,900	4,800	9,600	16,300
FRG	5,000	22,900	45,800	73,700

* NATO reductions were adjusted as necessary to compensate for reductions not taken by France.

WARSAW PACT REDUCTIONS

	Stage I	Stage II	Stage III	Total
USSR	10,000	26,750	53,500	90,250
GDR	2,200	7,050	14,100	23,350
POL	5,000	14,100	28,200	47,300
CZECH	2,800	9,050	18,100	29,950

The total reductions show that - as expected with an equal percentage reduction - the nations which have the largest standing forces take the numerically greater cuts.

MAGNITUDE OF NATIONAL REDUCTIONS

UNDER 1973 EASTERN PROPOSAL

NATO		Warsaw Pact	
FRG	73,700	USSR	90,250
US	44,200	POLAND	47,300
NETH	16,300	CZECH	29,950
BEL	13,800	GDR	23,350
UK	11,400		
CAN	850		

The above also illustrates the fact that the nations which play the key roles in the military equation in Central Europe - the United States, West Germany, and the Soviet Union - together would contribute close to 60 percent (208,150) of the total reduced forces. Despite Eastern claims that symmetrical reductions would not be destabilizing, the withdrawal or demobilization of over 200,000 of the best troops in Central Europe, not to mention the total reduction of 354,000 within a three-year period, would certainly have to be classified as a very real risk to stability, and raises the question of just how serious the East would have been in carrying through all three stages of its 1973 proposal.

The Soviet reduction, although surprisingly large, would have had less impact on Eastern security than the US and FRG reductions on Western security. The Soviet forces would simply have been withdrawn some 1,000 kilometers eastward to the western Soviet Union. In the case of the United States, some 46,000 US soldiers, or 20 percent of the US forces, would have been required to be withdrawn with all of their equipment some 10,000 kilometers back to the continental United States. This would represent a much greater problem for the United States than the Soviet Union if either side wanted to reintroduce these forces in time of crisis. This asymmetry has become known in MBFR parlance as the "geographical disparity" issue.

But the greatest impact would have been on the forces of the Federal Republic of Germany. As an indigenous nation, the FRG would have been required to completely demobilize the 74,000 soldiers being reduced. With the vast majority of the FRG active duty forces being combat forces, a 74,000-man cut would have resulted in a severe cut of

NATO's conventional force strength.

Of course, the initial Eastern proposal supported the goals of the Soviet Union in Central Europe. The insistence on taking symmetrical reductions across the board strongly supported the thesis often implied by the Soviet Union that it was content with, and wished the retention of, the balance of forces in Central Europe. By taking symmetrical percentage reductions the various force ratios which contribute to the "correlation of forces," as the Soviets call it, remain the same. Of particular concern to the Soviets is the ratio between East and West. To the Soviets, stability comes through having primacy in strength. They feel the balance is favorable to them from the standpoint of maintaining the status quo in Central Europe and influencing events in that area. Thus, they are emphatic that the status quo be preserved and violently attack the West as seeking to upset the existing "correlation of forces" in Central Europe which, of course, is exactly what the West wants to do. (10)

Besides maintaining the status quo, the Soviets wished to take the opportunity to further their long-standing goals of reducing the armed forces of West Germany; to secure limitations and a voice in the future of the Bundeswehr and, for that matter, all of NATO. The FRG forces comprise roughly 45 percent of NATO's strength. This factor, coupled with the historic fear of the Germans, makes reduction of the Bundeswehr an important and logical goal of the Soviets. (11)

THE EASTERN PROPOSAL OF FEBRUARY 1976

On 19 February 1976 Reuters reported from Vienna that the Soviets had introduced a new initiative at the 94th Plenary Session. Quoting a Soviet spokesman, the proposal "combined in a constructive manner principles and ideas embodied in previous proposals by Warsaw Treaty countries with certain elements of the Western proposal." (12) The article further quoted diplomats' statements that the Warsaw Pact seemed anxious to make its proposals before the Soviet Communist Party opened its 25th Congress the following week, when Brezhnev would deliver a keynote speech on Soviet policies. (13)

On 16 December 1975 the West made its first substantial change to its reduction proposal of 22 November 1973. It tabled a proposal which included aircraft and nuclear systems, two forces the East had insisted on including in the reductions from the beginning. The nuclear offer consisted of a one-time reduction of US tactical nuclear capability in Central Europe. As reported in the Frankfurt Allegemeine on February 14, 1976, the reduction would consist of 1,000 nuclear warheads, 54 F-4 nuclear capable fighter-bombers, and 36 Pershing surface-to-surface tactical nuclear missile launchers. (14)

The purpose of the Western initiative was to add weight to its original offer to withdraw 29,000 US soldiers in exchange for the withdrawal ofa Soviet tank army consisting of 68,000 troops and 1,700 tanks. The 1,000 nuclear warheads of unspecified type would be withdrawn from the approximate 7,000 maintained in Western Europe. The initial Eastern reaction to the Western proposal was to label it "inadequate" because it did not contain Allied, especially West German, nuclear launchers. Nevertheless, the offer proved to be sufficiently attractive to the East to incorporate in their 1976 proposal.

As had been predicted, Brezhnev did say something about MBFR. In his speech on 24 February 1976 to the assembled Party faithful, he stated:

> Political detente needs to be supplemented by military detente. The peace program (15) advanced the clear aim: to reduce armed forces and armaments in Central Europe. Talks on this question have been going on in Vienna for more than two years. However, no tangible progress has been made. The sole reason for this is that the NATO countries still do not want to stop trying to use the talks to insure for themselves unilateral military advantages.
>
> Striving to shift the matter from this stalemate, the socialist states recently submitted new proposals in Vienna. We are prepared to begin with reducing this year the troops of the USSR and the United States only and to leave the level of the armed forces of other participants in the talks "frozen" for the time being. They would then be reduced during the second stage in 1977-78. We have also submitted concrete proposals on the reduction by both sides of the number of tanks, aircraft capable of carrying nuclear weapons, and rocket launchers, together with a certain quantity of nuclear ammunition for these carriers.
>
> We build our proposals on a solely realistic basis - to preserve in Central Europe the prevailing balance of forces, an equilibrium in fact. It is to be hoped that all this will find an appropriate response in Western Countries so that it will be possible to go over at last from discussions to taking concrete measures for the reduction of armed forces and armaments. (16)

After Brezhnev's announcement, the Eastern press began an orchestrated release of some details of the new proposal. Significantly, articles and broadcasts all referred to the East having incorporated "considerations and concepts of the NATO countries." (17) More specifically, the Polish press release implied the East considered and adopted portions of the Western nuclear initiative in the new proposal.

The proposal lists concrete figures and spells out in detail the Soviet readiness to reduce the potential of the strategic nuclear weapons from the very beginning of the negotiations. To begin with, the Soviet Union would be prepared to reduce a certain number of warheads and their carriers, namely 54 bombers and a definite number of medium-range, ground-to-ground missiles. This proposal, combined with the reduction of the same percentages of Soviet and American armed forces and armaments in Central Europe, accords with the general desire of the European nations to lessen the dangerous stocks of nuclear weapons. (18)

A description of the new Eastern proposal was given by Vienna's <u>Die Presse</u> in its 28-29 February 1976 edition. <u>Die Presse</u> quoted Warsaw Pact spokesmen as saying that, in the first place, the United States and the Soviet Union would reduce their forces by 3 percent - approximately 30,000 Americans and 33,000 Soviets. The other direct participants would freeze their troop strengths at the 1976 level and accept a binding commitment to reduce in a second phase. In addition to reducing manpower, both the Soviet Union and the United States would reduce two to three tank regiments with 200-300 tanks. Fifty-four nuclear weapon carriers, as well as nuclear warheads and rocket launchers, would also be withdrawn. The article also pointed out the East's intention to reduce the armed forces of both sides by 15 percent by the end of 1978. (19)

The East was obviously incorporating elements of the Western position into their new proposal. In addition to adopting the element on nuclear weapons, an East German report stated that the "plan makes an important concession to the basic element of the Western two-phase plan by accepting that in the first phase only Soviet and American armed forces and arms be reduced." (20)

A significant point of the new proposal was brought to light in a Polish press article of 5 March which reviewed the proposal and disclosed that the withdrawing US and Soviet units would be "disbanded after returning to their homelands." (21)

Disbanding withdrawn US and Soviet forces appeared to be a Soviet concession to the NATO flank countries (Norway, Greece, and Turkey), which had expressed the fear that Soviet forces withdrawn from Central Europe would be repositioned opposite their countries. Such a concern of the flank countries was, and still is, somewhat unrealistic. A glance at any unclassified Soviet troop list shows they have more than enough forces opposite the NATO flanks. Furthermore, it is only logical that the Soviets would want to retain the withdrawn forces in the western Soviet Union, where they could be quickly returned to Central Europe in a crisis situation. Announcing only that the units would be disbanded would allow the Soviets to play a shell game with the personnel. The units could be inactivated, then the personnel could be assigned to existing understrength units, which would then be brought to full strength to replace the disbanded units. On the other hand, such a shell game would be difficult for the United States to attempt. Once the units were deactivated, budget considerations would make it difficult to create new units to replace them. Thus, the offer to disband units was a clever propaganda move on the part of the East.

The most complete description of the 1976 Eastern proposal was given in an article in the 22 May 1976 edition of <u>Die Welt</u>. (22) Quoting a secret Federal Defense Ministry study which purportedly had analyzed the plan, the article made the following points:

● The Soviets and the United States would reduce their ground and air forces by 2 to 3 percent of the total strengths of NATO and the Warsaw Pact.

- Both sides would reduce 300 tanks.

- 54 nuclear-capable aircraft would be withdrawn. The United States would withdraw F-4 fighter-bombers and the Soviets, Fitter fighter-bombers.

- The same number of tactical surface-to-surface missile launchers of the US Pershing and Soviet SCUD B type would be withdrawn.

- Nuclear warheads of an undetermined number would be withdrawn.

- 36 surface-to-air missile launchers of the Nike-Hercules and Soviet SAM-2 would be withdrawn.

- Both sides would remove an army corps headquarters with combat support and supply units.

- Reductions would be carried out in units.

- US and Soviet forces would withdraw to their homelands where they would be disbanded.

- The remaining direct participants would agree to freeze their forces at their 1976 level and make a binding commitment to reduce by 15 percent in 1977-1978.

The most eye-catching aspects of the 1976 proposal were the incorporation of the US offer to withdraw certain elements of its nuclear arsenal in Central Europe and a Soviet offer to match it. Whether or not these were concessions can be debated. (23)

The new proposal also showed more Eastern sensitivity to the size of the US manpower withdrawal. Such accommodation seemed out of character for the Soviets, except for the fact that one of the reasons the Soviets came into MBFR was to insure at least for the mid-term the American presence in Western Europe. Dropping their reduction percentage from 17 percent to 15 percent brought the actual reduction of US ground forces down to the size identical to that volunteered by the United States under the 1973 Western Proposal - 29,000. The actual withdrawal would have been slightly higher - some 34,000 - because the Eastern proposal still contained the demand to reduce air forces, and a 15 percent reduction of the 35,000 US airman stationed in Central Europe would have added 5,000 to the ground withdrawal, (24) an increased reduction the United States did not wish to take.

While showing consideration for the size of the US ground reduction, the 15 percent reduction naturally allowed the Soviets to reduce the size of their withdrawal. In retrospect, it could be deduced that by February 1976 the East had already settled on the data base they were to table that June.

An Eastern official stated the size of the first-phase Soviet withdrawal would be "approximately" 33,000. The figure the East advanced in June 1976 for the Warsaw Pact ground and air personnel strength in the proposed area of reduction was 987,000; 33,000 is 3 percent of this figure. This coincides with the size of the first phase of the January 1976 proposal. Applying Western estimates of the Warsaw Pact strength of 1,162,000 to the 1976 Soviet proposal would have resulted in a slightly greater Soviet reduction of about 35,000. (25)

The East had not seen fit, however, to accommodate the West European desire to take only 10 percent reductions. In fact, the West Europeans would have had to take half again as many reductions as they thought prudent. Even though, in the new proposal, the East was only demanding a FRG reduction of 69,000 ground and air personnel - vice their 1973 proposal which demanded a ground/air reduction of 78,000 - the demand was considerably greater than a 10 percent reduction of 34,000 ground-only FRG personnel, which NATO felt was the maximum allowable.

The 1976 proposal also required a freeze of non-US NATO and non-Soviet Warsaw Pact forces at their present levels while the United States and Soviets were withdrawing the forces designated. In 1977-78, these remaining direct participants would reduce their forces by 15 percent and the United States and the Soviets would reduce an additional 12-13 percent. (26)

It was not made clear in any descriptions of the 1976 Eastern proposal whether the second stage would be split into two sub-stages, or that each country would have two years in which to take a 15 percent reduction. In agreeing to US and Soviet first stage reductions, the East made it plain that this was a significant concession, which must be accompanied by an ironclad guarantee by the West Europeans of their intentions to take reductions in the second stage.

The East demonstrated its concern in the following explanation of the second stage commitments it expected from the West:

> The envisioned commitments for the remaining nine participating states in the second stage are aimed at achieving an equivalent reductions contribution by all participants within a precisely defined period of time. The socialist states are proceeding from the premise that the reduction of all types of armed forces and arms must be equivalently continued in the second stage of the reductions. The reduction of the nuclear delivery vehicles and nuclear warheads must not remain a "one time action" and must not be confined only to the Soviet Union and the United States. The West European states including Great Britain and the FRG with together nearly 60 percent of the NATO forces in the reduction area, must not be able to evade this reduction. All participating states should bindingly accept, together with this reduction, a clear time limit, namely 1977-78 - so that their reduction cannot be postponed indefinitely. (27)

While the East was concessionary in its approach to US personnel withdrawals, it displayed a rigid symmetrical approach toward tank withdrawals. The withdrawal of 300 main battle tanks on each side introduced reciprocal arms reduction as a key element of the Eastern proposal. It did nothing, however, toward satisfying the Western desire to reduce the wide disparity between NATO's 6,700 tanks in units compared to the Pact's 16,200. (28)

A reduction of 300 US tanks would have represented only 4 percent of NATO tank strength in active units but over 15 percent of the US tank strength. (29)   This would have caused a considerably greater impact on the Western tank ratio than on the East, in that a Soviet 300-tank reduction would have resulted in only a 2 percent reduction in Soviet tank strength.

A US tank battalion consists of 54 tanks; hence, such a reduction would have resulted in the withdrawal of 5½ US tank battalions. In the case of the Soviets, who have 31 tanks in a tank battalion, (30) it would have required a withdrawal of over 9½ tank battalions or slightly over three tank regiments. If the Soviets had insisted on strict adherence to the proviso in their 1976 proposal to withdraw in complete units of battalion size, the United States would have had to withdraw 324 tanks (6 battalions), while the Soviets would have withdrawn 3 regiments plus 1 battalion for a total of 316 tanks. (31)

By proposing equal reductions of specific weapons systems, the East introduced an even stricter reduction concept than the 1973 proposal contained.   In that proposal the East envisioned equal percentage reductions, which would mean that those nations which had more of a given type of weapons system (e.g., tanks) would reduce proportionately more of that type of armament as part of the reduction of units. However, under the 1976 proposal, the United States and the Soviets would have specifically reduced equal numbers of tanks and certain nuclear weapons systems. Thus, the East would have gained further numerical superiority in these weapon systems than under their original proposal, because the United States would have had to reduce proportionally more than the Soviets.

The 1976 proposal also stipulated that both sides would withdraw an army corps headquarters with combat support and supply units. With the United States having only two corps headquarters in Europe, the V and VII, such a reduction would seriously impair the command and control of the Seventh Army's combat units. Published troop lists of the Soviet forces in the proposed area of reductions do not show a Soviet corps headquarters.   Perhaps the Soviets were referring to the withdrawal of one of their army headquarters in the Group of Soviet Forces in Germany (GSFG); however, this seems highly unlikely. Another possibility is the activation of a Soviet corps as a device to bring about the withdrawal of a US corps. The rationale behind focusing on the withdrawal of a US and Soviet corps, as opposed to other combat formations, has never been publicly explained by the East.

In summary, the Eastern negotiating position of February 1976 did not represent the substantive move toward Western positions that the East claimed. Even though the East accepted the Western position of a first phase consisting only of US and Soviet forces, they continued to insist, as they had since 1973, that before US and Soviet reductions could begin, the West Europeans must commit themselves to specific reductions in Stage II and freeze their forces in the interim.

The dropping of the reduction percentage to 15 percent could be viewed as a concession to the United States, in that it made the size of the US ground reduction demanded by the East coincide with the programmed US withdrawal. No such concession was made to the West Europeans who wanted to take a 10 percent reduction. But by scaling down their reduction percentage, it did indicate the East's flexibility on the size of reductions, and their interest in getting reductions started as a process rather than in the size of the reductions. Hence, one could conclude that residual limitations might be more important to the East than the reductions themselves.

In the case of weapons reductions, their 1976 proposal was even more hard-line than the 1973 proposal, by its insistence on numerically equal equipment reductions of the US and Soviet tanks and surface-to-air missile launchers. By their surprising offer to reduce nuclear weapons and warheads, the Soviets demonstrated, to an extent greater than they probably later found to be prudent, their eagerness and desire to set reductions and limitations of Allied nuclear systems.

But most significantly, the East made no changes in its basic MBFR objectives of equal percentage reductions, and did not show any movement toward the Western position of parity and collectivity, thus guaranteeing its rejection by the West.

THE EASTERN PROPOSAL OF JUNE 1978

On the 8th of June 1978 at the 172d Plenary Session, the Soviet Union, speaking for the East, tabled a new reduction proposal. (32) Hailed as "an important breakthrough," it was described as the first major move Moscow had made since the start of the negotiations. (33)

The first details of the proposal came from Moscow on 9 June in Pravda. In what appeared to be a major concession, the East announced acceptance of the Western position of parity - reductions to a common ceiling of 700,000 ground force personnel and a combined ground and air personnel ceiling of 900,000. (34)

Other elements of the proposal listed by Pravda included acceptance of the Western desire to limit reductions to ground force personnel, "to make a selective reduction and limitation of armaments of types that were named by the Western side," (35) and to limit first-stage reductions to the United States and Soviet Union only.

At first glance it would seem that the East had made fundamental changes in their negotiating position in an attempt to move the negotiations forward. But an examination of the details of the new proposal will demonstrate that changes in the Eastern position were not yet of a fundamental enough nature for it to be acceptable to the West.

Limiting first-stage reductions to US and Soviet forces was not a new concession. However, no longer insisting on Air Force reductions could be classed as a concession. On the other hand, the Soviets may have recognized, as the West had done earlier, the futility of any meaningful limitations on air forces, given the close proximity to

Central Europe of thousands of aircraft and the short flying times to get there. Furthermore, it must be remembered the Soviets have just completed a massive force improvement program of their forward-based tactical air forces, which considerably increased the capability of these air forces in both the air defense and ground attack roles, especially that of nuclear attack. Thus, they might have had second thoughts about having any of these aircraft withdrawn or limitations placed on those remaining.

A recognition of the Western viewpoint that requiring reductions and limitations on a multitude of weapon systems would overly complicate the negotiations probably contributed to the East further reducing the scope of armaments reductions and limitations from their February 1976 proposal. Another contributing factor was probably the belated realization that it would not be in the Soviets' best interest to accept reductions and limitations on their tactical nuclear forces.

By stating that they were willing to accept reductions and limitations of weapon systems "of the types that were named by the Western side" (this would be the Option III element--54 F-4's, 36 Pershing launchers, and 1,000 nuclear warheads, and on the Eastern side, 1,700 Soviet main battle tanks), the Soviets appeared to be making a concession to the West when, in reality, they were withdrawing an earlier offer to accept reductions. But not wanting to lose the opportunity to secure reductions and limitations on US and Allied nuclears, the East kept the Option III in their new proposal.

It should be remembered that the US nuclear offer was specifically conditional on the withdrawal of a Soviet tank army. Then, in April 1978, it was tied to a reduced Western demand to withdraw any five divisions, 1,700 tanks, and 68,000 troops. However, the Soviets refused to meet this scaled-down Western demand in the new Eastern proposal. Instead, they only offered to withdraw three Soviet divisions and 1,000 tanks. In what might appear to be a concession, the Soviets also volunteered to withdraw 250 infantry combat vehicles (BMP). (36) The 1,000 tanks and 250 infantry combat vehicles, however, simply approximate the number of tanks and BMP's found in a total of three Soviet tank divisions.

More details of the new proposal became known at the end of the Fifteenth Round in July 1978. It was reported at that time that the East had again reduced the reduction percentage it demanded, from 15 percent to 13-11 percent. The East would reduce its forces by 13 percent and the West by 11 percent. Soviet and US forces would reduce by 7 percent of these forces in the first stage. This would result by Eastern calculation in a reduction of 30,000 Soviet ground force personnel. (37) The United States would initially reduce 14,000 personnel. (38)

The most important aspect of the 1978 Eastern proposal, the one which undermines the basis for a real negotiation, was the Soviet caveat that the reductions could only be carried out if based on Eastern data.

In the original Pravda release, a statement was made that clearly signalled this fact:

These proposals from the Socialist countries retain the fundamentally important elements without which a truly effective and equal reduction of armed forces and armaments in Central Europe cannot be implemented. These include, above all, the recognition as a point of departure for reaching agreement, of the real fact that an approximately equal correlation with respect to numbers [emphasis added] has been formed and exists in the center of the continent between the Warsaw Pact and NATO countries. (39)

To guarantee no misunderstanding on this point, it was reiterated in Pravda on 27 June 1978:

The real basis for an agreement on troop reduction is recognition of the real fact that an equilibrium between the forces of NATO and Warsaw Pact...has now existed for many years...as of 1 January 1976 the Western States had 981,000 men...and the Socialist states had 987,300, while the ground forces totaled 791,000 and 805,000 respectively. (40)

The whole problem of data will be discussed in depth in Chapter 7. But briefly, what the Soviets had done was to table data on 10 June 1976 that were only slightly above those the West had tabled earlier of 981,000 Western ground/air active duty personnel. This ploy supported the Eastern contention that there was a numerical balance in Central Europe.

An application of the Eastern data to the proposal will illustrate that the 1978 Eastern proposal is nothing more than another iteration of the original proposal of November 1973, and that the basic objectives of the East remain - preservation of the status quo through symmetrical reductions, while securing reductions and placing a ceiling on the Bundeswehr.

As before, the most significant point of this latest Eastern proposal is continued refusal to change their position concerning asymmetrical reductions. In this proposal, as in their two previous, the concept of symmetrical reductions is based on their perception that the correlation of forces in Central Europe must be preserved. Time and again Eastern spokesmen have emphatically stated that under no circumstances will the East take asymmetrical reductions to the extent demanded by NATO.

When Western estimates of Warsaw Pact strength are applied to the 1978 Eastern proposal, one can easily understand why the West would find it impossible to accept Eastern data. Using the Western estimate of 962,000 total Warsaw Pact ground force personnel, (41) and the figure of 475,000 for Soviet forces, (42) the East would have to reduce a total of 262,000 ground personnel to reach the common ceiling of 700,000. Instead of a 13 percent reduction, it would be a 27 percent reduction of Warsaw Pact forces. With the East's agreement to a common ceiling of 700,000, the total Eastern reduction, if Western estimates were used, would be identical to that required under the

TABLE 1. 8 JUNE 1978 EASTERN PROPOSAL

	Stage I (First Year)	Stage II (Second & Third Years)	Total
Soviet	30,000*	25,700**	55,700
Other Warsaw Pact	0	49,300	49,300
Warsaw Pact Total	30,000	75,000	105,000
US	14,000	7,700***	21,200
FRG	0	37,500	37,500
Other NATO	0	32,300	32,300
NATO Total	14,000	77,500	91,000

*By calculating that 30,000 is 7 percent of 428,000, the Eastern figure for the strength of the Soviet ground forces in the area of reductions can be determined.

**Stage II Soviet reductions were calculated by taking 6 percent of 428,000.

***Stage I reduction was based on US tabled numbers of 193,000 US ground force personnel. Stage II reductions were calculated by taking 4 percent of 193,000

Source: Based on official East/West data.

Western proposal except for the ratio between Soviet and East European residual forces. However, it is interesting to note that considerably more Soviet ground personnel would be withdrawn under the Eastern proposal than under the Western proposal, if Western estimates were used.

WARSAW PACT REDUCTIONS UNDER
1978 EASTERN PROPOSAL USING WESTERN ESTIMATES

	Stage I	Stage II	Total
Soviet	66,500	62,000	128,500
Non-Soviet Warsaw Pact	0	133,500	133,500
Total	66,500	195,500	262,000

The key to a reduction proposal lies in the resolvement of the data issue. But if the Allies accepted the Eastern figure, 157,000 active duty Eastern direct participant ground force personnel would escape MBFR reductions and limitations. The Allies would reduce 91,000 to a residual ceiling of 700,000 but the Pact would only reduce 105,000, leaving them by Western estimates still in a position of numerical superiority with 857,000 ground force personnel versus 700,000 for NATO.

The 8 June 1978 proposal also gave an interesting twist to the question of national ceilings. The East has held the position since the beginning of the talks that once reductions were taken, individual national ceilings must be placed on the residual forces. This, they have openly admitted, is to prevent the FRG from expanding back to or past its pre-reduction strength should one of the other NATO nations make subsequent unilateral reductions. (43)

FORCE RATIO MAINTENANCE

The force ratio of most concern to the Soviets is the Soviet/FRG ratio. It is of even more importance than the ratio vis-a-vis US forces. Historically, the Russians have reason to respect the military potential of the Germans. Twice in this century they have been badly hurt by German military power; hence, they find the Germans' present military strength a residual threat which, given the historic capability of the Germans to mobilize quickly, could present a threat under certain conditions to the current status quo in Central Europe. Hence, in the

Russian view, the Bundeswehr, not the United States Army, is the principal counterpart to the Soviet forces stationed in Central Europe. Therefore, they insist that if Soviet strength is to be reduced, then the Bundeswehr must also be reduced. (44) The East shows little interest in the magnitude of the UK, Canadian, Belgian, or Dutch reductions, provided some reductions take place in order to set post-reduction national ceilings. But because the East has accepted the special linkage between US and Soviet reductions demanded by the West in a separate first phase, this primary Soviet concern to gear the magnitude of their withdrawals to FRG reductions is obscured.

At first glance the size of the Soviet reductions proposed by the East, using their data, (45) appears to be quite generous and quite asymmetrical when compared to the reduction the East demands of the United States in a first phase. For example, in the 1978 proposal, the Soviets are willing to take out a total of 55,600 to only 21,200 US; more than a 2 to 1 ratio in favor of the West. This appears to be a significant concession, but when the Soviet reduction is compared to the combined US and FRG reductions demanded by the East, a different ratio results, much more favorable to the East:

EASTERN REDUCTION PROPOSAL OF 1973

US	44,200	USSR	72,250
FRG	73,700		
TOTAL	117,900		72,250

Reduction ratio is 1.6 to 1 in favor of the Soviets.

EASTERN REDUCTION PROPOSAL OF 1976

US	35,000	USSR	63,750
FRG	69,000		
TOTAL	104,000		63,750

Reduction ratio is still 1.6 to 1 in favor of the Soviets.

EASTERN REDUCTION PROPOSAL OF 1978

US	21,200	USSR	55,700
FRG	37,500		
TOTAL	58,700		55,700

Reduction ratio is 1.1 to 1 in favor of the Soviets.

Thus, by successively scaling down the percentage of the overall reductions, the East can demonstrate apparent flexibility and seeming willingness to accommodate Western desires for greater Soviet reductions than US in the first phase, while at the same time giving up none of its basic position that the force ratio status quo be maintained.

In demonstrating a willingness to take an overall 2.6-to-1 Soviet reductions for US reductions, the East gives the appearance of accommodating the West, when in actuality the size of the reductions of the Soviet Forces (55,600) are less than the reductions of the forces seen by the Soviets as their greatest threat, those of the United States and FRG (58,700).

SUMMARY OF EASTERN REDUCTION POSITIONS

The Eastern proposal of 1978 adopted in principle several key features of the Western position at that time as follows:

- The provision for a first phase consisting only of US and Soviet ground personnel, (46) in which Soviet withdrawals would be greater than US withdrawals.

- Reduction by both sides of ground personnel to a common ceiling of 700,000 personnel. Air personnel would not be reduced but would be subject to an air subceiling of 200,000 within a combined air/ground common ceiling of 900,000.

- Mixed package equipment withdrawals consisting of US nuclear launchers and warheads in exchange for Soviet tanks and tank divisions. (47)

- Acceptance of the principle of collectivity under a common ceiling even though the Eastern formula actually results in modified national ceilings.

- Of major significance was the acceptance of the NATO desired size of the Western reductions. The East had scaled down its reduction percentage to 15 percent in its 1976 proposal, a percentage that accommodated the US desire at that time to withdraw only 29,000 ground personnel, but it did not accommodate the West European desired 10 percent reduction.   The 1978 proposal, however, did demand only an 11 percent Western reduction.   This is identical to the percentage the West has agreed upon since June 1976 (48) as the size of the Western reduction; an indication that the East is more concerned with maintaining the status quo and securing binding limitations than insisting on large NATO reductions.   The East hopes that symmetrical reductions will become more palatable.   By accepting certain Western views on parity and collectivity, as well as the size of the Western reduction, the East has given the impression of making a significant concession to the West.   However, the concessions were contingent upon acceptance of the Eastern data.   Thus, by making the entire proposal contingent on this point, the East could give the appearance of making significant concessions, while at the same time holding their basic position of maintaining their numerical superiority by taking symmetrical reductions.

The Eastern package is designed primarily to maintain the military status quo in Central Europe; hence, the actual percentage is not as important to the Soviets as the data baseline.   As Brezhnev stated when interviewed during his trip to the West in May 1978:

> We are ready at any time to sign in Vienna a reduction agreement by 5, 10, 20, or if you wish, 50 percent. But let's do it honestly so as not to impair the existing correlation of forces and so as not to favor one side over the other. Let us implement steps which are realistic and acceptable to both sides right now and not attempt to utilize the talks in order to achieve one-sided military advantages. (49)

The Eastern proposal of 1978 did move toward the Western approach in three respects: agreeing to parity of outcome, agreeing to reductions of Soviet armored strength, and accepting residual collective ceilings by adopting the structural aspects of the Western approach. But despite these moves the main substantive differences between the two approaches remained essentially unchanged. Specifically, the East has made its acceptance of the common ceiling, a form of collectivity, withdrawal of 1,000 tanks (vice 1,700), and withdrawal of 3 divisions (vice 5) contingent on the West accepting the East's claim that approximate parity in manpower currently exists in Central Europe and, therefore, asymmetrical reductions of the extent demanded by the West are totally unnecessary. By not confronting the data issue, i.e., offering some compromise, the East had demonstrated that it was not yet ready to bring MBFR to a decisive plateau.   But most importantly, by accepting for the most part the structure of the Western approach, it placed the outcome of the data issue squarely in the spotlight as the central problem. This sets the stage for a possible compromise between East and West, in which the East could trade acceptance of Western

Table 2. Comparisons of the Three Eastern MBFR Proposals

November 1973	February 1976	June 1978*
1. Reductions Reductions in three stages of ground air manpower in units with corresponding armaments and equipment to include nuclear weapons Stage I (1975) Total of 20,000 ground and air personnel of each side Stage II (1976) 5 percent reduction in personnel by each direct participant Stage III (1977) 10 percent reduction in personnel by each direct participant 2. Limitations Ceilings placed on each direct participant's residual personnel and equipment.	1. Reductions a. Stage I (1976) US/USSR reduce air and ground manpower by 2-3 percent of NATO/Pact respective total strength in units and with equipment US/USSR each reduce: • 300 tanks • 54 nuclear capable aircraft • 36 surface-to-air missile launchers • Equal number of surface-to-surface missile launchers • Equal number of nuclear warheads • One Army Corps HQ with supporting units b. Stage II (1977-78) All direct participants would take reductions totaling 15 percent of pre-1976 strength in units to include arms and equipment. 2. Limitations Ceilings placed on each direct participant's residual personnel and equipment.	1. Reductions a. Stage I (1 year) Soviets • 7 percent ground manpower (30,000) • 3 tank divisions • 1,000 tanks • 250 infantry combat vehicles • One Army Corps** HQ and supporting units US • 7 percent ground manpower (14,000) • 2-3 brigades • 1,000 nuclear warheads • 54 F-4's • 36 Pershing launchers b. Stage II (2-3 years) All reduce 11-13 percent to reach common ceiling of 700,000 ground and 900,000 air ceilings 2. Limitations Ceilings placed on US/USSR equipment reduced. Modified national ceilings on manpower within a collective ceiling.

*Contingent on acceptance of Eastern data. The East has stated that "all aspects of the 1973 and 1976 proposals not changed by the 1978 proposal remain valid." (Sovietskaya Russiya, 29 June 1978, p. 3.)

**May still be offered but status unclear.

positions on collectivity and parity for less demanding asymmetrical Eastern reductions.

1979 SOVIET UNILATERAL WITHDRAWAL

Any analysis of the Eastern MBFR proposal would not be complete without a discussion of the unilateral withdrawal of a small fraction of Soviet forces from East Germany, which began on 5 December 1979, and its potential impact on the MBFR negotiations.

In East Berlin on 6 October 1979, in a speech marking the 30th anniversary of the formation of the German Democratic Republic, Brezhnev made three arms control offers. The one that was most striking was his offer to reduce Soviet medium-range nuclear missiles if the United States deployed no additional medium-range systems, i.e., the Pershing II and cruise missiles. Another offer made in the context of CSCE was to reduce the level of exercise notification from 25,000 to 20,000, and to ban all exercises in excess of 50,000 troops.

It was his third offer which had the most direct impact on MBFR. Brezhnev proposed a unilateral withdrawal of Soviet forces from East Germany during the next year:

> Motivated by a sincere desire to take out of the impasse the efforts of many years to achieve military detente in Europe, to show an example of transition from words to real deeds, we have decided, in agreement with the leadership of the GDR and after consultation with other member-states of the Warsaw Treaty, to unilaterally reduce the number of Soviet troops in Central Europe. Up to 20,000 Soviet servicemen, a thousand tanks and also a certain amount of other military hardware will be withdrawn from the territory of the German Democratic Republic in the course of the next twelve months. (50)

It was immediately recognized by knowledgeable observers that the magnitude of the withdrawal, when compared with the overall Soviet strength in the GDR, made it truly a "token" reduction that did little to diminish overall Soviet combat capabilities. Nevertheless, the West in general welcomed it as a step in the right direction.

Of interest to the Western participants in MBFR were the objectives behind the announcement and the impact it would have on the Eastern negotiating position at Vienna. In the words of the NATO participants:

> We look forward to hearing clarifications as to how this announcement may relate to the Eastern position in the Vienna negotiations and to the agreed objectives of the talks in establishing parity in military manpower. (51)

Despite an early report of Soviet assurance to the US State Department that the unilateral withdrawal was an unconditional offer, (52) there were numerous indications from Eastern sources that the withdrawal would be related to the MBFR process, specifically to the size and composition of the Phase I Soviet withdrawals. There were also hints that the Soviets saw unilateral withdrawals as a way of circumventing the data stalemate: " [The withdrawals are] related to the Socialist countries' efforts to rescue the Vienna negotiations from their present difficult situation." (53)   Significantly, the Brezhnev statement on announcing the withdrawal began with an apparent allusion to MBFR: "Motivated by a sincere desire to take out of the impasse the efforts of many years to achieve military detente in Europe." (54)

By late November 1979 the East was making very clear that they saw the "unilateral" withdrawal as being intimately involved with the MBFR process, specifically as a method to get around the data problem.

> The Soviet Union at once and unilaterally will withdraw 30 percent of the personnel and 60 percent of the quantity of tanks which the NATO countries demanded from the USSR in their proposals....this quantity is equal to two thirds of the ground force personnel the United States has stated its willingness to withdraw....a favorable influence can be made on our talks if the NATO countries followed the example of the Soviet Union. (55)

The East also was giving indications during late November 1979 that the withdrawal was not to be considered over and above what the East had offered in the way of Soviet withdrawals in their 1978 MBFR proposals:

> Despite that, the West intends to withdraw 13,000 American soldiers from Central Europe in exchange for the Soviet reduction of 30,000 servicemen without taking into account the fact that the USSR has already announced the withdrawal from the GDR of about 20,000 of its servicemen. It is nothing but an attempt to upset the balance of forces in favor of NATO. (56)

On 5 December 1979 the Soviets put into motion their withdrawal plan. Western correspondents are invited to Wittenberg, East Germany, to witness the withdrawal of a contingent of 18 T-62 tanks and 100 Soviet soldiers from the 6th Guards Tank Division. (57)

By undertaking this unilateral withdrawal, the Soviets appear to be concluding that there is little chance of achieving an outcome to the data problem which they would find satisfactory. It gives them considerable propaganda value and, furthermore, gives the erroneous impression that the East is more interested than the West in conventional arms control in Central Europe. Whether the Soviets will actually withdraw a total of 20,000 personnel and 1,000 tanks remains to be seen. It appears that they have decided to make the withdrawals piecemeal in division configurations.   If so, then it is likely the withdrawal would consist of two tank divisions each of about 10,000 soldiers and 325 tanks, (58) plus an additional 350 older tanks due for withdrawal in any event.

If Eastern statements made prior to the withdrawal hold up, Western negotiators may receive a modified Eastern MBFR proposal in the future that takes maximum advantage of this unilateral withdrawal.

THE WESTERN REDUCTION PROPOSAL OF 1973

The circumstances surrounding the tabling of the Western reduction proposal on 23 November 1973, and its basic content, have been discussed above. (59)

The 1973 Western proposal called for reduction in East/West ground force manpower to a common ceiling of 700,000 on each side. Reductions would take place in two phases.   The first phase would consist of a 15 percent reduction of US and Soviet ground manpower. The United States would withdraw 29,000 individual soldiers, leaving their equipment behind.   It was initially proposed that the Soviets withdraw a complete five-division Soviet tank army consisting of 68,000 soldiers (approximately 15 percent of the Soviet manpower) and 1,700 tanks.

The first phase was obviously designed with the Mansfield threat in mind.   It presented Congress the tempting possibility of getting the Soviets to withdraw a five-division tank army from East Germany in exchange for only 29,000 US soldiers.   Such an exchange, it was reasoned, would go a long way toward blunting the calls for large unilateral US withdrawals.   By confining the first phase to US and Soviet reductions only, the West focused on the Mansfield threat and give the impression it wasn't overly concerned about reducing East European forces, nor for that matter, West European forces.   State-ments were made that Phase II would be contingent on the successful accomplishment of Phase I, and that the Western direct participants would commit themselves to specific reductions only after a Phase I had been completed.   Such vague assurances were totally unsatisfactory to the Soviets, who were much more concerned with securing reductions and limitations on the Bundeswehr than on US forces.

On 19 April 1978, as a further concession to the Soviets, the West stopped insisting on the withdrawal of a complete five-division Soviet tank army.   Instead, the new Western position was that the Soviets could withdraw any five divisions consisting of 1,700 tanks and 68,000 personnel. The United States also partially accepted the Soviet demand that US soldiers be withdrawn in units, rather than be thinned out, and agreed to withdraw a portion of the 29,000 in small units as well as by thin-out. (60)

Trumpeted by the West German press as an initiative of Chancellor Schmidt, the April 1978 proposal also committed the West European direct participants to take reductions in Phase II instead of waiting until the conclusion of Phase I to make such a commitment. But the West European direct participants stopped short of doing what the East wanted most, making specific numerical reduction commitments before the start of a Phase I. This principle of collectivity with respect to reduction quotas is a basic West German position which is supported by the rest of the Alliance. (61)

Commenting on the April concession, the Eastern press admitted that while some of the "Socialist states' just demands" had been met, the West had failed to meet the East's serious concern over reduction commitments of the FRG:

> NATO continuously demands that the determination of the specific share of each Western direct participant in the reduction should be exclusively within the competence of NATO's highest bodies and not the subject of the Vienna talks. Such a form of internal division of the reduction quota contains in itself the potential danger that the troops of some states totalling three-fourths of all Western states' troops in the reduction area will not have to participate in the reduction process at all. (62)

As the following statement illustrates, the 1978 Western modification, like the 1976 nuclear option and air/ground common ceiling of 900,000, was not significant enough to overcome the refusal of the East to take 3-to-1 asymmetrical reductions, as demanded in the original Western proposal of 1973.

> The unrealistic assessment of the current balance of power in Central Europe has been the basis of the NATO states procrastination tactics and delays for more than 4 years of the talks duration. This is no different with the changes and amendments of Western proposals submitted on 19 April 1978. (63)

In short, the Eastern proposal was unacceptable to the West because of the caveat that it must be based on Eastern data, and the Western proposal was unacceptable to the East because the Western data estimates showed the East must take 3-to-1 reductions to reach the common ceiling of 700,000.

By the fall of 1979 the stalemate over data was so complete the East decided to try to circumvent it through unilateral withdrawals. Coincidentally, at the same time the West was preparing a major revision of its proposal in the hope of getting the talks moving.

THE WESTERN PROPOSAL OF DECEMBER 1979

Early in November 1979 the FRG Foreign Minister Hans-Dietrich Genscher indicated that the Federal Republic of Germany would soon approach NATO with a new MBFR proposal, the objective of which was "to lead to an interim result as soon as possible, whose essential element is a US-Soviet agreement on troop reduction." (64) In a speech on 13 November 1979 Chancellor Helmut Schmidt also reported that the FRG had submitted a new proposal to NATO intended to bring an interim result to MBFR from which the negotiations could proceed further to a second-phase agreement. (65)

The new proposal was approved at the 13 December 1979 meeting of the NATO Foreign Ministers in Brussels. (66) As described in Western press accounts, the new proposal confirmed that the West had revised its Phase I proposals to such an extent that it now was almost identical to the manpower elements of the 1978 Eastern Stage I proposal. The December 1979 Western proposal consisted of a Phase I reduction with the following elements:

- Withdrawal of 30,000 Soviet ground personnel in three divisions

- Withdrawal of 13,000 US ground personnel, two-thirds in units, one-third by thin-out

- Ceilings on residual US and Soviet personnel

- Option III is withdrawn in total

- No specific armament reductions in Phase I and, therefore, no residual ceilings on specific types of equipment, e.g., tanks. Discussion of reductions/limitations on specific armaments deferred to Phase II.

- Withdrawals must be preceded by achievement of an agreed data base on the strengths of US and Soviet ground force personnel in the reduction area.

- Agreement to implement a comprehensive package of confidence-building measures to monitor residual manpower levels and military movements, with the aim of reducing the capability to conduct a surprise attack.

- A reaffirmation of the declaration that West Europe direct participants are to commit themselves to take adequate reductions, in accordance with the size of their armed forces in a Phase II, but not prior to agreement between the two sides on the strengths of the involved nations' forces. (67)

On 17 December 1979, the above proposal was formally presented to the East in Vienna. (68)

Several factors led the West to modify its MBFR proposal late in 1979. The most important of these was the NATO decision to proceed with a modernization of their theater nuclear forces. Part of the modernization package was the decision to convert US Pershing Ia to Pershing II, and another was the decision to withdraw unilaterally 1,000 US nuclear warheads. The latter decision was reached to demonstrate that the new weapons being introduced were part of a modernization

Table 3. Comparisons of the Three Western Proposals

November 1973

1. Reductions

   a. Phase I

   Soviets withdraw a five-division tank army including 68,000 soldiers and 1,700 tanks

   United States withdraws 29,000 individual soldiers

   b. Phase II

   Pact and NATO reduce to a ground common ceiling of 700,000 each

2. Limitations

   Residual ceilings on US and Soviet manpower and Soviet tanks common collective ceiling of 700,000 with no national ceilings for rest of direct participants

December 1975

1. Reductions

   a. Phase I

   Soviets same as Nov 1973*

   United States withdraws 29,000 individual soldiers plus 1,000 nuclear warheads, 54 nuclear capable F-4's, and 36 Pershing launchers

   b. Phase II

   Pact and NATO reduce to ground common ceiling of 700,000 within an air/ground common ceiling of 900,000

2. Limitations

   US/Soviet ground air manpower, Soviet tanks, US warheads, nuclear capable F-4's, Pershing launchers, common collective ceiling of 900,000 ground air manpower

*On 19 April 1978 the West modified this demand from a tank army to any five divisions as long as they totaled 68,000 men and 1,700 tanks.

December 1979

1. Reductions

   a. Phase I

   Soviets withdraw 30,000 soldiers in 3 divisions

   United States withdraws 13,000 soldiers 2/3 in units, 1/3 as individuals

   b. Phase II

   Pact and NATO reduce to ground common ceiling of 700,000 within an air/ground common ceiling of 900,000

2. Limitations

   Ceilings placed on US/Soviet ground manpower; common collective ceiling of 700,000 ground manpower within a 900,000 ground/air manpower. No national ceilings

3. Associated Measures

   Agreement to implement the following measures before Phase I withdrawals:
   - Prior notification of movement into the MBFR area.
   - Designated Exit/Entry points manned by inspectors from the other side
   - Up to 18 air/ground inspection trips to other sides MBFR area per year
   - Periodic exchange of data
   - Non-interference with National Technical Means
   - Establishment of a Standing Consultative Committee
   - Prior notification of division size (10,000 personnel) movements throughout Europe to include western Russia
   - Right to send observers to such movements.

process, and not a buildup of nuclear systems.   In addition, the unilateral withdrawal of 1,000 nuclear warheads was described also as an answer to the unilateral withdrawal by the Soviets. (69)

The net effect of the NATO nuclear modernization on Option III was to spell its demise. With the 1,000 nuclear warheads being unilaterally withdrawn, and with Pershing Ia being converted to Pershing II, the retention of 54 obsolete F-4's as a meaningful bargaining chip was unrealistic. (70) With Option III no longer on the table as compensation for the smaller US personnel withdrawal, it was obvious that the West would have to reduce its demands on the East in Phase I.

The Western proposal of December 1979 moved significantly closer toward the Stage I elements of the Eastern 1978 proposal, by considerably reducing their demands as to size and composition of the Soviet withdrawal.   Understandably, for the long-held NATO position that greater asymmetrical Eastern reductions must be taken, the same 2.3-to-1 Soviet-to-US withdrawal ratio demanded in the original 1973 Western proposal was retained in the latest proposal. This would result in 1,000 fewer US soldiers withdrawn than demanded by the East. Of course, without Option III the West could no longer realistically demand specific tank withdrawals or residual ceilings. This resulted in a Phase I which focused exclusively on US and Soviet ground manpower withdrawals and limitations.

Perhaps if the Soviets had not decided to take a 20,000-soldier unilateral withdrawal, the new Western proposal would have been more acceptable to the East, because the size of the Soviet withdrawals called for by the West was identical to those volunteered in the 1978 Eastern proposal.   Instead, the Eastern press began to attack the provision calling for a 30,000-soldier withdrawal even before the new proposal had been advanced in Vienna, implying it was too excessive in light of the on-going 20,000-soldier unilateral withdrawal.   Once officially submitted, the Eastern press began an even more vigorous and wider-ranging attack on the new proposal.

Concerning the size of the reduction, the East stated "the Atlanticists suggest that the Soviet Union withdraw 30,000 troops. Evidently NATO chooses to remain blind to the already proceeding withdrawal from the GDR of 20,000 Soviet soldiers." (71)

The East was also unhappy over the fact that Option III had been withdrawn. Furthermore, they did not like the idea that the West was still insisting on an agreed data base (albeit only on US and Soviet manpower) before reductions could take place, while the East wanted to get around the data issue through unilateral withdrawals.

But the greatest criticism was voiced over what the East claimed was an attempt to revive the old "Quick Fix" concept which had been popular in the West earlier in the negotiations. The "Quick Fix" or symbolic reduction had been contemplated as a way to placate Congress in the issue of US unilateral withdrawals, by securing a quick agreement on US and Soviet withdrawals and then letting the MBFR process either drag on indefinitely or expire without a Phase II. If there was no Phase II then the East would not be able to achieve one of its main goals of limitations on the Bundeswehr. Such an outcome was then and still is unacceptable to the East. Fearing that the West had just such an approach in mind in their December 1979 proposal, the East stated:

> The socialist countries want to be sure that the process does not end with Soviet withdrawals but that those West European participants to the talks whose armed forces account for 75 percent of the NATO potential in Central Europe will also reduce their strength.... The present Western proposal, however, draws apart the two stages of the talks and from the point of view of our security does not provide sufficient guarantees. (72)

The Soviet ambassador to the MBFR talks, Nikolai Tarasov, was even more blunt in his choice of words: the West "is steering matters toward leaving the troops of the FRG, Britain, and other European NATO countries, which constitutes 75 percent of the bloc's armed forces, outside any cutbacks and toward leaving open the possibility of their further buildup." (73)

While it is true that the Western direct participants did not give specific commitments on the size of reductions each would take in Phase II, they did reaffirm their collective commitment to each take adequate reductions in Phase II in relation to the size of their armed forces. Hence, the vituperative Eastern reaction may have been based more on long-held doubts over Western seriousness about a Phase II than on anything specific in the new proposal itself.

Despite the Eastern complaints, they did not reject the new Western proposal outright, but instead declared they would examine the proposal, even though the "elements essential for concluding a mutually acceptable agreement were not visible in it." (74)

In summary, the 1979 Western proposal, while formally reducing its demands on the size and content of the Soviet withdrawal, continued to press for long-held Western demands; refused to make commitments on specific national reductions in Phase II; continued to demand meaningful solutions to the data problem; and closed any opportunity to reduce US nuclear systems within the context of MBFR, a net result which the East found unsatisfactory. Thus, the deadlock continued.

HOW NATO MIGHT REDUCE

Except for the United States, the West steadfastly refuses to specify the amount of reductions each individual Western direct participant will take. But barring some unforeseen desire on the part of one of the Western direct participants to take more than its fair share of the reduction, the most likely approach taken by NATO would be to reduce by common percentage, based on the size of each direct participant's ground strength, to the 700,000 ground common ceiling. The effect of such a reduction on the individual Western direct participants is explained below.

The assumption will be made here, for the purposes of this analysis, that the United States will withdraw additional manpower in a Phase II if the Soviet Union agrees to do so also. Whether the United States will continue to be agreeable to withdraw its previously announced maximum total of 29,000 ground personnel, or whether they would decide to take less or more, would probably be based on the size of any additional Soviet withdrawals. This analysis assumes, in order to show the minimum reductions Canada and the West European direct participants would have to take, that the US withdrawals would total 29,000. If it proves fewer than 29,000, even greater West European reductions would be required to achieve the common ceiling of 700,000.

In order to reach the common ceiling, NATO must reduce 91,000 ground personnel (791,000 - 91,000 = 700,000). Of these 91,000, it is assumed 29,000 are to be withdrawn by the United States. This would leave 62,000 to be reduced by Canada and the West European direct participants. Each of the individual direct participant's share of the 62,000 reduction would probably be computed based on the NATO strength less that of the United States and France: 791,000 - (193,000 + 60,000) = 538,000. Sixty-two thousand is 11.5 percent of 538,000. Therefore, each Western European direct participant and Canada would take roughly an 11.5 percent cut of its existing strength to allow NATO to reach the common collective ceiling of 700,000.

NATO PHASE II[75]

	Strength Before	Reduction	Strength After
UK	58,000	6,670	51,330
CAN	3,000	345	2,655
BEL	62,000	7,130	54,870
NETH	74,000	8,510	65,490
FRG	341,000	39,215	301,785
TOTAL (Rounded)	538,000	62,000	476,000

TOTAL NATO REDUCTIONS

US	193,000	29,000	164,000
Non-US NATO	538,000	62,000	476,000
TOTAL (less France)	731,000	91,000	640,000
FRANCE	60,000	0	60,000
TOTAL	791,000	91,000	700,000

It should be kept in mind that the West has agreed to make allowances for the fact France has roughly 60,000 personnel stationed in West Germany. Those French forces would fall under the common ceiling and therefore the other direct participants would have to take additional reductions to compensate for no French reductions. It is ironic to note how vital it is for NATO to include the French forces in their data. If the 60,000 French troops stationed in the FRG were not counted (and the French don't like the idea of them being counted), it would result in a total NATO ground strength of 731,000. The West then would only have to take a 31,000 reduction, of which 29,000 could be US, to reach the 700,000 ceiling. A 2,000 West European reduction would obviously be totally unacceptable to the East.

IMPACT OF WESTERN PROPOSALS AND
DATA ON WARSAW PACT REDUCTIONS

Under the original Western proposal of 1973, Phase II was described as an "indigenous" phase. That is, reductions would be taken in this phase by West and East European forces. The possibility of further US and Soviet reductions in Phase II was left open-ended. As desirable as further Soviet withdrawals might be, it is clear from past Soviet statements that they are going to limit the size of their withdrawals to those of the United States Army and the Bundeswehr. Given the geographical advantage the Soviets possess to quickly reintroduce forces into Central Europe, any further withdrawals of US forces or further cuts in the Bundeswehr beyond those currently envisioned by NATO would not appear to be in the best interests of the West. The West might be successful in negotiating further Soviet withdrawals in a

Phase II, but the size of the reductions given Soviet linkage would have to be quite small in order not to jeopardize Western military security any further.   Hence, Phase II would in effect still be as the West originally intended it to be, an indigenous reduction.

For the purpose of the following analysis three assumptions were made. First, the West would be successful in securing a 30,000-soldier Soviet withdrawal in Phase I.   Second, the Soviets would indeed unilaterally withdraw a total of 20,000 soldiers before there was an MBFR agreement.   Third, the Soviets would agree to withdraw an additional 6,000 personnel in Phase II (the last assumption is included because in their 1978 proposal, which was based on their data, the Soviets indicated a willingness to withdraw a total of 56,000 personnel in MBFR).   By including the maximum Soviet withdrawals deemed realistically possible, the analysis can thereby demonstrate the minimum reduction the East European direct participants would have to take in order for the East to reach the 700,000 common ceiling. A lesser Soviet reduction than 56,000 would, of course, require greater East European reductions.

Assuming the Soviets would withdraw 30,000 in Phase I and 6,000 in Phase II in addition to the 20,000 unilaterally withdrawn, the required reduction of East European personnel (using official Western estimates) to reach the 700,000 common ceiling would be 206,000:

$$962,000 - (56,000 + 206,000) = 700,000.$$

The East European direct participant's share of the 206,000 Phase II reduction is computed here based on the Western estimate of Eastern strength less that of the Soviet Union's of 475,000; 962,000 - 475,000 = 487,000. Two hundred and six thousand is approximately 42 percent of 487,000. Thus the three East European direct participants would each have to reduce its forces by 42 percent in order to reach the 700,000 common ceiling.

EASTERN REDUCTIONS UNDER WESTERN PHASE II

	Pre-Reduction Strength	Reduction	Residual Strength
Soviet	475,000	56,000	419,000
Non-Soviet	487,000	206,000	281,000
Total	962,000	262,000	700,000

The Western proposal would have the following numerical impact on the forces of the two alliances:

TOTAL REDUCTIONS

US	29,000	Soviet	68,000
FRG	39,000	Other Eastern	194,000
Other Western	23,000		
TOTAL	91,000		262,000

The reduction required of the East is almost triple that required of the Western direct participants. This, of course, as pointed out before, is totally unacceptable to the East. They have stated in many instances that such an asymmetrical reduction can never be agreed upon.

From the NATO point of view, the magnitude of such a reduction demanded by the West would accomplish the objective of reducing the Pact to numerical parity with the West. It would not, however, result in large withdrawals of the forces which the West considers to be the most threatening - Soviet combat manpower. The assumed maximum Soviet withdrawals (of 56,000) would equal only 21 percent of the total required Eastern reduction. This is much less than that required of the United States, which would be taking 32 percent of the NATO reductions. Interestingly enough, the combined US/FRG reduction of 68, 000 is greater than the 56,000 reduction of the Soviets. Hence, under the Western proposal, rather than having a framework which causes large scale Soviet withdrawals, NATO seems content with a US/FRG-to-Soviet reduction ratio similar to that of the Eastern proposal.

Hence, the Western Phase II objective seems to be a massive reduction of East European ground forces as the key to achieve parity. The impact of the Western Phase II proposal on the East European direct participants' ground forces illustrates this in a startling way:

IMPACT ON EAST EUROPEAN GROUND FORCES
(Figures Rounded)

	Pre-Reduction Strength	Reduction	Residual Strength
GDR	105,000	44,000	61,000
Poland[76]	220,000	92,000	128,000
Czech[76]	135,000	57,000	78,000

Such a massive reduction of East European standing armies would certainly accomplish the announced Western objective of a "stable military balance in Europe," (77) through reductions to a numerical balance in the categories of active duty ground and air manpower in central Europe. A reduction which results in a 61,000-man East German army, a 128,000-man Polish army, and a 78,000-man Czech army, would require either national mobilization in Eastern Europe or a massive introduction of Soviet forces from Western Europe before a major attack on Western Europe could be undertaken. Thus, it would virtually preclude a meaningful surprise attack.

Such an approach also has the coincidental negative effect of increasing the Soviet force ratio in Eastern Europe. Using Western estimates, the present Soviet-to-East European ground force ratio is roughly 1 to 1. After a Western Phase II described above, it would be a 1.6 to 1 ratio in favor of the Soviets.

The obvious question is, does NATO really want to see an increase in the ratio of Soviet manpower in Central Europe vis-a-vis East European manpower? Given the acknowledged hostility of East Europeans to the Soviets and their serious reliability problem, is it really in the best interest of NATO to have the armies of Poland, Czechoslovakia, and East Germany reduced by 42 percent? Isn't there some Western and Eastern European benefit vis-a-vis Soviet hegemonistic control over Eastern Europe to have East European standing armies of a strength that must be taken seriously by the Soviets should they deem further internal control necessary? The answers are obviously affirmative, but NATO must realistically look after its primary concern, that of a surprise attack.

This problem has been recognized by the West German Chancellor Helmut Schmidt, who has proposed that no direct participant should maintain more than 50 percent of the residual 700,000 on each side. (78) While there is no problem for the West - even the pre-reduction strength of the West German ground forces is less than 350,000 - it would cause problems for the Soviets and require additional Soviet withdrawals of between 22,000 (using Eastern data) to 69,000 (using Western estimates). This would, of course, be more in keeping with Western objectives of lowering the Soviet presence in Central Europe. But it is obvious that without further FRG and US reductions of a magnitude currently unacceptable to the West, there will be no further Soviet withdrawals in Phase II that would meaningfully improve Western security. Furthermore, there is clear evidence that the Soviets would not agree under any circumstances to such massive reductions of East European manpower. All Eastern statements strongly point out the unacceptability of the Western Phase II approach.

If the West is serious about increasing stability in Central Europe by decreasing the chances of a surprise attack, the achievement of parity through massive reductions of East European armies is the only current Western MBFR proposal which, if implemented, would accomplish that objective.

Over the years since negotiations began, the East has gradually reduced the size of the US withdrawal it finds acceptable, to the point that in the Eastern proposal of June 1978, the size of the required withdrawal was actually less than the United States had stated at the start of the negotiations it was prepared to take.   These gradual reductions in the required size of the US withdrawal have been linked with numerous Eastern statements calling for some type of interim agreement as soon as possible, in order to show progress and to further military detente in Central Europe. (79) Furthermore, their unilateral withdrawals, as the East has stated, were designed to put additional pressure on the West to show progress in Vienna and to help resolve the data issue. (80)

The East has thus positioned itself to take, should it choose to do so, a symbolic type of reduction designed to achieve an interim result that does not require the East to be forthcoming on data.

During the early period of the talks, when the US administration was under heavy pressure to undertake unilateral reductions, the symbolic reduction was contemplated to placate Congress and to forestall large cuts in US forces.   However, the disappearance of congressional pressure for such unilateral reductions has not rendered the symbolic reduction concept obsolete.   With the current data impasse, such a solution seems once again to be attractive to the West. By reducing the size of the Soviet withdrawal to that compatible with Eastern desires; by no longer requiring explicit tank withdrawals and ceilings in Phase I; by reducing the need for a data agreement only to US and Soviet forces; and finally, by deferring difficult problems to a Phase II negotiation, the 1979 Western reduction proposal certainly seems to suggest that the West may be rethinking the attractiveness of symbolic reduction.

The West German leaders who initiated the 1979 Western Proposal in NATO have stated it was designed "to lead to an interim result as soon as possible." (81)   But the West has retained one element which automatically precludes an early result: the requirement for an agreed data base on US and Soviet ground manpower before any reduction can take place. How demanding the West will be in such a data discussion remains to be seen, but statements made by West German officials that the data problem should be placed in the hands of politicians (82) further indicate the West might decide in the future to seek an interim agreement more in line with the Eastern approach, in order to show progress in MBFR.

6 The Role of Nuclear Weapons in MBFR

Nuclear weapons play a critically important role in the force balance in Central Europe. Because of their vast destructive power, it has always been impossible to treat them strictly within the military context as simply another weapons system. In reality, nuclear weapons are not merely military weapons, but political weapons as well, and the emotional responses to their presence makes them an issue of the highest political as well as military significance.

Since the mid-1950s, tactical nuclear weapons have been the mainstay of NATO's defense. They were introduced at a time when the United States possessed clear nuclear superiority over the Soviet Union. They were there to counter the large superiority of conventional forces the Warsaw Pact held in Central Europe and thus deter the Soviets from launching an attack on Western Europe. If, by some set of desperate circumstances, the Soviets decided to attack, these tactical nuclear weapons would serve as the inextricable link to the American strategic nuclear forces. If NATO was unable to deter or defeat the invasion, the United States would escalate the nuclear response to a massive strike on the Soviet Union.

In the late 1950s, the Soviets began seriously to develop a strategic nuclear capability. This effort was spurred by the loss of prestige suffered by the Soviets during the Cuban missile crisis of 1962. By the mid-1960s, it was generally recognized that the Soviets had developed a strategic nuclear strike force which possessed an assured destruction capability. (1)

The realization that the United States was no longer immune to nuclear attack caused US officials to begin rethinking the strategy of automatic escalation. A search for a modified decoupling or firebreak led NATO in 1968 to adopt a three-part strategic concept consisting of deterrence, forward defense, and flexible response. The concept envisioned that these elements would be employed sequentially. First, peace would be preserved by presenting a credible deterrence of conventional forces, tactical nuclear weapons, and strategic nuclear forces. Should these forces fail to deter Soviet aggression, NATO would respond with "forward defense." Forward defense was considered to be essentially a conventional defense up close to the FRG border. NATO was, however, prepared to fight from the onset at the level of conflict chosen by the Soviets, i.e., nuclear if need be.

If the Soviets chose to attack conventionally, flexible response sought to defeat the Soviets by deliberately escalating the intensity of combat to include, if required, the selected use of tactical nuclear weapons with the primary objective of "terminating the war in terms acceptable to the United States and its allies at the lowest feasible level of conflict." (2)

Flexible response thus changed the basic role of tactical nuclear weapons from one of a war-fighting and winning role to one of deterrence and last resort. The Germans put it quite bluntly:

> The initial use of nuclear weapons is not intended so much to bring about a military decision as to achieve political effect. Our intent is to persuade the attacker to reconsider his intention, to desist in his aggression and to withdraw. At the same time, it will be impressed upon him that he risks still further escalation if he continues to attack. (3)

To have effective deterrence one must have either superiority or, at a minimum, parity. What put the viability of the new NATO doctrine into question almost from the start was the fact that, at the same time as NATO, the Soviets had also been building up their theater nuclear capability. The Soviets have maintained nuclear-capable delivery systems in Eastern Europe for decades, both aircraft and surface-to-surface rocket and missile launchers known as FROG and SCUD. Backing up these systems in Western Russia were other surface-to-surface missile launchers, the tactical SCALEBOARD, some 600 intermediate- and medium-range ballistic missile launchers, and almost as many medium bombers capable of carrying nuclear weapons.

As long as the United States possessed strategic nuclear superiority, this formidable Soviet theater nuclear force could be checkmated. However, the attainment of strategic parity by the Soviet Union made the Soviet tactical nuclear force a viable threat and one that was soon to be considered the equal or better of the Western theater nuclear capability.

As part of their overall force improvement program, the Soviets have increased the number of tactical surface-to-surface missile launchers in their field armies to roughly three times as many systems as NATO possesses; the Soviets are also replacing older launchers with newer, more capable ones. There is increasing evidence of a Soviet nuclear artillery capability, which has long been an area of NATO monopoly. (4) The Soviets have, in addition, undertaken a massive modernization of their tactical aircraft stationed in Central Europe, so that now all of their aircraft stationed there have the capability to deliver nuclear weapons. (5)

Two other systems recently deployed in Western Russia are the Backfire bomber and the SS-20 mobile intermediate-range ballistic missile. The Backfire is a highly capable supersonic bomber primarily designed for use as a theater weapon but with sufficient range to reach the United States. Soviet refusal to codify restrictions on it within the SALT II treaty itself was one of the most emotional issues of those negotiations. The SS-20 has three highly accurate independently targetable warheads and a range of 4,900 kilometers, which puts all of Western Europe well within its range. These two weapons are at the heart of the argument about the so-called "Gray Area Systems" because they possess tremendous capabilities but fall under neither SALT nor MBFR.

The introduction of these two new systems dispelled any lingering hope that the West still held superiority over the Warsaw Pact in Central Europe in theater nuclear systems. (6) In fact, there is a growing consensus that the Soviets have superiority over the West in theater nuclears at least to the extent that makes the tactics of flexible response, as described above by the Germans, clearly question-able as a viable strategy for NATO.

While all West European nations fear the outbreak of a nuclear war in Europe, it is primarily the Germans who are the most concerned and take the greatest interest in NATO's theater nuclear employment policy. This is understandable, for in a tactical nuclear exchange resulting from an outbreak of hostilities between the East and West, it is the Germans who will likely suffer the most casualties and destruction. Numerous NATO exercises over the years have fueled German fears that the casualties and destruction in Germany would be massive, particularly using the high yields found in earlier and some present generations of tactical nuclear warheads. (7) Helmut Schmidt, before becoming Chancellor of the FRG, wrote in 1962:

> The use of tactical nuclear weapons...would lead to the most extensive devastation of Europe and to the most extensive loss of life amongst its people.... Those who think that Europe can be defended by the massive use of such weapons will not defend Europe but destroy it. (8)

Official West German views on the role of theater nuclear weapons have undergone a significant change since their first introduction into the Alliance in 1958. As pointed out earlier, the initiation of the Rapacki plan was in response to NATO's decision to deploy tactical nuclear weapons and particularly to give tactical nuclear launchers to the Bundeswehr. The Allies and the West Germans (although with some strong domestic opposition) welcomed their introduction. They saw theater nuclear weapons as giving NATO the capability to redress the conventional imbalance between East and West and to use them early in the case of a deliberate large-scale Warsaw Pact attack. Most of all, they saw these weapons as providing an additional and even more valid linkage commitment between the US conventional presence in Western

Europe and the massive US strategic retaliation capability. (9)

Subsequently, however, the achievement by the Soviet Union of strategic nuclear parity with the United States in the mid-1960s and the US pressure on NATO to accept the doctrine of flexible response gave the Europeans, especially the West Germans, cause for considerable concern over whether there would be such an automatic escalation to strategic nuclear war. To the Germans, the primary purpose of nuclear weapons is to deter. The achievement of strategic parity and the adaptation of flexible response indicated a change they did not relish. For deterrence to be effective, reasoned Bonn, the Soviet Union proper must be threatened with nuclear destruction; otherwise, the Russians will have no inhibition against waging a nuclear war in Europe, especially on the territory of their hated enemy, the Germans. The Germans therefore continuously stressed over the years the critical role that US theater nuclear weapons stationed in Western Europe played as the escalating link to the US strategic nuclear force that could reach the USSR.

Against this background it is easy to understand the considerable West German misgivings when the United States first proposed that NATO consider reduction and limitation of US theater nuclear weapons in MBFR. The purpose was to add weight to the original and obviously unbalanced Western offer to withdraw 29,000 individual US soldiers in exchange for the withdrawal of a five-division Soviet tank army consisting of 68,000 troops and 1,700 tanks.

Known as Option III, this offer was to consist of a one-time withdrawal of 36 Pershing surface-to-surface tactical nuclear missile launchers, 54 F-4 Phantom nuclear-capable fighter-bombers, and 1,000 nuclear warheads. (10) The 1,000 nuclear warheads of a type unspecified would be withdrawn from the 7,000 maintained in Western Europe. Limitations would then be placed on the residual in each category.

It should also be noted that pressure had been building in Congress during that period of time as part of the post-Vietnam malaise to reduce the 7,000 nuclear-warhead arsenal maintained in Western Europe. The fact that Option III contained an offer to remove 1,000 of these warheads may have lent impetus to the US pressure on NATO to propose Option III to the East at that time.

The West Germans were fearful that the US nuclear offer would be seized upon by the East as a method to bring West European, especially West German, nuclear delivery means under MBFR. (11) The United States, however, managed to overcome West German reluctance and consensus was achieved by NATO on 17 September 1975 to make the offer to the East. (12)

On 16 December 1975 the West presented Option III. Ambassador Resor of the United States made the proposal conditional as a one-time offer. (13)

The Pershing I missile launcher and the F-4 Phantom are both classified as deep-interdiction or deterrence weapons in contrast to battlefield nuclear weapons such as nuclear artillery or the Lance missile. (14) The Pershing I can deliver a nuclear warhead some 720 kilometers and the F-4 can deliver a nuclear bomb at the range of 1,145 kilometers. It is envisioned that these weapons would be used to attack railheads, air fields, and other lines of communication in Eastern Europe, either selectively as part of the flexible response scenario or massively as part of an all-out nuclear war. The FRG also possesses 72 Pershing I launchers, (15) but the warheads are maintained under US control. It is also important to realize that the Pershing I does not have the range to reach the Soviet Union. The F-4 could reach the Soviet Union but only on a one-way mission.

The East immediately attacked the new Western proposal as an inadequate although positive step: inadequate, because Allied nuclears were not included; positive, because it recognized the Eastern position that nuclears should be included. In a press interview the Polish MBFR representative, Dabrowa, stated:

> The socialist states have from the beginning been for the reduction of all kinds of the armed forces and armaments including nuclear weapons. However, one cannot help noticing that the possibilities for constructively using the Western proposal of 16 December 1975 are greatly curbed by the fact that it has been made dependent on the Socialist states acceptance of the Western reduction scheme in its entirety, a scheme that as we have already explained so many times is unacceptable.... The new proposal provides for reduction of only a certain part of the American carriers of nuclear weapons. It does not concern the carriers possessed by the armed forces of the other NATO states in Central Europe.... [emphasis added] We consider the proposal of 16 December 1975 as a step that is tantamount to recognizing the need to include nuclear weapons in reductions, but we also consider this step inadequate. (16)

Other Eastern press articles echoed Dabrowa's statement on agreeing the Western proposal was a half-hearted measure that failed to break the impasse in Vienna. They also pointed out comments in the Western press such as those made by General Steinhoff, former head of NATO's Military Committee, who stated in reference to the nuclear option, "It is a question of whether the Soviets will accept this trade of somewhat outdated NATO equipment." (17)

General Steinhoff's comment may have been an attempt to weaken the Allied offer, which had come under attack by the conservative West German political faction, the Christian Democratic and Christian Social Union (CDU/CSU), which maintained that:

> Western concessions are going far beyond earlier German expectations. The West has abandoned its firm starting position on all three levels by making tactical nuclear weapons and their carrier systems subjects of the Vienna negotiations. The fact is not being considered at all that Europe is as before threatened by Soviet medium range missiles which cannot be matched by the West. (18)

Obviously Option III was not proving to be a panacea for moving the talks forward, and it appeared to be setting some precedents which could turn out to be dangerous for the West. The East was upset because it was only a one-time offer; because it required them to accept other tenets of the Western proposal such as asymmetrical reductions to a common ceiling; and above all because it did not include Allied nuclear systems, especially those of the West Germans. In the West, principally in the conservative circles of West Germany, NATO was being accused of offering too much with its nuclear option.

Given the very obvious weakness of the initial Allied proposal, that is, the offer to trade 29,000 American soldiers chosen at random for a five-division Soviet tank army, it was evident something further had to be added to strengthen that offer; hence, Option III - which initially resulted only in an Eastern promise to study its contents.

The East, after considering the Western proposal, apparently did see some benefit in it, most probably as a possible link to future inclusion of West German nuclear launchers, for they did incorporate Option III into their 1976 proposal, and surprisingly enough matched it with an offer to withdraw Soviet nuclear weapons as well.

In the 1976 proposal the East matched Option III as follows:

- 54 nuclear-capable aircraft would be withdrawn. For the United States they would be F-4 fighter-bombers and for the Soviets, Fitter fighter-bombers.

- An equal, but unspecified, number of tactical surface-to-surface, nuclear-capable missile launchers would be withdrawn, Pershing by the United States and SCUD by the Soviets.

- Nuclear warheads of an unspecified number would be withdrawn.

Not a part of Option III, but included in the Eastern proposal, was an additional provision that the United States would withdraw 36 Nike Hercules surface-to-air missile launchers and the Soviets would withdraw 36 SAM-2 surface-to-air missile launchers. (19)

Even though the Soviets subsequently pulled back their offer to withdraw nuclear elements, it is well to review the content of that offer to evaluate its real meaning.

In the offer to withdraw 54 Fitter fighter-bombers, the East did not specify which model of the Fitter it intended to withdraw in exchange for the F-4's. In 1976 the Soviets were conducting a vigorous upgrading of their tactical air forces in Central Europe, and the older Fitter A aircraft were in the process of being replaced by the newer and more capable Fitter C. As of spring 1976 it was reported that the Soviets had approximately 180 of the older Fitter A's still in Eastern Europe. Some 90 newer Fitter C's had already been introduced into the area. (20)

The withdrawal of 54 of the older Fitter A aircraft would have been relatively painless for the Russians. The Fitter A was a 20-year-old fighter-bomber with a limited capability to carry slightly under 1,000 kilograms of ordinance out to a range of 555 kilometers. The Fitter C, introduced in 1971 to replace the Fitter A, has a more powerful engine which permits the delivery of a 5,000-kilogram payload out to a range of 700 kilometers. (21)

Neither aircraft is the equivalent in capability to that of the US F-4. The Phantom, introduced in the late 1950s, has served as an interceptor, fighter-bomber, and reconnaissance aircraft and is considered to be old by aircraft standards. Nevertheless, it has a range greater than Fitter C. It can carry 7,000 kilograms of ordinance to a range of 1,145 kilometers. (22)

The Soviets, therefore, would have lost little by withdrawing Fitter A's which were being replaced by Fitter C's. Even withdrawing the Fitter C would have meant little. The geographical disparity works even more in favor of the Soviet Union when it pertains to aircraft. Returning the 54 F-4's to Europe would require a long over-water flight involving mid-air refueling. For the Soviets, Fitters based in western Russia could be back into the area literally in a matter of minutes.

The Soviets maintain approximately eight SCUD brigades in Central Europe, each having 12 launchers. (23) The SCUD B, unlike the Pershing, can fire conventional as well as nuclear warheads to a range of 280 kilometers, but with an accuracy much less than the Pershing, which has a range of 720 kilometers. (24) It is also known that the SCUD system will shortly be replaced by a much more capable follow-on system. (25) Hence, in a weapon-for-weapon comparison, the SCUD, like the Fitter, is inferior to the corresponding US system.

The 1976 proposal was, however, more significant when it came to nuclear warheads. Although vague as to the number of warheads to be withdrawn, the Soviets, by offering to withdraw warheads, did for the first time officially admit that they maintained nuclear warheads in Eastern Europe. No figure as to the number stored has been given by the Soviets, but it is estimated that the Soviet Union stockpiles about 3,500 nuclear warheads and bombs in Eastern Europe. (26) It is doubtful that the Soviets would take out 1,000 of these warheads, which would be 29 percent of its estimated stock, whereas the United States would only withdraw 14 percent of its stockpile of 7,000 stored in Western Europe. By not mentioning definitive numbers for nuclear warheads, the Soviets apparently did not wish to commit themselves to matching the number of nuclear warhead reductions the United States indicated it would be willing to withdraw unilaterally.

The Soviets proposed an additional weapon category not included in Option III, that of surface-to-air missiles (SAM). The rationale for such an inclusion from the Soviet point of view is understandable. The Nike-Hercules has a nuclear warhead which can be used crudely in a surface-to-surface role. Of particular concern to the Soviets is the fact that not only does the United States have both Nike-Hercules launchers and warheads located in West Germany, but the West German Luftwaffe also has 216 of these launchers. (27) Hence, the Eastern proposal called for a reduction of 36 US Nike-Hercules launchers in exchange for 36 Soviet SA-2 systems.

The Soviet SA-2 is also classified as nuclear-capable. Both the

Nike-Hercules and the SA-2 are old SAM systems. But the Nike-Hercules is the superior of the two systems. The very poor kill ratio of the SAM-2 vis-a-vis the US B-52 bomber in the Vietnam war was indicative of the value of the SA-2, and the Soviets have been rapidly replacing the SA-2 with the more capable and newer SA-4 system in Central Europe. (28) Consequently, withdrawing SA-2's in exchange for Nike-Hercules would have dovetailed into Soviet replacement plans and thus could not be viewed as a concession.

The real purpose behind the suggestion to withdraw 36 Nike-Hercules and SA-2's appears to have been not to reduce surface-to-air systems per se, but rather to set a precedent of bringing all nuclear-capable systems in possession of the United States, and eventually those of West Germany as well, under MBFR limitations.

The reasons behind the Soviets' voluntary introduction of their nuclear systems into MBFR have never been explained publicly. It appears that they saw an opportunity by matching the US nuclears with Soviet nuclear weapons to establish a linkage that would make withdrawal of the Option III offer difficult for the West if the Soviets chose not to fulfill the Western demand to withdraw a Soviet tank army. Thus, by offering Soviet nuclears as compensation for the failure to withdraw a full Soviet tank army, the East had its own "nuclear sweetener," one that perhaps could create a situation leading to reductions and limitations on Allied, especially West German, nuclear systems. Furthermore, the weapons offered were all expendable systems, either in the process of being phased out or soon to be, and they were all inferior to the corresponding Western systems. Considering the very large Soviet theater nuclear threat, the proposed withdrawal would have had virtually no impact on the Soviet capability to fight a theater nuclear war.

The reason the East withdrew the nuclear segment of its 1978 proposal has never been explained. Again one can only speculate. One reason may have been internal misgivings among the Soviet leaders concerning the possibility of limitations being placed on Soviet theater-nuclear systems, especially given the ongoing force improvement programs. Furthermore, there was growing indication that by 1978 the West was willing to make Option III a permanent part of its proposal, thus obviating the need for a Soviet counter-link. The West had also wanted a mixed-package arms reduction; that is, US nuclears for Soviet tanks in order to get residual limitations on Soviet tanks. Thus, with the West apparently willing to give Option III a permanent status in the negotiations, it appeared the opportunity would remain for the East to continue to press and perhaps eventually secure reductions and limitations of Allied nuclear systems without having to pay the price of limitation on Soviet nuclear systems. Instead, the Soviets could exchange tanks for nuclears. They had a large superiority in tanks and their vigorous tank upgrade program was creating a surplus of older T-55 and T-62 tanks eligible for withdrawal. Consequently, the Soviets probably saw no further need to risk Soviet nuclear weapons in their attempts to get limitations and reductions on Allied nuclear weapons.

The question then became whether the Allies would still be willing to trade the full Option III package for the 1978 Soviet offer to withdraw only 3 tank divisions, 1,000 tanks, and 56,000 soldiers; (29) or whether the Allies should modify the package or withdraw it entirely.

Also by 1978, events which eventually impacted on the future of Option III were beginning to gather momentum. These were: the growing realization of the failure of Option III to achieve the desired objectives; a consensus in the West that the Soviets had achieved superiority in theater nuclear systems, as epitomized by the Backfire bomber and SS-20 missile; and uncertainty over the viability of the US nuclear commitment to Western Europe.

The credibility of the NATO nuclear deterrent had also been questioned within both official and unofficial circles for quite some time. (30) The theory of flexible response had been critically questioned, especially its "light and late" tactics and the increasing vulnerability to a Soviet first strike of NATO's nuclear warheads and launchers. It is not within the scope of this study to probe the various possible alternatives to the present NATO nuclear doctrine, or to conduct an in-depth review of NATO's nuclear forces. But some details need to be sketched out in order to discuss the future of nuclear systems in MBFR.

In 1979 the realities of strategic parity were brought home to the West as the details of the SALT II Treaty were released. In Western Europe, debate and doubt increased over the credibility of an automatic United States escalation to the use of strategic nuclear weapons in the event of a Soviet attack on NATO. Additionally, the growing Soviet theater nuclear threat, led by the continued deployment of the SS-20, was putting the NATO nuclear capability at growing risk.

In response the United Stated decided to revalidate its nuclear commitment to NATO and to respond to the Soviet threat by producing the Pershing II surface-to-surface ballistic missile and the ground-launched cruise missile, both of which would have the capability to strike the western Soviet Union. (31)

In accordance with the desire of the West to move long-range theater nuclear weapons into an arms control forum, discussions of reductions and limitations, on both the new US systems as well as Soviet systems, particularly the SS-20, would begin as soon as possible. If by 1983, the year the US systems would be ready for deployment, there were no satisfactory results to the arms control efforts, the two US systems would be deployed. This plan was approved by the NATO Foreign Ministers meeting in Brussels on 12 December 1979. (32)

The United States intends to convert all 108 of the US Pershing I's stationed in West Germany to 108 Pershing II's. It is also planned to deploy 116 ground-launched cruise missile launchers, each having four cruise missiles, in the FRG, the United Kingdom, Italy, and perhaps Belgium and the Netherlands as well. Thus, a total of up to 572 new US nuclear weapons capable of hitting the Soviet Union from West Europe could be deployed to counter the growing Soviet threat should the arms control initiative fail. (33)

Another part of the plan approved by the NATO Foreign Ministers was to unilaterally withdraw 1,000 US nuclear warheads from Western Europe. Such a withdrawal would be considered a response to the Soviet announcement to unilaterally withdraw up to 20,000 Soviet troops and 1,000 tanks from East Germany. It also was designed to underscore the NATO contention that such a deployment would be a modernization rather than a quantitative increase in the NATO nuclear arsenal. Over two-thirds of the 7,000 nuclear warheads stored in Western Europe have a range under 160 kilometers. Possible employment of these warheads, constrained by their short range to NATO territory, would increase West European fears of nuclear destruction. (34) Such a withdrawal of battlefield warheads would put the United States more in line with the West German position that deterrence is more viable with weapons that can hit the Soviet Union, rather than with battlefield weapons where collateral damage of friendly territory make their use less plausible.

Despite the understandably strong reluctance of the West Germans toward first use of nuclears in the event of a Soviet attack, it is doubtful that NATO will modify the existing concept of flexible response. As Helmut Schmidt put it:

> Flexible response is reasonable and credible. There is no alternative to it. A return to massive nuclear retaliation would be incredible, as would a fallback on purely "tactical" nuclear defense - the former being unimaginably cruel to the Americans, the latter to the Europeans. (35)

Another German official candidly points out that the real reason NATO keeps the strategy of flexible response deliberately vague is in order to straddle the interests of the Germans - who would want to escalate the conflict to the strategic level as quickly as possible - and the Americans - who would wish to keep the military conflict confined to Europe as long as possible. (36)

It should be realized that European distress voiced over the SS-20 and Backfire are to a great extent manifestations of more deeply rooted concerns about the future of the US nuclear commitment in Europe. This has been exacerbated by the Allied frustration in having a voice in the SALT II process. Thus, the Europeans see the SS-20/Backfire threat as an opportunity to have a say in subsequent US/Soviet negotiations on controlling strategic nuclear weapons. (37)

Two events occurred in December 1979 that made the future of any such subsequent negotiation uncertain. First, the NATO foreign ministers decided to proceed with the production of the Pershing II and the ground-launched cruise missile (GLCM) over strong Soviet objection, leading to a Soviet declaration that they would not enter any arms control negotiation on medium-range nuclear delivery means until the NATO Ministers reversed their decision. Secondly, the Soviet invasion of Afghanistan severely damaged the detente process and led to a decision by the United States to put the SALT process on an indefinite hold. (38)

If any future negotiation which involves both US and Soviet theater nuclear systems ultimately convenes, it is well to keep in mind that under any circumstances, the Soviet Union will always retain the capability to target Western Europe with nuclear ballistic missiles and bomber aircraft. The SS-20 and the Backfire bomber, despite their greatly increased capabilities, are to a great extent follow-on weapons systems programmed to replace older SS-4, SS-5 MR/IRBM's, and Badger/Blinder medium bombers. In other words, the threat of nuclear missile and bomber attack against Western Europe is not new; it has existed for many years. Therefore, one should be realistic as to what degree the threat posed by these Soviet systems could be reduced.

The fact that Western Europe will always be targeted by Soviet missiles of one type or another makes it extremely important that Western systems used as bargaining chips in any theater nuclear arms control negotiation be carefully evaluated from the standpoint of criticality in carrying out the missions of deterrence and defense. The Soviets, with their greater redundancy in medium-range systems, obviously consider limiting or even entirely preventing the deployment of a GLCM and/or an extended-range Pershing, as well worth taking reductions and accepting limitations on some Soviet IRBM/MRBM's or medium bombers. Brezhnev confirmed this on 6 October 1979 in Berlin, when he offered

> to reduce the number of medium range nuclear means deployed in western areas of the Soviet Union as compared to the present level in the event that no additional medium-range nuclear means are deployed in Western Europe. (39)

For those critics who often accuse NATO of being a paper alliance, it was significant that the Alliance ultimately rejected this Brezhnev offer along with other Soviet accusations and threats.

The events described above - especially the decision to convert US Pershing Ia to Pershing II, the unilateral withdrawal of 1,000 nuclear warheads, the deferral of discussions of any specific weapons reductions or limitations to a Phase II of MBFR - removed the last vestiges of viability from Option III and left the West with no choice but to remove it from the table at Vienna.

Dropping Option III thus put the focus of the Western proposal strictly on reductions of ground force personnel. No US/Soviet specific equipment limitations would be possible in Phase I because without Option III there could be no tradeoff of US nuclear systems for Soviet tanks. While 1,000 Soviet tanks are to be withdrawn unilaterally and others would probably go out in withdrawals of units in a Phase I, no limitations or ceilings could be placed on the residual, because Soviet tanks would no longer be a specific category. Option III was initially presented as a nuclear sweetener to compensate for just such asymmetrical reductions. However, given the position of the East on data, there was no indication whatsoever that the East would prove willing to take asymmetrical reductions of any meaningful magnitude, Option III notwithstanding. The East, on the other hand, had tied Option III to a nuclear-for-tanks trade. Such a trade - the Option III package for a ceiling on Soviet tanks - would have been considerable Western overcompensation.

Achieving consensus in NATO to drop Option III was not difficult. The Allies were reluctant to see it introduced in 1975 and their reservations over the years toward it remained. They saw Option III as a possible open door to large-scale reductions and limitations of Allied nuclear systems. This fear had been increased when the East again demanded in its proposal of 1978 that the Allies must take equipment reductions in Phase II to include nuclear systems. (40) This demand of the East has been a consistent one ever since the West initially proposed Option III in 1975. The East has always termed Option III "inadequate" because "it does not concern the [nuclear] carriers possessed by the armed forces of the other NATO states in Central Europe." (41)

Even though Option III proved to be a failure and was eventually withdrawn, it would not make a subsequent offer, long demanded by the East, of reducing and limiting NATO nuclear systems any less viable as a possible device to achieve greater Warsaw Pact conventional force reductions.

In contemplating such an offer, it is well to remember that the original rationale behind the development of NATO tactical nuclear systems was to negate the large superiority of Warsaw Pact conventional forces in Central Europe. They were introduced at a time in which the United States possessed clear nuclear superiority. Now, with the Soviets achieving strategic nuclear parity and building a very large theater nuclear force as well, the NATO tactical nuclear forces can no longer effectively serve as a checkmate to the greater conventional strength of the Warsaw Pact. In fact, they have become de facto substitutes for the lack of sufficient NATO conventional forces.

For the doctrine of flexible response to be as effective as possible, it must create doubt in the minds of the Soviet planners as to the probability of a successful Soviet attack. For the purpose of deterrence, the threshold of nuclear weapons must be seen to be low. For the purpose of warfighting, i.e., battlefield use, it must be quite high because the battlefield will be in Western Europe.

Phrasing it another way, for deterrence to be effective, the capability of conventional forces must appear less than optimal in order to give credibility to the nuclear deterrent. For the purposes of warfighting, the conventional forces must be capable enough to stop and turn back a conventional attack without having to resort automatically to nuclear weapons. This concept is called deterrence by "conventional inadequacy." (42)

Conventional inadequacy, however, is in reality more of a recognition of economic fact than a deterrence policy. The Allies simply have not wanted to maintain standing armies of the size required to guarantee defeat of any conventional Warsaw Pact attack. Conven-

tional inadequacy, on the other hand, does not preclude the moderniza-
tion or the strengthening of conventional forces as currently done by
NATO. It simply means that the Allies are not going to match the
Warsaw Pact "man for man" in active duty forces.

NATO's decision in 1973 that it could accept only a 10 percent
reduction under an MBFR agreement (43) was recognition of the fact
that the size of NATO active duty forces was barely adequate:
absolutely no fat could be trimmed to allow reductions beyond 10
percent. Whether or not NATO can still afford a reduction of roughly
10 percent in the face of the vigorous Warsaw Pact force improvement
program should be a matter of great importance and study in Brussels.
The reason it is raised here is to recognize that Allied tactical nuclear
weapons might prove effective in the same role in which US nuclears
failed; that is, to serve as substitutes for additional conventional
reductions.

There is ample evidence of strong Eastern desire to incorporate
Allied, particularly West German, nuclear launchers into MBFR reductions and limitations. Belgium, the FRG, the Netherlands, and the
United Kingdom forces stationed in the reductions area all possess
nuclear-capable battlefield systems. These are the 203mm (8-inch) and
155mm howitzers and the Honest John rocket (being replaced by the
Lance surface-to-surface missile). In the category of theater strike
systems, only the FRG possesses the Pershing I of which it has 72
launchers. However, all of the West European direct participants
possess nuclear-capable aircraft based in the reduction area that can
perform theater strike missions. (44)

The West Europeans so far have strongly resisted Eastern efforts to
restrict their nuclear systems, despite their less-than-enthusiastic
feelings toward these weapons. Anti-nuclear feeling has always been
strong in the Netherlands. (45) It was the Dutch who raised objections
at the NATO Foreign Ministers Meeting on 12 December 1979 on the
decision to go ahead with modernization plans before starting arms
control negotiations. They further insisted that such nuclear weapons
modernization must be linked to a reduction in the overall number of
existing warheads. (46)

The West Germans shared the Dutch view toward reducing warheads.
Chancellor Schmidt also insisted that the modernization must not lead
to "the further amassing of nuclear warheads in Europe," (47) and during
the development of the NATO plan, called for the reduction of the
existing inventory of warheads as a response to the Soviet unilateral
troop and tank withdrawal. (48)

The West German support of the element of impreciseness in the
strategy of flexible response, the fear of their nation being destroyed by
nuclear weapons in the event of war, and their renunciation of the
development and maintenance of nuclear warheads, all underscore their
mixed feelings toward nuclear weapons. Chancellor Schmidt, who in
1962 proposed a denuclearization of East and West Germany, has stated
on several occasions that the FRG is not a nuclear power and does not
wish to give the appearance of becoming one. (49)

On the other hand, the FRG recognizes the need, from the deterrence standpoint, for possession of nuclear launchers in order to have a voice in NATO nuclear planning. The West Germans are also particularly sensitive that they possess the same nuclear-capable weapons as East Germany, which is equipped with the dual (conventional- and nuclear-) capable SCUD missile launcher and the dual-capable FROG rocket launcher as well as dual-capable aircraft. (50) While the West Germans have some control over the US warheads dedicated for use by their launchers, it is a virtual certainty, given the historical distrust of all Germans by the Russians, that the nuclear warheads for the East European launchers (if any have even been so dedicated) are securely in the hands of the Soviets.

One result of the NATO decision to go ahead with the Pershing II and cruise missile development was a clear message from the FRG that because of its Ostpolitik relationship, it did not wish to be put out in front of the Alliance on nuclear matters. The FRG does not want to be portrayed as ever seeking a greater or more provocative nuclear role. This was especially important in the case of Pershing II and cruise missiles which can strike the Soviet Union.   During the Alliance consultations in the fall of 1979 on the modernization plan, both Chancellor Schmidt and the FRG Defense Minister, Hans Apel, bluntly stated that deployment of such systems only on German soil was out of the question.   The FRG would allow deployment only if there was Alliance consensus to deploy the systems in other NATO countries as well. (51) Largely in deference to West German desires, other NATO nations agreed to the stationing of the US cruise missiles on their soil. (52)

A perceptible shift in West European thinking took place during the modernization debate which indicated a growing preference for longer-range, deterrence-type of theater nuclear weapons over shorter-range battlefield weapons. While the Alliance did not reject the need for such weapons, some nations within the Alliance, primarily the Netherlands and West Germany, obviously saw the debate as an opportunity to reduce warheads of short-range weapons whose employment would probably be on their soil. This suggests that with the reaffirmation of the US commitment to defend NATO with nuclear weapons through the modernization program, West European reception to an offer in MBFR to reduce and/or limit their short-range nuclear system might not be as impalatable as it has been previously. The clear desire of the East to limit and reduce Allied, chiefly West German, nuclear launchers remains. Within the current MBFR approach, Allied nuclear weapons are practically the only realistic bargaining strength left to the West which has not been used. Two factors that should make the playing of the Allied nuclear card attractive to the West are:

1. Despite the failure of Option III, the West has, outside of nuclear weapons, little if any realistic bargaining strength left under the current approach to achieve significant asymmetrical reductions of Eastern ground power.

2. In 1973 NATO drew the line at a reduction of no more than 10 percent. In 1976 there was a de facto modification to 11 percent (91,000 personnel). If NATO no longer believes a reduction of such a magnitude is tolerable in the face of the ongoing Warsaw Pact force improvement program, or if it wishes to achieve additional Soviet withdrawals in Phase II without incurring further reduction of US and FRG conventional forces, offering reductions and/or limitations on Allied nuclear launchers may prove a very attractive alternative to the East, especially since the East is well aware of how quickly the indigenous Allies (especially FRG) could mobilize the approximate 55,000 personnel they would reduce under the present concept.

The combination and makeup of such a nuclear package are quite numerous with pros and cons for each. For example, to mention only a couple, it could be made up of an additional 1,000 US nuclear warheads as desired by the Dutch in combination with limitations on Western nuclear launchers, or it could consist of reductions and limitations solely of Allied nuclear launchers (UK, Dutch, Belgian, and FRG). Because of the long history of Eastern attempts to denuclearize West Germany, it would seem that just about any Western nuclear package that offered reductions and/or limitations on Allied nuclear launchers that included some belonging to the FRG would be attractive to the East.

It must be recognized that the subject of Allied nuclear systems is a delicate one. In the face of Soviet upgrading of theater nuclear weapons and with the United States and USSR at strategic nuclear parity, the Allies may believe that any voluntary diminution of even their limited nuclear capability would unacceptably weaken the viability of deterrence - even if it resulted in increased Eastern conventional reductions. Yet, when all is considered, it is the only realistic option the West has left to offer if there is to be any chance of achieving asymmetrical reductions of a magnitude that would enhance NATO security. Therefore, if the West intends to continue to insist on three-to-one East-to-West reductions, an Allied nuclear option needs to be actively considered. If it is deemed in the best interest of the Alliance not to propose a package that includes Allied nuclear systems, then it would appear that the West has run the course of viable options it could offer under the present approach.

7 Two Key Problem Areas

The preceding chapters have shown that, despite considerable differences between the two original proposals, MBFR negotiations have achieved consensus on a number of points. However, in two areas critical to an overall agreement, both sides are still far apart: the scope of the limitations to be put on residual forces and the data base which determines the size of the Eastern reductions.

LIMITATIONS ON RESIDUAL FORCES

Post-reduction limitations are, next to data, the most contentious issue of MBFR. This is principally because of their impact on national sovereignty as well as on the future structure of the forces in Central Europe, especially those of the Western indigenous countries. The subject of limitations is a complex one which both sides approach from different viewpoints - viewpoints which lend support to the overall objectives of each side and their perceptions of the other side's objectives.

The West has called for asymmetric reductions to eliminate the gross disparity existing in active duty ground manpower in Central Europe. Reductions would take place to a common collective ceiling of 900,000 air and ground manpower which would include a ceiling of 700,000 for ground forces personnel on each side.

In keeping with the Western viewpoint that it is the Soviet forces which pose the greatest threat to the NATO, the West has called for a ceiling on the residual number of Soviet manpower and has offered a like ceiling on residual US manpower. Indigenous direct participants are to fall under the common collective ceiling without having additional national ceilings placed upon their forces. The concept of reductions to parity and then a contractualization of this parity is a cornerstone of the Western position.

The Eastern position has reflected a long-standing desire to achieve a contracted ceiling on future peacetime expansion of the Bundeswehr. Their 1978 proposal accepted in principle the Western position of a common collective ceiling but, through a convoluted formula, required de facto national ceilings. This proposal remains unacceptable to the Allies because of their opposition to national ceilings for indigenous forces and of the Soviets' announced refusal to accept a subceiling on residual Soviet forces.

The Eastern press did not discuss the issue of ceilings during the first two years of MBFR, preferring instead to attack the West for its insistence on asymmetrical reductions on the part of the Warsaw Pact and for the lack of commitment to specific reductions by the West's European direct participants. When accused of using national ceilings to put a cap on the West German expansion, Eastern spokesmen denied such a goal.

Beginning in 1976, however, Eastern spokesmen were more candid in expressing the Eastern rationale for national ceilings, indirectly admitting that the rationale was to get limitations on the Bundeswehr.

> By sponsoring the concept of the collective ceiling, the Western states are trying to exclude the Bundeswehr from the program of reductions in armed forces and armaments although everyone knows that the Bundeswehr accounts for about 50%, of the numerical strength of NATO. (1)

An equal percentages reduction proposal would hit the Bundeswehr the hardest of the Western armed forces because of its size and because the majority of its troops are in combat units. Thus, the combination of percentage reductions and national ceilings on the residual forces supports the objective of the Eastern proposal to reduce and then limit the forces of the Federal Republic of Germany. The announced decision of the FRG to increase (through restructuring) the number of combat brigades in the Bundeswehr may have been the Eastern motive to go public. (2)

Izvestia on 25 January 1976 included an article on MBFR which stated in part:

> The idea of collective ceilings represents a trap. In NATO no such ceilings exist. If it were introduced, certain members could, by referring to the reduction of forces by one or the other partner, increase its own armed forces. In practice this would develop into a reduction of forces on the part of the weak partners and buildup of the arms race on the part of the strong ones. The concept of ceilings would, for example, legitimize an increase in the numerical strength of the Bundeswehr.... As it happens the West German newspaper Frankfurter Allegemeine has been writing about this. It openly expresses satisfaction at the constant growth of the Bundeswehr's firepower and it complains only of its inadequate

numerical strength. The newspaper comes to the conclusion that the introduction of collective ceilings for the East and West Europe would provide broad possibilities for the further strengthening of the Bundeswehr. Need one spell out the fact that the common ceiling idea can only be a retarding factor for the real implementation of military detente. (3)

Following this opening attack, the East European press dutifully began to publish articles expounding on this theme. First the Poles:

So called common ceilings would allow the apportioning of individual state limits as each side devises. This could bring about a situation which various national armies would continue to increase. There is no need to make a secret of the fact that to most Central European nations this brings to mind the Bundeswehr above all. (4)

An identical attack by the Czechoslovakian press stated, "The proposed common ceiling would not prevent, for example, increasing within the framework of these ceilings the effectiveness of the Bundeswehr which is the main striking force of NATO." (5)

A similar comment was made by the Hungarian press:

It is no secret that with the help of the common ceiling NATO politicians are aiming at the fact that the weaker members of their bloc could reduce their armed forces while the militarily strong countries would be able to pursue the arms race with even more intensive vigor. Thus, the apparently innocent-sounding formula would make it possible to further strengthen the West German Bundeswehr. (6)

Eastern fear of a Bundeswehr increase was probably heightened by the fact that other NATO countries were under pressure to reduce their active forces. It was well known at the time that the Dutch wished to reduce their army and refrained only because of last-minute pressure from NATO's Secretary General. Belgium was indicating a wish to take cuts and the economic situation in Britain looked like it might force the British to take cuts in the British Army of the Rhine (BAOR). (7) Moreover, because of the continuing shortage of British troops, London has been forced to draw units out of Germany for temporary duty to Northern Ireland.

Should such reductions occur, feared the East, it could lead to both external and internal pressures on the West German government to compensate. Chancellor Schmidt, however, publicly stated in Bonn in July 1976 that the Federal Government had no intention of expanding the Bundeswehr and that "this would be the case even if other NATO partners reduced their defense contributions." (8) This position was reiterated by Hans Apel, the Federal Defense Minister, who stated in a press interview, "Increasing the numerical strength of the Bundeswehr would be politically wrong and inadvisable with regard to the policy of the Alliance and the arms control negotiations with East Europe." (9) However, without a codification in MBFR, the East may feel such assurances may not hold up over the years. They obviously want definitive, binding commitments which not only reduce the Bundeswehr but put a cap on any future expansion. The Western rationalization given for a common ceiling, as opposed to individualized national ceilings, is generally explained along the following lines: The countries of Western Europe must retain their territorial sovereignty as well as the freedom to structure their forces and armaments as they see fit. They will not allow any international control to exist which would prevent the taking of required action in defense matters. Furthermore, NATO does not want a ceiling put on the Bundeswehr as it is the backbone of Western conventional defense. (10)

It should be recalled that in order to regain influence in European and world affairs after World War II, the FRG had to accept restraints on its sovereignty. Through the help of the West and their own spectacular economic recovery, the West Germans have largely succeeded in once again becoming a dynamic power on the world scene. Accepting a national ceiling on the Bundswehr is considered by the Germans to be another impingement on their hard-won national sovereignty and a surrender to one of the main objectives of the Soviet Union in these negotiations.

The question of national ceilings brought the West German problem into open discussion in the press. On 14 January 1976 the West German newspaper Frankfurter Allegemeine warned that one of the Soviet's objectives in attempting to reduce the Bundeswehr was to shake the security of NATO and create pressure among the NATO Allies to reduce their forces. The article quoted German Defense Ministry officials as believing that "the Kremlin would not object if the Americans were to stay in Europe for the time being and instead operational units of the Bundeswehr were reduced." (11) The article concluded by stating the West German tactical position on MBFR was not to make any advanced concessions in Vienna but to strengthen the negotiating position by "continuously enhancing the capabilities of the Bundeswehr." (12)

In the American press, the discussion continued. Michael Getler in the Washington Post observed that both West Germany and the United States remained steadfastly opposed to any limitations on the West German armed forces. (13) East bloc diplomats were quoted in another article conceding that the old fear of the Wehrmacht was partially to blame for this, but more realistically the East regards the West German forces as the most formidable of the conventional Allied armies facing them in Central Europe. (14)

The German Foreign Minister, Hans Dietrich Genscher, expressed the view in Der Spiegel that the Soviet objective in Vienna was to bring "the Bundeswehr - the second strongest military power in NATO after the United States and the strongest conventional army of Europe - under Moscow's control." This would be done by "blocking closer cooperation between the Allies by establishing an armament control zone, including the Federal Republic of Germany and Benelux and subordinating the Bundeswehr to direct national reductions." The Foreign Minister also stated his belief that under the Eastern proposal the Soviets planned to weaken the strong combat capability of the Bundeswehr by introducing national ceilings. (15) He went on to state bluntly that the reason NATO wanted a common collective ceiling, as opposed to national ceilings, was in order to have the flexibility "to equalize the weaknesses of individual partners by special efforts of others." (16)

The Eastern press also began promulgating the view that the United States and the FRG were cooperating in building up the strength of the Bundeswehr. An article by the East German ambassador to the MBFR talks, Dr. Ingo Oeser, declared: "The five year concept of equipping the Bundeswehr with new precision weapons systems of all kinds is aimed at intensifying the arms race and to obtain greater political leverage for the FRG." (17) The FRG program to strengthen itself in order to play "a leading role in West European military union directed against the socialist countries," would be blocked by an MBFR agreement and this is why, according to Oeser, the FRG has intensified its resistance to the concept of the Vienna force reduction talks: "The reason is the fear that the FRG armaments and their nuclear delivery vehicles will be reduced." (18)

The Soviet press, in discussing the unwillingness of the West Germans to reduce, clumsily attempted to demonstrate a split in the Allied position:

> ...the Netherlands, Belgium, and Denmark (19) were not against truncating their military expenditures and using the means thus released for measures against inflation and unemployment whereas the US, Britain, and the FRG who are considered the backbone of NATO zealously stand guard on NATO's defense potential. (20)

The article then points out that appropriations for the purchase of armaments for the Bundeswehr have increased by 50 percent from 1970 to 1976, and that "even more active ties are being established between the military-industrial complexes of FRG and US and therefore it is quite natural that the FRG is now in the front ranks of those who prevent progress at the Vienna negotiations." (21)

The attack on West Germany as the main obstacle to a successful MBFR negotiation was accelerated by the East in 1978. Speaking of the Eastern view of national ceilings a Soviet spokesman stated:

> The military men who object to any regulation that could complicate or offset the Bundeswehr's NATO status now and in the future are involved. [It] indicates striving to secure a dominant part for the Bundeswehr in the North Atlantic bloc. This is why one wants a free hand without accepting any reduction in commitments. They are using this and other things to delay Western response to the Warsaw Pact proposals. (22)

The East is quite concerned about the possibility of the West increasing their forces to compensate for unilateral reduction of other West European direct participants. This is one reason why the East has summarily rejected the Western proposal to put a ceiling on Soviet forces.

> The West is insisting upon the establishment of national restrictions on USSR forces - which are the basic defensive power of the Warsaw Pact - and at the same time does not admit national restrictions of troops in West European countries. (23)

The realization that a ceiling would no doubt have to be accepted on Soviet forces, if there was to be any chance of ceilings being placed on the West Germans as well as the other Western direct participants, may have been instrumental in the East developing a convoluted ceilings proposal as part of the 8 June 1978 proposal; the Eastern formula appeared to accept the limiting concept of the West but, in reality, was nothing more than national ceilings labeled as collective ceilings.

The fact that the East had offered this compromise to its previous stand on national ceilings was reported at the press conference held at the end of the 174th Plenary. There the GDR representative, Oeser, announced that under a common ceiling of 700,000, a nation could increase its ground forces by the equivalent of half the reductions made unilaterally by another ally. But as the Eastern formula was explained to the press, it became apparent that the East had made only a small step toward the Western position and had for all intents and purposes retained national ceilings.

As Eastern diplomats explained it, if Belgium took a 40,000 unilateral cut, the FRG could only replace 20,000, or 50 percent of the cut. The remaining 50 percent must come from other Western direct participants as long as they did not return to their pre-reduction strength. (24) The probability of such unilateral NATO reduction appears at this time to be remote. Nevertheless, times change and NATO believes that it is in its best interest if it is left unfettered for future force structure changes. Naturally the East sees it differently.

It should be recognized that the formula also contains a capability for abuse. For example, by forcing their allies to take several time-phased unilateral cuts, the Soviets (and theoretically the United States as well) could legally build back up their strength to a figure that was only one soldier below their prereduction strength. This could not happen under the Western limitation proposal because of specific residual limits on Soviet and US forces.

Figure 7.1 illustrates the complex Eastern formula. The left side shows the magnitude of required reductions under a Phase II MBFR reduction for the Netherlands, Belgium, the United Kingdom, and the FRG.

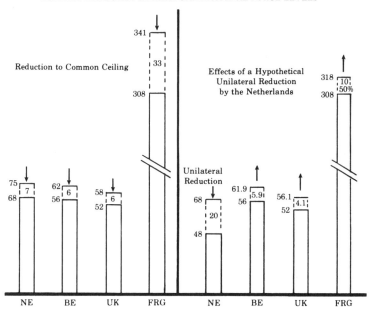

EASTERN FORMULA FOR RESIDUAL NATIONAL FORCE LEVELS

Data from *Military Balance 1977-78.*

Note: All figures indicate thousands.

Fig. 7.1.   The Eastern reduction formula.

The right side of the chart illustrates the impact of the restrictions the East proposal of 1978 makes on NATO's freedom to make up a hypothetical unilateral reduction of 20,000 Dutch personnel.

Because only 50 percent of the reduction can be made up by any one nation, the most that could be made up by the FRG is 10,000 (50 percent of 20,000). No nation can build back up to its previous strength although it can theoretically go up to a strength of only one soldier less (for these illustrative purposes, the strength is held at 100 less). Therefore, the most the Belgians could add on would be 5,900, thus requiring a third NATO direct participant to make up the remaining 4,100; in this illustration it is hypothetically the United Kingdom.

On 28 June 1979 the East again repackaged its limitation proposal. Hailing it as a "new step that has taken account of Western ideas," the East claimed it recognized that "the FRG and other West European states only want to enter into a collective reduction obligation." The so-called new proposal would allow each direct participant "to determine its own contribution within the overall alliance reduction." However, the East would insist that each state make a reduction proportional to its overall strength and that each direct participant announce the size of its reduction before the treaty is signed. (25)

In comparing the limitation proposal of 28 June 1979 with that contained in the 8 June 1978 proposal, it is readily apparent there had been no substantive change to the Eastern portion on Western, particularly FRG, limitations. In fact, the East admitted as much when they stated that the new proposal only meant that the East no longer insists on a codification of the individual state's reduction commitment in the treaty proper. (26)

Limitations are important adjuncts to reductions because they make the reductions meaningful by prohibiting a return to the pre-reduction levels and they also furnish a baseline for verification. A possible additional benefit is that limitations would not only serve as ceilings, but could also serve as de facto floors for the strength of the residual forces. Each country's post-reduction strength contributes to the overall alliance maintenance of the common ceiling. Citing the need to maintain this residual strength as part of the MBFR common ceiling would serve as a strong counter-argument to any future drive by elements within a particular Western country to make further unilateral reductions in its national army.

The subject of limitations is more emotional than that of reductions because of the relative permanency of limitations, and especially because of their impact on national sovereignty. Accepting ceilings on one's forces is in effect a renouncement of a degree of one's sovereign right over these forces. In the case of the indigenous countries, such limitations are total as opposed to the United States, Soviet Union, Britain, and Canada where only a portion of their forces would fall under a limitation. As illustrated above, the evidence is strong that the primary Eastern objective in the use of limitations is to put a cap on the Bundeswehr. The acceptance of such a limitation, given the history of the Eastern attempts over the years to limit the Bundeswehr would, in the perception of the FRG, impinge upon the sovereignty regained after World War II. Consequently, the concept of national ceilings is very unattractive to the FRG.

The Western negotiators realize, however, that without residual ceilings the impact of reductions will be negligible, and it leaves them open to the criticism that they are conducting a partial and meaningless negotiation. Yet, if ceilings are proposed that are so restrictive they seriously impair a side's present or future plans to restructure or realign the organization of its military establishment, they could prove equally unacceptable not only from the standpoint of sovereignty but from the standpoint of security as well. Hence, the search for the proper balance of limitations with both sides trying to put more restrictions on their opponents than they themselves are willing to accept. This naturally tends to lead to ultimate agreement on minimal ceilings that can be acceptable to both sides. Common collective ceilings will allow for the freedom to restructure internally within each alliance. Realistically, when considering FRG statements on no manpower increases, even national ceilings would probably not interfere with the restructuring contemplated under the NATO Long-Term Defense Plan, or with the current Bundeswehr reorganizaiton. But the West underatandably does not want to take the chance that a sudden shift in a Western direct participant's government could lead to a unilateral reduction requiring an increase in the forces of another NATO nation. In the search for militarily acceptable limitations, the problem of verification must also be considered. Stringent ceilings placed on manpower, and possibly specific weapons systems, will definitely increase the problem of monitoring and verifying Eastern compliance.

Despite the complicated ramifications, the tradeoffs in limitations are reasonably clear-cut. If the West wants a ceiling on the Soviets, then the East will insist on national ceilings. If the West wants a collective limitation, then the East wants de facto restraints on the FRG within the collective limitation.

Limitations were originally thought to be only of Western interest. But the negotiations over the years have given ample evidence that the East is intensely interested in the use of limitations to restrict the Bundeswehr. Such interest could be used by the West in a variety of ways to gain Eastern concessions on other points. For example, the FRG might agree to implicit codification of limits that they themselves have no intention of exceeding in return for desired Western objectives. The subject of limitations is a critical one. While it has military impact, it is ultimately more of a political problem and, as such, there is more flexibility in arriving at a solution than is available for the other key problem area of data.

THE DATA BASE PROBLEM

The problem of an agreed data base for MBFR has become the Gordian Knot of the negotiations. Both sides have traded accusations concerning the validity of the data they have introduced. The West maintains that the East must take three to one reductions to compensate for the Eastern superiority in active duty ground manpower. The East claims that a balance in active duty manpower already exists; therefore, reductions should be symmetrical. Consequently, an impasse has developed in the negotiations with both sides accusing each other of malfeasance and deliberately stalemating the negotiations. At first glance it appears that the negotiators have a seemingly impossible task to resolve. This is not necessarily so.

An arms control negotiation that contemplates reductions and/or limitations must have initially agreed data on which to base both the reductions and with which to monitor residual limitations. This data base can be composed of a variety of categories but as the name implies, it deals with quantities. The categories can, for example, be types of equipment, military organizations, or manpower.

In the case of SALT there is an equipment data base. An equipment data base made sense in that negotiation because it dealt with specific large weapons systems. MBFR, on the other hand, encompassed numerous weapons systems as well as military units of all sizes and various organizational schemes. Both sides, in preparing their negotiating positions, chose manpower as the measure by which reductions and limitations would be carried out. At first glance manpower seems to be a good choice, for it is the common denominator on which units and pieces of equipment are based. A soldier is a soldier is the concept and what is more simple than that? But the idea that manpower is a simple denominator can be misleading. Estimating the manpower in an opponent's combat forces is not too difficult because combat forces have a highly visible structure. However, estimating the number of personnel serving in less easily identifiable rear services, schools, and staff organizations is more difficult. Be that as it may, the West chose to base its MBFR proposal on the active duty ground manpower stationed in the countries of Belgium, the Netherlands, Luxemburg, West Germany, East Germany, Czechoslovakia, and Poland. (27) By active duty, the West meant those individuals who soldier on a full-time, 24-hour basis. In effect, the West was counting all active duty soldiers from the rifleman in the field to the military clerk in the Office of the Ministry of Defense.

In support of the Western contention that a destabilizing disparity in active duty ground force manpower existed in favor of the East, the West presented six figures in conjunction with its reduction proposal of 22 November 1973. According to NATO at that time, there were 925,000 Warsaw Pact active duty ground force personnel in the proposed area of reductions, of which 460,000 were Soviet. In contrast, the West stated that they had 777,000 active duty ground force personnel of whom 193,000 were American. In order to demonstrate the need for large Eastern tank reductions and to support their objective of getting the Soviets to withdraw a tank army, the West also claimed that the East had 15,500 main battle tanks in active units to only 6,000 for the West.

When the East introduced its initial proposal in 1973, it did not submit any supporting data. Stage 1 was to be a reduction of 20,000 and percentages were used to illustrate the magnitude of Stages 2 and 3 but none of the stages was tied to a data baseline.

Once the Western proposal was set forth, the East attacked its contention that the Warsaw Pact had a superiority in personnel. To the contrary, Eastern spokesman insisted there was a balance of forces in the area. The East charged that the counting rules used by the West were artifically contrived, and by doing so implicitly admitted that by Western counting rules, the Warsaw Pact had a superiority in active duty ground manpower. For example, writing in the London Times in 1974, Komlev, a Soviet arms control specialist, stated:

The attempts made by Western states in assessing the balance of forces of the two sides [do not take] into consideration... other branches of the ground forces [thus] giving a false picture of the real state of affairs in Central Europe.... For instance when estimating the overall strength of the NATO ground forces, the West does not include their air defense forces which number thousands of men. (28) At the same time they include the air defense troops of the ground forces of the Warsaw Pact states. It is also known that 120,000 West German civilians are employed in the foreign armed forces stationed on West German territory and the majority of them perform the same functions as are performed by servicemen in the Soviet armed forces stationed in the area in which reductions are proposed. (29)

Komlev seemed to be saying that if the West had not counted the forces along traditional service lines, i.e., as the forces were so administratively organized by each of the nations involved, (30) but rather along functional lines, there would be no disparity. Komlev implicitly acknowledged there was a disparity when he called for the adding of 120,000 West German civilians to the Western count. Putting it another way, Komlev was saying that while the East has more active duty soldiers than the West, they are performing tasks that were being performed by civilians (presumably housekeeping functions and peacetime rear service duties) and air force personnel (air defense) in the West. It is significant that when the 120,000 civilians are added to the number of Western air force personnel assigned to air defense duties, the disparity the West was claiming of roughly 150,000 would be virtually eliminated. Hence the East, as illustrated by the Komlev article, implicitly recognized that the West was indeed correct in claiming there was a significant disparity in ground manpower in their favor under the active duty counting rule. Explicitly, however, the East could not admit such a situation existed because to do so would lend credence to the Western negotiating position that the East should take greater reductions than the West. Admitting to such a disparity would have put the onus on the East to accept the Western negotiating position. It was indicative of the Eastern desire to move the talks forward that they were bold enough to go public with such an implicit admission. The intention was to get the West to modify its counting rules by either eliminating those Eastern soldiers counted by the West who were performing housekeeping functions and homeland air defense duties, or to get the West to include the 120,000 West German civilians as well as Western air force air defense personnel.

The second option would obviously be more to the East's liking, as any additional integration of West German personnel into MBFR would be in line with Eastern goals.

From the Western point of view, neither option was attractive. Exempting personnel who were active duty soldiers, even by the East's own implicit admission, simply because in peacetime - taking the East at their word - they were performing housekeeping duties, would be self-deluding as nothing would preclude them from being quickly transferred to combat duties in the event the East decided to attack NATO. Nor would it be in the best interest of the West to bring West German civilians into MBFR. Such a move would have far-ranging political implications and would radically change the nature of the negotiations. In reality, it illustrates deep Eastern respect and concern with the mobilization capability of the West Germans.

The West had been pushing the East since the start of the negotiations to present data, but the East had been resisting such a move probably for the reasons behind the Komlev article - that by Western counting rules, there was a numerical disparity. By 1976 the East had obviously developed counting rules and a data base which they believed would stand up to Western attack. On 10 June 1976 after two and a half years of negotiations, the East finally provided data on their troop strength in Central Europe. (31) Pravda's announcement of the event follows:

> On 10 June the Socialist countries presented figures concerning the total numerical strength of the armed forces of the Warsaw Pact countries in Central Europe including the numerical strength of ground forces stationed there. (32)

Not surprisingly, but no doubt disappointing to the West, the East tabled figures which showed almost numerical symmetry in active duty manpower.

DATA TABLED 10 JUNE, 1976

	Western	Eastern[33]
Ground	791,000[34]	805,000
Air	193,000	182,300
TOTAL	984,000	987,300

Even though the Eastern data showed none of the numerical disparity claimed by the West, the East still seemed to be implying that the differnces in the data probably resulted from using different counting rules. No less an authority than Brezhnev alluded to this probability when addressing the Conference of European Communist and Workers Parties shortly after the tabling of the Eastern data:

If we are speaking of Central Europe, there are no great differences here between the size of the armed forces of the Warsaw Pact countries and NATO countries. Their level has been more or less equal for many years now - with a certain difference in configuration on each side. (35) [Emphasis added]

While the Pact accepted Western data on Western forces as accurate, the West found Eastern data on Eastern forces unacceptable. The revised Western estimate of Eastern forces showed an increase from 925,000 in 1973 to 962,000 in 1976. Western estimates of Eastern air manpower were also higher at 200,000 (36) for a total of 1,162,000 Warsaw Pact active duty air and ground personnel in the proposed area of reduction.

WESTERN ESTIMATES VERSUS EASTERN CLAIMS IN WARSAW PACT MANPOWER

	Western Estimate	Difference	Eastern Claims
Ground	962,000	157,000	805,000
Air	200,000	17,700	182,300
TOTAL	1,162,000	174,700	987,300

Admitting a disparity of 175,000 was simply too much for the East to accept. They immediately began to attack the Western estimate while defending their own claim of symmetry in active duty forces. An example of the numerous Eastern press articles on the subject:

The delegations of the NATO countries, however, stubbornly refuse to acknowledge the figures submitted by the Socialist countries and continue to assert that the Warsaw Pact forces in Central Europe exceed the NATO forces by approximately 150,000. (37)... In this connection it must be stressed that the NATO states have so far not produced any concrete proof of this claim. We state that 150,000 men constitute a complete army of a medium size state. It is simply impossible either to conceal or temporarily hide such a number of soldiers with appropriate weapons in an area the size of Central Europe. Since the Western participants in the negotiations are constantly referring to the precision of their information, there should be nothing simpler for them to show where the Warsaw Pact has their 150,000 men. (38)

Such challenging of the West to prove its estimate invokes the counter challenge for the East to explain its counting rules and to back up its claims with further data disaggregation. (39)

This seeming impasse has evolved through a series of events which could be called putting the cart before the horse, the cart in this case being data and the horse - agreed counting rules.

An agreed data base is essential to the negotiations in order to verify adherence to the terms of the treaty. This means that both the data and what the data represent (counting rules) must be agreed upon before any terms of the treaty are carried out. Otherwise, neither side can be sure of what the other side's data actually represents.

In the case of MBFR, data were introduced before counting rules were agreed upon. The West presented data to support its reduction proposal of November 1973. This data was useful from the Western standpoint in order to demonstrate its claims. As long as the East did not reciprocate, there was still the opportunity to develop agreed counting rules. However, with the tabling by the East in 1976 of its data (at Western urging), the issue of what the East had counted and how, became infinitely more difficult to determine. Once the East had provided data it was then committed to defend those figures. With national prestige behind publicized numbers, attempts by the West to get the East to change these numbers (i.e., significant increases) through a data discussion is proving very difficult.

The East and the West both introduced further disaggregated data in March 1978. (40) The Eastern data, not surprisingly, supported the gross totals tabled in June 1976. The new data obviously was on individual direct participants for it was reported that the discrepancy between Eastern data and Western estimates was greatest in Soviet and Polish forces. (41)

The West is thus on the horns of a dilemma. It naturally finds it totally inadmissible to accept the Eastern data because to do so would undercut Western security by destroying the long-held Western position that there is a considerable disparity in active duty manpower in Central Europe. The perception of the threat as envisioned by NATO would also be substantially altered with a consequent negative impact on defense budgets and NATO defense programs. On the other hand, if Eastern data are not accepted, MBFR in its present form appears stalemated.

Figure 7.2 graphically illustrates the problem. The West has got to determine the status of the 157,000 troops the East says are not there; otherwise, the 700,000-man common ceiling would, in effect, be a ceiling only for the West with the East having a de facto ceiling of 857,000.

In accordance with the announcement made by Brezhnev in Berlin on October 6, 1979, to withdraw unilaterally up to 20,000 soldiers and 1,000 tanks from the GDR within a year, the Soviets began to withdraw elements of the 6th Guards Tank Division on December 5, 1979. Given Soviet press statements made in late 1979 and early 1980, it should be assumed that no matter how many Soviet soldiers are unilaterally withdrawn, the East will correspondingly reduce its announced ground

BEFORE REDUCTIONS   **AFTER REDUCTIONS**

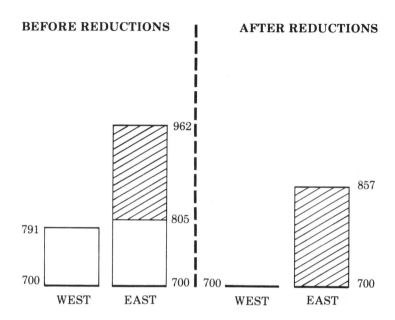

(Note: cross hatched areas show amount and effects of disputed
force levels;   all figures indicate thousands)

Fig. 7.2.   The data discrepancy before and after reductions.

force figure of 805,000 downward accordingly. Assuming that 20,000
were in fact withdrawn, the East could then claim that their strength
was only 785,000 and therefore would only need to take an 85,000-
instead of a 105,000-man MBFR reduction to reach the 700,000 common
ceiling.   Ironically, this would result in a reduction of some 6,000
personnel less than the NATO required reduction of 91,000.

If the West determines to its satisfaction that the Soviets did indeed
withdraw 20,000 Soviets, Western estimates would be lowered. Accordingly, the present disparity of 157,000 between East and West data
would be reduced to 137,000.

If the East continues to hold fast on its numbers, the logical
objective of the West would be to try to find, through a counting rules
discussion, an acceptable explanation as to why those personnel in
dispute should not be included in the MBFR data base.

The East continues to stress the point that there are differences in
the structure of the forces on each side and by doing so seems to be
implying that the West's counting rules have been incorrectly applied to

Eastern forces. For example, the Eastern press continues to echo the statement of Brezhnev concerning the difference in configuration in the forces of each side:

> It is natural that certain differences have evolved in the structure of the individual types of armed forces of the states participating in the Vienna talks. This applies above all to the ground forces, to the proportions between conventional and nuclear weapons, to the organizational structure, number of men in divisions, and other formations.... In spite of these particularities and differences, there exists a balance of power between the Warsaw Pact and NATO in Central Europe. (42)

One could conclude from the above that the East had not counted its forces exactly as the West had done, hinting that perhaps the East had kept out some types of personnel which the West considers to be active duty, but which the East believes they can defend as not being active duty.

Adding confusion to this issue are other Eastern statements which maintain that:

> The socialist states explained in detail their principles and methods for computing data about the number of their troops in Central Europe. All troops are included in these figures except for those excluded after agreement with Western diplomats (civilian employees, reserve soldiers, border guards, and military personnel assigned to ministries other than defense). (43)

Such statements lead to a reaction by some Western officials that the East is lying about its figures. (44)

Hints as to what types of personnel the East might have deleted have also appeared in the Eastern press:

> The West might possibly include reservists who are only in service temporarily in its count of Warsaw Pact forces. Moreover, the military administrative personnel serving in the Warsaw Pact - NATO uses mostly civilians for administrative work - are included in the military personnel ceilings. (45)

Such statements appear to be implicit admissions that the East realizes it has more active duty personnel than the West and is looking for Western agreement to delete a portion of Eastern personnel from the count, or if the West would agree, to have additional Western forces added to the count rather than Eastern forces being subtracted.

The East has always been disappointed in the fact that the French did not join MBFR. The East points out the fact that the West "distorts the real correlation of forces by only counting those personnel committed to NATO." (46) In Soviet eyes the French Army is considered to be a part of the NATO military organization. (47) They have insisted, and the West has agreed, to count the 60,000 French soldiers stationed in West Germany. But because France refuses to participate in MBFR, no French territory is included in the proposed area of reduction; consequently, only 60,000 of the 330,000-strong (48) French standing army are included in the count of Western forces. The East has bluntly indicated unhappiness with the situation: "Armed forces of France are usually omitted in East/West comparisons although France is still a NATO member." (49) Including 270,000 additional French soldiers in the MBFR data base would, of course, eliminate the disparity and actually put it in favor fo the West.

Another Eastern concern was the exclusion of the majority of the Territorial Army of the FRG because it is largely a reservist organization. The Territorial Army includes 63,000 active duty personnel which are counted in MBFR and some 400,000 quickly mobilizable reserves which, of course, are not. While assigned primarily to support functions such as logistics and transportation, the Territorial Army also contains six home defense brigades and motorized infantry regiments which are well equipped with tanks and antitank weapons. (50) It is only natural for the Soviets to want reductions in the Territorial Army because it would be facing this formidable force in addition to the active NATO troops in the event of a PACT attack.

Reservists may be one area which East and West could explore to find a possible answer to the data discrepancy problem. At the 1978 Bonn Congress of Reservists, a West German reservist, Colonel Rudolph Woller, suggested that the discrepancy might be because the West counted certain Warsaw Pact personnel as active duty when they are, in fact, reservists called up for periodic training. (51)

If a precise military/technical solution cannot be found - and if there is a desire on the part of the West to move forward in MBFR as it is currently formulated - a political solution which accepts Eastern claims to some degree on faith might prove attractive. (52) West German Chancellor Helmut Schmidt has suggested that a precise data solution may not be required. Referring to the joint German-Soviet statement of 6 May 1978 issued at the conclusion of Brezhnev's visit to the FRG which in part said: [Both sides] proceed from the premise that approximate equality and parity are significant for guaranteeing defense," Schmidt stated that a data solution was possible if "absolute accuracy is renounced," (53) and indicated a return to a counting rules discussion might bring a solution. (54) Mr. Apel, his Defense Minister, stated that he was in favor of making the "counting a bit more political so that politicians would be able to take care of the counting." (55) Solutions, whether they be military/technical or political, which in some way result in diminution of the Warsaw Pact threat for the purposes of solving the data problem, will have to be carefully constructed for them not to damage Western security. Modifying Western intelligence estimates without concrete contrary evidence, in order to reach an MBFR agreement, would do serious damage not only to the credibility of the Western intelligence community but to Western defense budgets and the US efforts to strengthen NATO.

While the Brezhnev unilateral withdrawal is a clear attempt by the

Soviets to circumvent the data issue, the Western proposal of December 1979 attempts to come to grips with the data issue through an interim solution of modifying the long-standing Western position that there must be an agreed data base on all direct participants before any reduction could be taken. Now the West is only asking for agreement on data on the Soviet and US forces in the reduction area prior to Phase I reductions. According to reports, the decision to split the data problem and address only Soviet forces in Phase I was made because the West had determined that the greatest part of the discrepancy lay in the data advanced on East European, particularly Polish, forces. (56)

However, as was pointed out previously, there is disagreement as well between Western and Eastern data on Soviet forces. The Soviets maintain they have 50,000 troops less in the area of reduction than NATO estimates. (57)   This statement squares with the existing difference in the NATO estimates of 475,000 Soviet ground personnel vice the implicit Soviet figure of 428,000 which can be deduced from the Eastern 1978 proposal. (The unilateral withdrawal will not help shrink this disparity as both East and West will simply subtract 20,000 from their respective data bases.) Thus, splitting the data base problem will not in itself make the solution any easier to find.

As long as the West insists (and properly, indeed mandatorily so) that an agreed data base is absolutely necessary prior to withdrawals, the basic problem which has stalemated the negotiations remains.

Nevertheless, there are solutions to the data problem. The acceptability of a particular solution to one side or the other is the question.   Solutions which undercut Western security and threat perceptions will be unacceptable to the West. Solutions which result in data that require the East to take other than rough symmetrical reductions will be unacceptable to the East. Somewhere among the various alternatives, there may be the makings of a compromise which would allow both sides to come to a face-saving solution which would not jeopardize Western security. (58)

At Eastern urging, updated data were exchanged in June 1980. No figures were made public but   a   NATO spokesmen stated they "differed only slightly" from the 1976 data and that the latest exchange had done nothing to settle the data dispute. (59)

For MBFR to move forward as it is presently structured, a solution to the data problem is absolutely essential in order that there can be an agreed data base with which to monitor residual limitations. The best approach to a data solution lies not in data update but in an agreement on counting values. If, on the other hand, either side wished to end the MBFR process or change its focus, the inability to solve the data problem is a very plausible rationale for doing so. If such a shift is contemplated by either side, it would have to be proposed before a data solution; for data as the key to the size of the Eastern reductions is the last real obstacle to an agreement.

8 Associated Measures

An important aspect of the negotiations which has received little publicity by either East or West is the subject of "associated measures." This Western-coined phrase appears in the official title of the negotiations because of Eastern refusal to allow the Western term "balanced" to be used. (1) By Western definition, "associated measures" means there are other matters besides reductions which must be discussed and agreed upon before a treaty can be signed. Agreed measures are needed, the West insists, for adequately verifying compliance with an MBFR agreement; also needed are confidence-building measures in the form of preannouncement of maneuvers, to enhance stability primarily by reducing the capability to launch a surprise attack. (2)

VERIFICATION

Verification of an MBFR treaty would be much more difficult for the West than the East. In the open society of the West, where military plans and strengths are publicly debated and discussed, it is relatively easy for the East to know what is going on. Furthermore, with the media and political opposition parties ever alert, it would be almost impossible for the West to cheat on any of the treaty provisions, remote as the possibility might be. The widespread (given the numerous press reports) penetration of Western governments and defense establishments by Communist spies furnishes the East with further information on the status of Western forces. Add to these sources the Soviet reconnaissance satellite capability, and the East's lack of concern for any additional negotiated verification measures is not surprising.

In the 8 November 1973 reduction proposal the East stated that "control over the fulfillment of a future agreement can be fully insured with the aid of national facilities." (3) "National Facilities" is the Eastern equivalent to the Western term "National Technical Means." Both are euphemisms for satellites. This, as far as is known, is still the official Eastern position. By implication, therefore, one can assume the East feels National Technical Means is the only type of treaty monitoring acceptable to them.

Discussion of verification has been almost nonexistent in the Eastern press. In a letter in the Danish paper, Aktuelt, a Novosti correspondent in discussing MBFR wrote, "The socialist countries advocate now as they have previously, that military reductions must be accompanied by a reliable and effective system of monitoring." The article then went into a rambling discourse that such monitoring could not, however, be carried out "openly" or by "democratic means" because of the CIA and Pentagon secret operations throughout the world. It implied that any proposed negotiated (i.e., on-site inspection) verification measures would be simply an excuse for Western spying. (4)   Another brief statement on verification was made in the Czech press to the effect that "Each state was to check adherence to agreements itself and if need be, it should demand consultations with all partners in the treaty." (5)

The East is on high ground in choosing National Technical Means as the vehicle to monitor and verify an MBFR agreement.   Both the Soviets and the United States rely greatly upon them for verifying the Strategic Arms Limitation Talks (SALT) Interim Agreement and the Anti-Ballistic Missile Treaty of May 1972.   Explicit provisions were made in both of these agreements to verify by National Technical Means.   Under Article XII of the AMB Treaty and Article V of the Interim Agreement, both the Soviet Union and the United States agreed to use of "national technical means in a manner consistent with generally recognized principles of international law." (6) They further pledged not to interfere with each other's satellites or to use deliberate concealment measures which impede verification by national technical means. (7) No on-site inspections or observers were thought necessary. These provisions have been carried over into the SALT II treaty as well. Thus, an important precedent was set by both sides to monitor future arms control agreements by National Technical Means and the Soviets are obviously attempting to capitalize on their precedent-setting initiative to restrict MBFR verification solely to National Technical Means.

While verification will probably be no problem for the East, even if it did not have reconnaissance satellites, the same is not true for the West.   With the East now agreeing to a common ceiling of 700,000 ground personnel within an overall ceiling of 900,000 ground and air personnel, there will be a requirement for NATO to be able to verify that the East is not violating these ceilings.   If other ceilings are also negotiated, such as the national manpower ceilings desired by the East or the US and Soviet manpower ceilings desired by the West, additional requirements will be placed upon Western intelligence to adequately monitor these ceilings so that NATO can verify Eastern compliance. (8)

MBFR verification looks like a formidable, maybe even an impossible, task at first glance. The problem of determining gross manpower levels with precision is a difficult and time-consuming one. Monitoring these levels for violations is also a challenge, but this task is only one part of the process of MBFR verification. MBFR verification is in reality a three-tier challenge for the West, each challenge more difficult than the one before. The first tier is to determine that the agreed-upon reductions have taken place. It would seem highly unlikely that the East would attempt any cheating in this phase, because the East, especially the Soviets, would have the opportunity to reap maximum propaganda benefit by announcing and publicizing the withdrawal of their forces. In its 1973 reduction proposal, the East suggested that both sides "inform each other of the start and the completion" of reductions. Determining that withdrawals of stationed forces and reductions of indigenous forces have been made, therefore, should not prove to be a problem. The wide publicity given by the Eastern press on 5 December 1979 to the first increment of the Soviet unilateral withdrawal from the GDR is indicative that the Soviets would be amenable to allow observation of at least the start of withdrawals.

The post-withdrawal or residual phase of verification presents a more formidable challenge, one that can be looked on as really two separate and distinct problems. The first is to promptly discover a massive reintroduction of Soviet forces and/or mobilization of East European forces that pose an immediate threat to NATO. Such an eventuality is no different than one that is faced today by NATO. A system to monitor for such a contingency currently exists and is considered quite reliable. It goes without saying that such a massive violation would automatically negate the MBFR treaty by its very enormity and gravity, and it would call for actions far more severe than East/West consultations within the MBFR forum.

The most difficult problem in monitoring post-residual limitations would be that posed by small incremental violations of the treaty which did not, in the short term, create an immediate threat to NATO security. Undoubtedly, small-scale re-introduction or increases in troop strength, made gradually over time, would be extremely difficult to detect. Such violations would have to be measured against the gross manpower residual ceilings, thus presenting a formidable challenge. Complicating the task is the long border between the area of reductions and the Soviet Union, which makes clandestine introduction of small units hard to detect. This problem led the West, in its December 1979 proposal, to again propose on-site inspection measures of the type discussed by both sides in earlier arms control proposals of the 1950s.

In order to understand Soviet reaction to the West's proposal in 1979, it might be beneficial to look back at previous Soviet positions on on-site inspection measures, beginning with the arms control talks of the 1950s. One should recall that in those days there were no satellites to perform verification. Aerial inspection in the 1950s could not furnish the level of monitoring capability that today's satellites can; hence, ground measures were seriously considered, even by the East, despite their intrusive nature.

At the 1955 meeting of the Foreign Ministers in Geneva such measures were first officially discussed between East and West; Soviet Foreign Minister Molotov proposed setting up a system of international control stations situated at ports, airfields, etc., through which troops must pass on their way to attack positions. (9) But he rejected earlier US proposals for aerial inspection and exchanges of information on the status of military forces as contributing to, rather than deterring, surprise attacks. In a reply to the Soviets by Henry Cabot Lodge, the United States representative welcomed the concept of control stations proposed by the Soviets, but pointed out that they had not clarified whether they would be fixed or mobile. If they were fixed, said Lodge, then the US proposal for aerial inspection would be even more valid. (10)

Later, in the Rapacki Plan of 1957-58, the Poles called for ground and aerial inspections and "adequate control posts with rights and possibility of action which would ensure the effectiveness of inspections." (11)

The subject of ground inspection and aerial inspection continued to be of interest to both sides. Largely at the urging of President Eisenhower, "The Conference of Experts for the Study of Possible Measures which Might be Helpful in Preventing Surprise Attack" was held in Geneva from 10 November to 18 December 1958. (12) The conference was notable in that for the first time, East and West addressed arms control measures at a level of preciseness greater than the previous general discussions. The conference failed to produce any concrete steps toward a treaty to diminish the threat of surprise attack but it did prove to be a useful exercise in determining Eastern views and approaches to negotiated inspection measures.

The East came to the 1958 conference prepared to discuss the technical aspects of only two measures: fixed inspection posts and aerial inspection. Unexpectedly, the Soviets had reversed their stand on aerial inspection and were calling for an 800-kilometer-wide zone of aerial photography on both sides of the East/West border. They were also agreeable to having 28 fixed ground control posts located on Warsaw Pact territory. (13) The West, on the other hand, put forth a whole series of technical papers. Among them was the Western concept of mobile ground inspection teams. In the West's view:

> Significant reduction of the danger of surprise attack by ground forces is practicable and technically feasible through the use of an adequate number of observer teams with properly defined rights, with proper technical vehicular and communication equipment and with unimpeded access to and over areas in which ground forces are located. (14)

But despite Western efforts, the mobile team proposal was ignored by the Soviets. Rather, they stuck to presenting only their detailed concepts of how fixed inspection posts and aerial inspection would function. "Ground Control Posts," as the East called them, would be established at railway junctions, major ports, and on main roads at agreed points within a zone extending 800 kilometers on both sides of the East/West border in Central Europe. (15)

No one expected that the Soviets would give Western inspectors carte blanche to roam Eastern territory at will. But to the dismay of the West, the Soviets placed restrictions on them that were so tight their usefulness as contributors to Western early warning would have been virtually nil. For example, according to the Soviets, the staff of each fixed post would consist of one-half NATO and one-half Warsaw Pact personnel with support personnel being provided by the host country. If located in the East, the Post Commander would be from a Warsaw Pact country and if in the West, the commander would be from a NATO country. Significantly, the post would not have its own communications but would be required to use host country communications to render their reports, which must be uncoded. (16)

In retrospect, such limitations are not surprising given the Russian fear that these posts would be used for spying. It is not hard to visualize how terribly restricted NATO members of a fixed post would be under terms of these Soviet 1958 proposals: surrounded by Warsaw Pact team members, host country support personnel, and above all, having to use host country communications to render reports. During a crisis, the Warsaw Pact could simply refuse to allow reports to be sent out or send fake reports to continue to lull NATO.

The Soviet concept for aerial inspection tabled at the 1958 conference also contained significant restrictions on freedom of operation. For example, to photograph Eastern installations, Warsaw Pact aircraft would be used, manned by mixed crews, and photography would be developed by a mixed staff within Eastern Europe. No actual photograph could be sent to NATO unless the East gave its permission. Uncoded verbal summary reports could be transmitted to the West but again only through host country communications. (17) Hence, like fixed posts, aerial inspection under such restrictions would result in little if any accurate information for the West in times of crisis. In effect, what one had was a self-policing system in which the West would have to place its trust in the Russians which, of course, would be unacceptable. Certainly it was not a system that would enhance Western early warning of a surprise attack.

Furthermore, the Soviets placed a caveat on the acceptance of even such a highly restricted system. In the course of presenting their concepts, the Soviets stated that such posts and aerial photography were not by themselves effective measures for reducing the danger of surprise attack unless they were linked to a one-third reduction of the forces in Central Europe and to a nuclear free zone made up of the two Germanies. (18)

By agreeing to NATO inspectors on Eastern soil, the Soviets believed they would be making a significant concession, for they were convinced that these inspectors would be used as intelligence gatherers. The Soviets reasoned that if they allowed such inspectors on their soil before reductions in the military capability of the West took place, the West would have no incentive to reduce its forces. In the East's view, Western inspectors on Eastern soil reporting on Warsaw Pact forces to an undiminished Western military capability would result in diminished Eastern security. (19)   As Chief US Delegate William C. Foster explained in his end-of-conference report, to the Soviets, surrendering any of their secrecy is a unilateral disarmament step that they believe must be compensated for by the West. (20) Nevertheless, even as late as July 1963, during the Partial Nuclear Test Ban Treaty discussions, Khrushchev proposed an exchange of inspectors and static control posts at ports, railheads, highways, and airfields. This proposal, according to the Soviets, was designed to assuage fears of a buildup for a military thrust against NATO. It did not, however, allow for mobile inspection which the Soviets deemed "obnoxious." (21)

The Russian penchant for secrecy is well known and predates the 1917 Bolshevik takeover. Thus, it was not surprising back in 1958, nor is it surprising in the current stage of the MBFR talks, that they would find intrusive types of inspections threatening. This is not to say that because of past Soviet rejection of mobile inspection teams and the proposal of emasculating restrictions for fixed posts and aerial inspection, the West should not attempt to negotiate such measures in MBFR in order to enhance verification and to increase early warning capability. But, as this brief historical review has shown, it will be difficult at best to negotiate effective inspection measures, especially in light of the apparent Soviet decision to rely solely on National Technical Means for verification. However, by agreeing to verification by National Technical Means in SALT, the Soviets have implicitly recognized the premise that attempting to maintain total secrecy has a destabilizing effect on arms control. (22)

In recognizing that some of their secrecy must be surrendered, the Soviets concluded that National Technical Means was the best method by which to accede to Western desires for verification measures without having to agree to intrusive negotiated inspection measures. By going on record that the MBFR agreement is to be verified by National Technical Means, the Soviets have implicitly stated that they do not need negotiated measures to verify MBFR, and indeed they do not.

Despite all the obstacles the Soviets have placed in the path of effective on-site inspectors, the concept of such measures maintained its attractiveness to the West over the years. The West realized how important entry/exit points, fixed inspection posts, ground inspection teams, and aerial inspection would be in providing continuous (but not blanket) coverage of the reduction area especially when periods of darkness and bad weather prevented surveillance by National Technical Means. Such measures would increase Western confidence in under-standing what was going on in the closed Eastern societies, and would furthermore give those direct participants who do not possess National Technical Means the opportunity to participate actively in some form in the monitoring and verification of the agreement. Misinterpretation would be less likely to flare into major political/military crises. Nor would the effectiveness of such observers be entirely negated should the East deliberately block observers or aerial overflights from carrying out inspections.   Such actions alone would indicate to the West the probability of something unusual taking place, such as large troop movements or mobilization.

Over the years since the start of the MBFR negotiations, there have been oft-repeated references to a Western desire to formally propose negotiated inspection measures as part of the associated measures provision agreed on by both East and West at the preliminary talks. But nothing transpired out of NATO over the years since then, largely because of sensitivity to West German concern that such measures would impinge on their sovereignty. (23)

It was not until the fall of 1979 that the West was able to achieve consensus on specific negotiated inspection measures to be advanced to the East.   These measures, along with several confidence-building measures (to be discussed later in this chapter), were included in the associated measures portion the new Western proposal presented in Vienna on 14 December 1979. (24)

The specific negotiated inspection measures proposed were: (25)

- The stationed direct participants (i.e., Canada, US, UK, USSR) must give prior notification of the movement of their ground forces into the area of reductions.

- Ground force units must enter and leave the area of reductions only through designated entry and exit points. These would be located at a fixed number of sea ports, railroad border crossings, highway border crossings, and airfields.

- Each side will have the right to place inspectors at each other's entry/exit points.

- Each side will have the right to make up to 18 air or ground inspection trips in the area of reduction belonging to the other side.

- There would be a periodic exchange of data and information on the forces in the area after the treaty becomes effective.

- The non-interference with the National Technical Means provision found in SALT would also be followed in MBFR.

- A Standing Consultative Commission, similar to that found in SALT, would oversee compliance with the treaty.

The inclusion of negotiated inspection measures as part of an overall associated measures package was an excellent piece of timing by the West, because it placed the most unattractive aspects of associated measures, from the Eastern point of view, on to the negotiating table in tandem with additional confidence-building measures of the type agreed to by both East and West at CSCE. The public Eastern support of the concept of confidence-building measures in general makes rejection by the East of the overall associated measures package, because of the inclusion of controversial inspection measures, politically more difficult.

Despite the fact that at long last negotiated inspection measures were formally made a part of the negotiations in 1979, their eventual codification was not at all assured. This was because of their basically intrusive nature and the fact that an internationally acceptable alternative already existed for verification in the form of National Technical Means. If such measures are not successfully codified, then Western negotiators will have to insure that the provisions of any MBFR agreement can be adequately monitored and verified solely through the use of national means before concluding an MBFR agreement.

CONFIDENCE-BUILDING MEASURES

Associated measures also include by Western definition "measures which will build mutual confidence and enhance stability by reducing fear of surprise attack and the risk of other misunderstandings...." (26) Measures which could accomplish such tasks without the permanent intrusiveness of negotiated inspection measures are of the type found in the Final Act of the Conference on Security and Cooperation in Europe. Those agreed upon at CSCE were: prior notification of major military maneuvers, prior notification of other military maneuvers, exchange of observers, and other measures such as promoting exchange visits of military personnel. (27)

The most significant of these provisions is the prior notification of major maneuvers, whereby all maneuvers exceeding a strength of 25,000 conducted in Europe and, in the case of maneuvers conducted in the USSR, within 250 kilometers of the western borders, will be announced 21 days in advance. Such announcements would contain among other things, the type and numerical strength of the forces engaged, the area, and the estimated time frame of its conduct. (28)

As far as the West was concerned, any Eastern preannouncement of maneuvers and the inviting of observers is precedent setting and welcomed. It should be emphasized, however, that such CSCE measures are strictly voluntary. In fact, it has been the consensus of those who observed them that the maneuvers announced by the East to which observers were invited were carefully orchestrated affairs designed primarily to show Eastern support of CSCE; that through modified adherence of the maneuver provisions, the Soviets were seeking to deflect the storm of criticism directed at them for nonadherence to the human rights provisions of CSCE.

Nevertheless, even token Eastern willingness to adhere to a type of confidence-building measures long favored by the West has raised hopes that such measures could eventually play a more significant role in arms control.

The East, as its initiative of the 1950s showed, has over the years maintained an interest in confidence-building measures, but for reasons different from those of the West. The West is concerned with confidence-building measures which enhance early warning and reduce the chance of surprise attack. The natural reaction among Westerners is to dismiss out of hand any Soviet fear of attack from the West and thus to expect the Soviets to have no interest in such measures. Such a conclusion may be erroneous. As the negotiations have demonstrated, the Soviets still are striving for as much control as they possibly can obtain over the Bundeswehr. It is quite apparent that the Soviets, having failed in getting a neutralized Germany under Soviet hegemony, have opted for a divided Germany whose partition is guaranteed by the overwhelming presence of Soviet military might. If the Soviets did not fear to some extent a possible West German attempt to reunite their country by force of arms, then such a military presence would not be required for maintaining Soviet internal control of East Germany. One may plausibly assume that the Eastern attempts to gain further control of the Bundeswehr are to insure that Germany stays divided. Soviet fears of a West German military reaction to turmoil in East Germany at some future date may seem ridiculous to Westerners, but such a prospect is a source of genuine Soviet concern. Hence, it is not correct to assume the East is not interested in confidence-building/stabilizing measures which, like reductions and limitations, place restrictions on the Bundeswehr. In fact, the East has already twice proposed such a measure in MBFR.

Shortly after the announcement by the FRG of the restructuring of the Bundeswehr that would add three additional brigades, the East proposed on 5 December 1974 that there be a freeze on "the numerical strength of the armed forces of each direct participant." (29) The West quickly rejected the Eastern proposal, arguing that without an agreed data base, such a freeze would be meaningless and, furthermore, would codify the numerical superiority of the East.

The US decision to increase the strength of its forces in Europe by adding two combat brigades, artillery, and aircraft, coupled with the NATO adoption of the Long Term Defense Plan, led to a renewed call by the East on 30 November 1978 for such a freeze. This time in deference to the Western position on collective ceilings, the freeze would be a collective one rather than a freeze of individual national forces. (30) The Soviets argued that if "the Western countries were really afraid of Soviet increases in Europe, they would have no reason to reject the socialist countries' proposal." (31) Even the prestige of Brezhnev was put behind the freeze proposal, which is indicative of the seriousness with which the Soviets viewed the NATO force improvement program.

Unlike the NATO countries [Brezhnev declared] we have not been building up our armed forces in Central Europe for a long time and we have no intention - I want to stress this with the utmost force - of increasing them in the future by a single soldier or a single tank. (32)

But once again the West rejected the freeze for exactly the same reason as before. (33)

The continued Soviet interest in other forms of confidence-building measures, which they supported in the 1950s and which are more compatible with Western concepts (i.e., of the CSCE type), was demonstrated in the speech by Brezhnev in Berlin on 6 October 1979. In it he proposed even more stringent reporting criteria for the current CSCE maneuver provisions by calling for a reduction in the ceiling to be reported from 25,000 to 20,000, and for a ban on all maneuvers involving over 50,000 troops. (34) Such continued Soviet interest, albeit to date only within the non-binding forum of CSCE, encourages the possibility that confidence-building measures of some type might be used to achieve an agreement in MBFR.

The lack of any progress toward meaningful Eastern reductions has led to a call for a new approach to MBFR. Some observers suggest placing emphasis on confidence-building measures in MBFR, or even restructuring MBFR away from its focus on reductions to one of enhancing warning time for the West through obligatory measures. One prominent figure who has gone on record for such an approach to MBFR is US Congressman Les Aspin. (35)

Congressman Aspin recognized the need for NATO to be able to protect itself from surprise attack. Instead of focusing on reductions, the Congressman suggested in August 1977 that the MBFR talks concentrate on negotiating confidence-building measures that would deter surprise attack and increase warning time.

> NATO continues to be preoccupied with the disparities of troops and tanks in the Central Region. This focus has simply not been fruitful. I am proposing instead of using the MBFR talks to negotiate a reduction in troops, we use it to negotiate measures to increase warning time and reduce the chance of a surprise attack. (36)

His criticism was followed by that of Senator Sam Nunn, who in December 1977 called for a redirecting of the MBFR negotiations away from manpower reductions which would be "meaningless" and "unverifiable" toward measures that would increase warning time. (37)

Support for such an approach grew in 1978 and 1979, and understandably so, given the stalemate with the reductions approach. Perhaps, it was argued, a switch to a confidence-building measures concept would prove more successful, that in fact, the cart was put before the horse when both sides went for an initial agreement on reductions rather than an agreement on confidence-building measures.

The French, who have long opposed MBFR and flatly refused to participate in it, called for a European Conference for Disarmament during the UN Special Session on Disarmament held in New York on 25 May 1978. Borrowing from early Western arms control proposals of the 1950s and 1960s, they suggested a three-phased approach of first, confidence-building measures which promote mutual trust and understanding, followed by implementation of measures to prevent surprise attack. Only after these measures were successfully implemented would force limitations or reductions be undertaken. (38)

The Soviets, in arms control proposals of the 1950s and 1960s, always placed implementation of confidence measures after actual reductions and limitations. Their position in MBFR toward such measures has given no indication of a willingness to change this priority. Yet, at the 5-6 December 1979 meeting of Warsaw Pact Foreign Ministers in Berlin, the Ministers, in supporting the call of the Pact's Political Consultative Committee made on 23 November 1978 to hold a conference on "Military Detente and Disarmament in Europe," suggested that the first stage of such a conference should be on confidence-building measures. (39)

Changing the approach in MBFR from one of reductions to one based on confidence-building measures may not be easy, nor should the types of confidence-building measures discussed above be considered adequate instruments in themselves to achieve the level of security from surprise attack desired by the West. Such measures as ceilings on the number of personnel allowed to participate in a maneuver are difficult to codify to an extent that cheating is meaningfully precluded. In sum, they must be considered effective only as supplemental or supportive to other arms control measures such as reductions and limitations.

Such a relationship is recognized in the December 1979 Western proposal which combines a call for reductions and limitations supported by negotiated inspection measures and confidence-building measures. The two confidence-building measures are of significance because it is the first attempt to codify confidence-building measures (as opposed to the CSCE approach) and to extend such codified measures outside of the proposed area of reduction, yet remain as provisions of an MBFR agreement. The two measures advanced to the East were prior notification of a full division (i.e., 10,000 personnel or more) moving out of garrison, and the right to send observers to monitor the maneuvers. (40)

What made these measures of extreme significance for MBFR was the Western requirement that they be adhered to not only within the area of reductions but throughout Europe as a whole, including a significant part of the western USSR. (41)

Since the negotiations began, all proposals made by both sides have been designed for implementation within the proposed area of reduction, i.e., the Benelux, FRG, East Germany, Poland, and Czechoslovakia. The fact that the 1979 Western proposal deliberately attempted to expand the geographic area of MBFR in the aspect of confidence-building measures is precedent setting and of potential significance to the future of MBFR.

The proposal was met with a quick note of Soviet protest which accused the West of "seriously" complicating the talks by submitting . . . control measures which transcend far beyond the limits of the agreed area of limitations." (42) While the Soviet Union finds nonbinding confidence-building measures acceptable on their territory, codified measures appear to be a different story.

The idea to expand the geographic area of MBFR was apparently of West German origin. The West German press reported in late September 1979 that:

> The Federal Government wants to extend the geographical framework of the confidence-building measures as broadly as possible beyond the MBFR area. Troop reduction in the MBFR area alone would not be worth very much if the Soviet Union accumulated just that much more offensive potential behind its border. The Federal Government wants to prevent a marked internationally controlled arms-control zone from emerging in central Europe. (43)

The last sentence of the above quote contains the rationale behind the initiative. The West Germans have long opposed the creation of an arms control approach that singled out the two Germanies as a special disarmament zone. The Benelux nations, Poland, and Czechoslovakia were included in the proposed area of reductions largely for that reason. West German Foreign Minister Genscher in a speech to the Bundestag on 14 December 1979 confirmed that such a rationale lay behind the expansion of the confidence-building measures geographical area when he stated, "Allowing the MBFR area to become an arms control zone with a special status ought to be avoided." (44)

In the same speech, while not repudiating MBFR, Genscher endorsed the French call for a conference on disarmament in Europe, especially, according to Genscher, because it "proceeds from the geographical indivisibility of confidence-building in Europe." (45)

The French proposal, the statements of Genscher, and the call of the Foreign Ministers of the Warsaw Pact in December 1979 for a conference similar to that proposed by the French, when taken together with the US statement that the Western associated measures package included in their 1979 proposal was "a new approach to arms control in Europe," (46) could certainly be construed as a trend in both East and West toward possible restructuring of MBFR. The lack of success in an approach that focuses on manpower reduction and limitation revalidates what James Dougherty said in his seminal piece on Zonal Arms Limitations in Europe, written in 1963:

> Each side perceives its military security problem as well as its long-range political objectives in such unique and incompatible ways that up to now, neither party has been capable of proposing a plan which the other could be expected to take seriously. (47)

Thus, in late 1979, at the close of almost a decade of ill-fated attempts to achieve arms control in Central Europe through reductions, both sides appeared to be seeking a new direction through confidence-building measures.

Besides the confidence-building measures discussed above, whose limitations preclude them from completely supplanting the present approach, there are other measures of a confidence-building type which could serve as alternatives to the current MBFR reduction approach. One such approach, which had been proposed in the 1950s, was dusted off in 1978 by Romanian President Nicolae Ceausescu, who called for establishment of a zone between the two blocs where no arms would be located and no maneuvers take place. (48)

Known as "disengagement" in the lexicon of arms control, this concept has been oft suggested through the years, especially by the Soviets. In its extreme form, it was a means of creating a neutral and demilitarized Germany through the total withdrawal of all foreign forces. The Rapacki Plan called for a form of disengagement in creating a nuclear free zone in Central Europe. In 1955 the West offered its version of disengagement as part of a plan to reunify Germany. The plan resembled in some respects the current MBFR proposal.

The West's disengagement proposal called for a control zone (depth unspecified) straddling the eastern border of a reunified Germany in which "levels for armed forces would be specified so as to establish a military balance." (49) For protection against surprise attack, a line of radar stations would be established, manned on the west edge of the zone by the Warsaw Pact and on the eastern edge by NATO. (50) To increase confidence and stability further, the Western proposal suggested a controlled zone of unspecified size on both sides of the border where "there might be special measures relating to the disposition of military forces and installations." (51)

Helmut Schmidt, the current chancellor of the FRG, proposed in 1962 a fairly extensive disengagement scheme for Central Europe. (52) Schmidt's first phase consisted of the implementation of confidence-building measures of the type which had been proposed by both East and West in the 1950s, i.e., fixed and mobile ground inspection and aerial inspection. This would then be followed by indigenous reductions. The second phase would consist of the establishment of two early warning lines, one in the West along the Rhine River manned by Warsaw Pact personnel and another in the East along the Bug River manned by NATO personnel. This would be followed by massive withdrawals of foreign troops (along the lines of earlier disengagement schemes of the 1950s until only small detachments of about brigade strength remained as "symbols along the dividing line." (53)

Schmidt openly acknowledged that his scheme was designed to reunify Germany. As he correctly observed, nothing is better calculated to perpetuate the division of Germany than the continued presence of Soviet troops on German soil. (54)

But since that time, many things have happened to the status of Central Europe that make such massive disengagement schemes totally impractical and all participants, both East and West, recognize this fact.

The reality of a distinctly separate East German nation, geographically the size of the state of Alabama, in which the Soviets maintain a massive military presence of close to 400,000 troops who are continually upgraded in capability, makes it perfectly clear that the Soviets have decided that the status quo is now preferable to any large disengagement scheme that could upset the current "correlation of forces." In fact, the similarity between disturbing the status quo through massive disengagement schemes and the Mansfield proposal can certainly be advanced as a possible reason, if not the key factor, for the Soviets agreeing to MBFR. Most would seem to agree that from the standpoint of military stability, it would be destabilizing to turn the ground over exclusively to the Bundeswehr and the Volksarmee. In 1958 Mr. Selwyn Lloyd made the following observation:

> The world is a much safer place if in critical areas there is a direct confrontation of the major parties and not an area of uncertainty. In Central Europe the two great nuclear powers do confront each other directly. As long as this situation prevails, a war triggered off by chance border incidents will be unlikely. (55)

A recognition of this fact can certainly be found in the Soviet desire to maintain the status quo and in the US Government's desire to keep a large viable American presence in Central Europe.

Despite the overall obsolescence of these massive disengagement schemes, certain aspects of them still have some potential application. A confidence-building measure proposal made by the West at the October 1955 meeting of Foreign Ministers in Geneva, as part of a plan for German reunification, which could presently contribute to an increase in early warning for NATO, was the idea to set up two surveillance early warning lines, one in the West manned by Warsaw Pact personnel, and one in the East manned by NATO personnel. (56) But without massive disengagement, the placing of such lines behind existing troop concentrations is valueless. Nevertheless, this scheme could be modified to fit into the current realities of the Central European situation.

Another Western suggestion made at the same Geneva meeting was to set up special control zones on both sides of the border in which restrictions (in the proposal they were unspecified) would be placed on the "disposition of military forces and installations." (57) Such an approach has been recently suggested by several specialists in security matters. Christoph Bertram, in arguing for a new direction for MBFR, like Congressman Aspin, suggests an approach that would focus on reducing the Eastern capability to launch a surprise attack. He proposes that measures be taken to reduce the capability of front-line units to launch such an attack through restructuring. (58)

Frederick Wyle, writing in 1976, correctly foresaw the current impasse on data. Instead of reductions which are data dependent, he proposed an alternative approach that would seek to restructure combat forces from offensive to defensive organizations. He noted that the Soviets are particularly vulnerable politically to this approach because of their numerous protestations to the effect that their forces are defensive in nature. (59) Senator Sam Nunn, in his December 1977 call for a refocusing of MBFR, suggested taking measures that would result in the removal of "forward deployed Soviet combat units." (60) A noted arms control specialist, J.I. Coffey, supports the concept of special zones which move offensive units such as armored divisions well to the rear. Such rearward basing not only makes the armored forces less menacing but it also improves the defensive posture of each side. (61) In the case of the West, such redeployment of offensive units to the rear could force NATO out of its layer cake cordon defense into an echelon defense with armor-heavy reserves, thus giving it more flexibility to block Warsaw Pact armored thrusts. (62)

The measures discussed above are representative of the additional possibilities in the area of confidence-building/stabilizing measures (as opposed to reductions) that appear to offer alternatives to the current MBFR approach. Other measures are possible and variants of these measures have almost no limits. But with any confidence-building measures proposed, two key questions must be asked. What measures are politically and militarily acceptable? And, given their acceptability, can the proposals be successfully negotiated in the MBFR forum?

9 Does MFBR Have a Future?

The negotiation on Mutual and Balanced Force Reductions (MBFR) have been underway since 1973. On October 30th of that year, 19 nations belonging to either NATO or to the Warsaw Pact gathered in Vienna, Austria. Their objective was to negotiate an enhancement of military stability through a reduction of the standing armies facing each other in Central Europe. In terms of tangible results, there is little to show for the thousands of hours and millions of words that have been expended in Vienna. This is principally because the two sides have not yet been able to agree on an arms control scheme acceptable to one another's perceived political objectives and/or military security concerns. Another contributing factor has been the pall thrown over detente and arms control by the Soviet invasion of Afghanistan in December 1979.

Having traced the tortuous path of the negotiations and sketched in some detail the stumbling blocks to agreement, it is now appropriate in this final chapter to stand back and make a summary assessment of MBFR and its future.

THE ROAD TO MBFR

Arms control proposals for Central Europe prior to the start of MBFR negotiations were neither attractive enough in themselves, nor were the pressures from outside the arms control spectrum strong enough, to bring the two sides to the negotiating table. In the 1950s, European arms control initiatives were essentially adjuncts to proposals for political solutions to the German reunification problem; others were general disarmament schemes proposed through the United Nations. What all these proposals had in common was the lack of a catalyst to turn them into actual negotiations.

By the middle 1960s, in the era of detente and the rise of the Soviet

Union to superpower status, events began to create a favorable political climate in which East and West could sit down at the conference table and negotiate an arms control agreement for Central Europe. The start of the Strategic Arms Limitations Talks (SALT) in 1969 set a significant precedent: for the first time, the Soviet Union and the United States were negotiating arms control measures over segments of their armed forces.

The Soviets had long desired a conference on European security which would recognize their hegemony over Eastern Europe, and the West wanted to negotiate reduction of conventional forces in Central Europe. With the precedent set by SALT no doubt contributing toward a more positive atmosphere for negotiations, the United States agreed in late 1972 to support the Conference on Security and Cooperation in Europe (CSCE) in exchange for Soviet agreement to participate in MBFR. It is generally believed this linkage was the primary motivator that brought the Soviets to the negotiating table in Vienna. While this linkage no doubt played a role, one should also remember that much of what the Soviets had sought in CSCE (especially recognition of the Oder-Neisse River as the boundary between East Germany and Poland) had already been realized in the West German treaties with the Soviets and with Poland in 1970.

To be sure, the Soviets clearly wanted a broader spectrum of recognition for their hegemony over Eastern Europe than the German treaties gave them. It is doubtful, however, that the desire for CSCE would have been strong enough to propel the Soviets to the table if they had not decided that participating in MBFR was in their best interests. In fact, the evidence shows that the Soviets had decided to participate several years earlier: the platform of the 24th Party Congress in 1971 called for MBFR participation and Brezhnev's speech in Tbilisi in May 1971 called for the start of the MBFR negotiations. The timing of the Tbilisi speech was significant. It came just before the congressional vote which defeated the controversial proposal by Senator Mansfield to reduce unilaterally US troops in Europe.

Viewing this series of events in retrospect, it is clear that the long missing catalyst for serious arms control negotiations in Central Europe had been found: the mutual fear of both the US administration and the Soviet Union concerning the uncertain impact a large and precipitous unilateral withdrawal of US ground forces from West Germany would have on the stability of Central Europe. The Nixon administration was fearful of what it would do to the defense of Western Europe and the viability of the NATO Alliance. The Soviets were fearful it could galvanize Western Europe into nuclear sharing with West Germany and lead to demands for increases in the strength of the Bundeswehr to compensate for the US withdrawals, thus increasing the possibility (in Soviet eyes) of West Germany revanchism.

WHY NO TREATY

The motivating factors which brought the two sides together to negotiate did not translate into an early and successful conclusion to the negotiations. Hence the lack of a treaty. Both sides shared the common objective of starting formal negotiations to block unilateral US withdrawals; beyond that, however, viewpoints split. The seeds of the current impasse were planted in the reduction proposals of the two sides. In making their proposals, both sides reverted to previously held perceptions of what the military equation should be in Central Europe from their respective viewpoints, viewpoints which had been unacceptable to one another long before the agreement to sit down and negotiate. Hence, it was not surprising that such viewpoints continued to be unacceptable once the negotiations began.

A factor which had a large share in creating the present impasse was that the initial proposals were designed around the central theme of manpower reductions and limitations. This was only to be expected because the driving force behind MBFR was the undesirability of massive US unilateral manpower withdrawals. But reductions and limitations have a finality about them that fosters a very cautious approach by the participants to insure that their security will not be jeopardized by the taking of such reductions and the agreeing to particular limitations.

In addition, the two sides differed fundamentally in their negotiating approaches prior to MBFR. In the 1950s and 1960s, Eastern arms control approaches called for reductions and limitations first, to be followed by confidence-building measures. Conversely, Western concepts (with the exception of MBFR) from the 1950s up to and including the 1978 French proposal made at the United Nations (1) suggested a more gradual approach, involving first the initiation of confidence-building measures, followed by measures to prevent surprise attack. Only after such measures were fully implemented would force limitations and actual reductions take place. But the realities of the situation in 1973 forced the West to develop a proposal using Eastern sequencing; in order to do what the administration had promised Congress it would do - seek withdrawals of Soviet ground forces in exchange for the withdrawal of US personnel - the Western proposal placed reductions first. Even if an approach had been contemplated along the Western lines of confidence-building measures first, it was obvious to all concerned that the mood of the Congress would have prevented the luxury of such an approach.

It would seem that by adopting Eastern sequencing out of necessity, the Western proposal should have been more acceptable to the East than it turned out to be. But it proved unacceptable because the West attempted, through calling for asymmetrical Eastern reductions, to alleviate its long-held fear of a Warsaw Pact surprise attack.

The original Western MBFR proposal called for a first-phase withdrawal of a Soviet tank army consisting of 68,000 soldiers in five divisions with 1,700 tanks. In return, the United States would withdraw 29,000 soldiers. A second phase would follow wherein both sides would reduce to the common ceiling of 700,000 ground personnel within a combined air/ground ceiling of 900,000. Using Western data estimates, this would require almost a 3:1 reduction of Warsaw Pact forces to NATO forces (262,000:91,000) to the common ceiling of 700,000. Such a reduction would greatly alleviate the capability of the Pact to launch a meaningful surprise attack. But such a reduction would be as disruptive to the Warsaw Pact as the Mansfield proposal of large US withdrawals would have been to NATO. And while a 3:1 reduction is a perfectly proper objective for the West to pursue, it would create a result which has been to date totally unacceptable to the East, for it does in reality change the peacetime ratio of forces in Central Europe from one in favor of the East to one of equality.

In response to Soviet charges that the proposed reductions were inequitable, and that nuclear weapons must be included in MBFR, the West added a nuclear package to its first-phase proposal in 1975. Known as Option III, it consisted of a one-time withdrawal of US nuclear systems consisting of 36 Pershing surface-to-surface ballistic missile launchers, 54 F-4 nuclear-capable fighter-bombers, and 1,000 nuclear warheads. The proposal was unsuccessful in achieving its desired objectives and was withdrawn in 1979.

A 3:1 reduction ratio would indeed negate the Eastern capability to use its preponderance of military force to intimidate the West in situations short of war. (2) However, by attempting to reduce the fear of a surprise attack through a reduction based on numerical parity, the West demands an Eastern reduction of a magnitude which is unacceptable in relation to the political and military objectives of the East.

In contrast, the Eastern proposal was and still is designed to maintain the Warsaw Pact advantage in active duty manpower through equal percentage reductions. It also incorporated long-held Soviet objectives vis-a-vis NATO and West Germany. To reduce and place limits on the Bundeswehr's size and on its nuclear launchers have been Soviet objectives since the 1950s. Another long-held objective has been the weakening of NATO. The opportunity through MBFR to attempt such was one that the Soviets could not resist. In the original Eastern proposal of 1973, the eagerness to obtain these objectives was clearly evident in their call for 17 percent symmetrical reductions and individual national ceilings on equipment, nuclear launchers, and personnel. Western acceptance of such a proposal was, of course, impossible because of its impact on the military security of the West and the sovereignty of the Federal Republic of Germany.

By succumbing to the temptation to strive once again for long-held political and military security objectives in Central Europe, both sides locked themselves into positions which even the momentum created by the desire to preserve the American presence in Western Europe could not overcome. Thus, the opportunity for early agreement on a precedent-setting arms control accord for Central Europe was lost by the presentation of obviously unacceptable proposals. The result has been a virtual stalemate while a search for common ground was undertaken. The search has been constrained by the parameters created by the basic positions of the two sides, yet nevertheless it has slowly staked out a commonality between the two positions (see Fig. 9.1) that leaves only two major obstacles - the size of the Soviet reduction and a commitment on the size of the Bundeswehr reduction in Phase II - before an initial East/West MBFR accord could be reached.

Over the years of negotiation, the Eastern participants have in principle gradually accepted much of the Western proposal. They have agreed to reduce to a common ceiling of 700,000 active duty ground force personnel within an overall common ceiling of 900,000 active duty air and ground personnel. The Eastern participants have agreed as well to Western data on Western forces and hence to the size of the Western reduction believed acceptable to NATO (91,000). But the East categorically rejects reductions of Warsaw Pact ground manpower of the magnitude demanded by the West and there is no evidence that the East would ever agree to such reductions in the future. The East has challenged the validity of the Western estimates of Eastern manpower by submitting data which supports their claim of parity in active duty manpower. Using their own data in getting down to the 700,000 common ceiling, the East would only have to reduce by 105,000 personnel instead of the 262,000-troop reduction they would have to make if Western estimates were used. Thus the existence of 157,000 Warsaw Pact troops is in dispute.

The West has ultimately got to resolve the status of the 157,000 troops the East says are not there. Otherwise, the 700,000 common ceiling would in effect be a ceiling only for the West with the East having a de facto ceiling of 857,000. It should be noted that if the Soviets indeed unilaterally withdraw a total of 20,000 soldiers, and if such were confirmed by Western intelligence, the Western estimate and hence the existing disparity would be reduced by 20,000. No doubt the East would correspondingly reduce its announced strength from 805,000 to 785,000. The East then could claim that it only needed to take an 85,000 instead of a 105,000 MBFR reduction to reach a 700,000 ground force common ceiling. Ironically, this would result in a reduction of some 6,000 less personnel than the NATO-required reduction of 91,000. This is the heart of the data problem that has brought the negotiators to a virtual stalemate. With the prestige of Eastern leaders up to and including Brezhnev now committed behind their figures, the possibility of the East eventually revising its data upward is highly unlikely.

The West has been calling for a meaningful data discussion in which counting rules could be reviewed to determine just what each other's data represent. So far the East has refused. This position is puzzling in view of the fact the East implicitly admitted early in 1974 that by Western counting rules there is a disparity in favor of the East. (3) Such a discussion must take place sooner or later because the West has insisted that no first phase agreement can take place without an agreed data base on Soviet forces. This is essential within the framework of the present approach, in order to verify adherence to the terms of the

Western Proposals

1. Reductions

    a. Phase I

       • Soviets withdraw three
         divisions (30,000
         soldiers)
       • United States withdraws
         13,000 soldiers, two-
         thirds in units

    b. Phase II
       Pact and NATO reduce to
       ground common ceiling
       of 700,000 within an
       air/ground common ceil-
       ing of 900,000

2. Limitations

    Ceilings placed on US/
    Soviet ground/air man-
    power

3. Associated Measures
   Agreement to implement the
   following measures before
   Phase I withdrawals
       • Prior notification of
         movement into the MBFR
         area
       • Designated exit/entry
         points manned by in-
         spectors from the other
         side
       • Up to 18 air/ground
         inspection trips to
         other sides MBFR area
         per year
       • Periodic exchange of
         data
       • Non-interference with
         National Technical Means
       • Establishment of a
         Standing Consultative
         Committee
       • Prior notification of
         division size (10,000
         personnel) movements
         throughout Europe to
         include western Russia
       • Right to send observers
         to such movements.

Eastern Proposals[*]

1. Reductions

    a. Stage I (1st year)

       • Soviets withdraw 7 per-
         cent ground manpower
         (30,000), 3 tank divi-
         sions, 1,000 tanks, 250
         infantry combat vehicles,
         and 1 Army Corps HQ and
         supporting units

       • US withdraws 7 percent
         ground manpower
         (14,000), 2-3 brigades,
         1,000 nuclear warheads,
         54 F-4's, and 36
         Pershing launchers

    b. Stage II (2nd-3rd years)

       • All reduce 11-13 per-
         cent to reach common
         ceiling of 700,000
         ground and 900,000 air
         ceilings

2. Limitations
   Ceilings placed on the US/
   USSR equipment reduced.
   National ceilings on man-
   power within a collective
   ceiling.

*Contingent on the Western
acceptance and use of Eastern
strength data on Eastern forces.

Fig. 9.1. Comparison of current MBFR proposals

treaty. It means that both the data (first Soviet and later East European) and what the data represent (counting rules) must be agreed to before the terms of the treaty are carried out. Otherwise, neither side can be sure of what the other side's data actually represent.

Obviously the worst option for the West would be to accept the East's contention that it has only 805,000 ground force personnel and therefore need only take a reduction of 105,000 personnel to reach the common ceiling of 700,000. To accept the Eastern figure of 805,000, either explicitly or implicitly, would do needless and untold damage to Western security. It would create the perception in Western societies that the threat caused by the numerical superiority of the Warsaw Pact was no longer valid when in reality the threat would still remain. (4) Portraying the Soviet forces as no longer a threat could result at some future date in calls from the left wings of Western parliaments for further cuts in defense budgets and armed forces. (5)

In sum, all indications are that the possibility of asymmetrical reductions of the magnitude necessary to enhance Western security now seems quite remote. With the likelihood of Eastern agreement to symmetrical reductions only, the present MBFR approach may no longer be in the best interest of Western security. This leads to the obvious question: should the West continue to seek reductions under the present concept?

CONTINUE TO SEEK REDUCTIONS

The current Western approach to MBFR seeks to diminish the threat of a surprise attack by the Warsaw Pact forces in Central Europe through large-scale reductions of these forces. To date, the West has been unsuccessful in this endeavor because of the lack of sufficient bargaining strength to overcome Eastern intransigence to taking such reductions.

Option III was not successful. According to the East the weakness of Option III was that it did not contain Western European nuclear systems, particularly those of West Germany. Throughout the negotiations the East has called for inclusion of Allied nuclear systems in MBFR. But the Allies, recognizing the Eastern objectives behind the demand, have been reluctant to do so. This reluctance was again evidenced by the Allied insistence that negotiations on the new mid-range US theater nuclear systems (the Pershing II and the cruise missile) and the Soviet "Grey Area" systems (the SS 20 and Backfire) be held outside of the MBFR arena. This would not however, preclude shorter range Allied nuclear missile and artillery systems from still being offered in the MBFR arena. As part of the NATO nuclear modernization program, the United States agreed to unilaterally withdraw 1,000 older tactical nuclear warheads. In addition, at Allied insistence, the United States agreed to withdraw one short-range tactical warhead for each Pershing II or cruise missile warhead deployed in Western Europe. Such a readiness on the part of the Allies to reduce battlefield nuclear capability suggests that they might be more receptive than in the past to such a proposal. It is the only avenue of bargaining strength remaining to the West within the present framework that has not already been explored. A proposal of Allied nuclear launcher reductions and/or limitations just might induce additional conventional Eastern reductions.

The original rationale behind the development of NATO tactical nuclear systems was to negate the large superiority of Warsaw Pact conventional forces in Central Europe. These tactical nuclear systems were introduced at a time when the United States possessed clear strategic nuclear superiority. Now, with the Soviets achieving strategic nuclear parity and maintaining an overwhelmingly large theater nuclear force, the NATO tactical nuclear forces as presently structured can no longer serve as an equal counter to the greater conventional strength of the Warsaw Pact. In fact, nuclear weapons - especially short-range battlefield types - have become de facto substitutes for the lack of sufficient NATO conventional forces.

With this in mind, reductions and/or limitations of Allied nuclear launchers could also be offered as substitutes for a portion of the required 91,000-troop Western reduction along the same vein that Option III was offered in lieu of greater US manpower reductions.

If the East continued to refuse to take other than symmetrical reductions, even if presented with the opportunity to get reductions and limitations on Allied nuclear launchers, the West would find itself at a critical crossroad. Acceptance of the Eastern proposal - that is, symmetrical reductions - would be an admission by the Western participants that they had failed in their objectives of reducing the Warsaw Pact capability of surprise attack and enhancing stability in Central Europe through parity in active duty ground manpower.

Moreover, the acceptance of Eastern symmetrical reductions would have a negative impact on the military preparedness of NATO, according to the former Commander in Chief of Allied Forces in Europe. Shortly before retiring in 1979, General Alexander Haig warned that symmetrical reductions would be destabilizing, and there should be no reductions unless they were asymmetrical to the extent that force levels became numerically balanced as a result. (6) Analysis done in 1972 prior to the start of the negotiations on the military impact of symmetrical reductions supports General Haig's contention that such reductions would put the West at a military disadvantage. (7)

A factor which also exacerbates the Western disadvantage in any withdrawal of US forces is "geographical disparity." This term, by Western definitions, describes the advantage the Soviets have in access to Central Europe as compared to that of the United States. Current MBFR proposals require US and Soviet troops to be withdrawn to their homelands. Soviet forces would be simply withdrawn to Western Russia only 1,000 kilometers away, while US forces would be withdrawn 10,000 kilometers, back across the Atlantic Ocean. Even if the East agreed to asymmetrical reductions of the size desired by the West, such a long-distance withdrawal is inherently unequal because of the ease of Soviet troop reintroduction when compared to that of the United States.

Because of this inherent Soviet advantage, irrespective of the size of the Eastern reductions, the military disadvantage incurred by any future US withdrawals could be substantially mitigated and the geographical disparity problems considerably diminished by restationing withdrawn US personnel outside of the reductions area but still within the European theater. This would contribute to reducing the military and psychological impact such a withdrawal would have on Western security. Because of the refusal of France to participate in MBFR and its previous dislike of US forces stationed on French soil, the only currently realistic possibilities would be either in the United Kingdom and/or northern Italy. Such stationing, of course, would have to be negotiated with the respective governments. If successful, it would place the US forces in a position for a much quicker return to West Germany in the event of crisis and thus remove one of the fundamental inequalities of any withdrawal process that is a genuine Western concern.

The Eastern use of symmetrical reductions could also result in an outcome similar to that which would be created with the "Quick Fix" (8) or symbolic reductions concept which the West has considered from time to time. While symmetrical reductions, as the East envisions them, involve all direct participants, the Quick Fix or a symbolic reduction is generally envisioned as consisting of US and Soviet withdrawals only.

During the early period of the talks when the US administration was under heavy pressure to undertake unilateral reductions, the symbolic reduction was contemplated as a way to placate Congress and to forestall large cuts in US forces. However, the disappearance of congressional pressure for such unilateral reductions has not caused the Quick Fix concept to be regarded as totally obsolete

Unless the East becomes uncharacteristically forthcoming, the data problem will probably continue to retard progress. Political leaders in both the East (if there were ironclad assurances that the Bundeswehr would reduce in a Phase II) and the West might see symbolic reductions as a way out of the data impasse and as a way of finally showing some results in MBFR.

From the Western standpoint and objectives, a symbolic US/Soviet withdrawal is not in NATO's best interest. A symbolic reduction would be concessionary to the East because it allows the East to defer a considerable portion of the data discrepancy to Phase II and it starts the process of reductions before the formalization of an agreed data base and other measures necessary to make MBFR a viable agreement. Once such withdrawals were made, the West could find it more difficult to return to a data/counting rules discussion so necessary if Western objectives of a militarily meaningful MBFR are to be realized. Trying to adjust data to satisfy Eastern desires to take symmetrical reductions allows the Warsaw Pact, in fact, to maintain its numerical superiority in active duty manpower. This then is an extremely dangerous tack for the West to follow, even if it is in theory confined to the MBFR arena. Artificial diminution of the Warsaw Pact's numerical superiority for the purposes of securing an MBFR agreement could very well backfire for the West by spilling over into other critical areas of NATO defense policy and lead to calls for reduced defense budgets and procurements.

Either a symbolic reduction or a symmetrical reduction type of agreement would clearly have a negative impact on Western security and would do nothing to reduce the Warsaw Pact numerical advantage in active duty ground personnel. Furthermore, it would leave a definite impression that the West has backed down under Soviet pressure, thus enhancing Soviet power projection capability in Central Europe. Militarily, within MBFR the Soviets would withdraw 3 divisions out of 27 (the number as of the June 1978 proposal) stationed in the area of reductions. However, Soviet comments concerning their 20,000-troop unilateral withdrawal indicate they may consider that withdrawal to compensate for two-thirds of the withdrawal volunteered in their 1978 proposal, thus leaving the Soviets (according to their own calculations) only an additional 10,000 personnel to withdraw to meet the Phase I MBFR requirement. A withdrawal of even the full 30,000 would not significantly reduce Soviet combat capability nor would it diminish the image of the Soviet forces in Central Europe as an offensive and threatening instrument of Soviet foreign policy. Of even more critical concern is the impact of either type of agreement on the United States program to strengthen NATO. Unlike the situation in 1973, there is now broad congressional support to strengthen US forces in Europe.

West European countries have also been strengthening their forces. Through restructuring, the West Germans have added three brigades. To enhance their combat capability the French are also restructuring their forces in West Germany and the UK has done the same. The new attitude of NATO is best examplified by the Long Term Defense Program (LTDP) endorsed by the member nations of the alliance in 1978 and designed to improve NATO defense capabilities. In support of this effort, NATO nations have pledged to raise their defense budgets. The program is part of the reaction to the large-scale Warsaw Pact force improvement program that began shortly before the MBFR talks began and has been continuing since then. Significantly, the Warsaw Pact force improvement program has been largely one of qualitative improvements as the East strives hard to close the technological gap. As a result, one can no longer assume that superior Western technology will offset the Warsaw Pact's decided numerical superiority.

Maintaining the momentum of the NATO response to this Pact drive to close the technology gap is a cogent reason why the West should not accept symmetrical or symbolic reduction agreements. Reductions result in visible and highly publicized troop movements. Such publicity would tend to distort the actual size of the reduction being taken and create the impression that the Warsaw Pact threat was actually being reduced. Furthermore, the sight of American troops boarding airplanes to return to the United States would no doubt undermine the momentum of the United States efforts to strengthen NATO. Therefore, it would seem for the foreseeable future that any Western reductions not matched by a significant reduction of the surprise attack capability of the Warsaw Pact would not be in NATO's best interest. In sum, taking any reductions - no matter what their size or ratio - would have to be carefully weighed in relation to the ongoing programs to strengthen NATO, and in relation to the rationale for this renewed commitment as well.

Considering all the negative ramifications of taking symmetrical or symbolic reductions, what should the West do if the East continues, as expected, to refuse asymmetrical reductions? One option would be to terminate the negotiations.

DISCONTINUE THE TALKS

The inability of the negotiators to come to any agreement since 1973 has often caused critics to label the MBFR talks a failure. While the MBFR talks have not yet resulted in an arms control agreement, they have succeeded in deterring US unilateral reductions that would have jeopardized the defense of Western Europe and the stability of Central Europe.

The viability of MBFR has been demonstrated in another way. The negotiations themselves provide a vehicle for the important exchange of East/West views concerning Central Europe. In this context, the talks up until December 1979 had certainly enhanced detente as the West conceived it and they continue to be a forum for a future dialogue and the possibility of an agreement. Hence, critics who complain about the lack of an MBFR accord fail to recognize the contribution of these talks to maintaining the stability of Central Europe and serving as an ongoing forum for NATO and the Warsaw Pact on the military situation in Central Europe.

Nevertheless the outlook for success of the current proposals appears dim because of the impasse over data. Of even more importance is the fact that the political factors and overall psychological climate which drove the West, and the United States particularly, into MBFR have changed radically since the talks began. No longer is there a Senator Mansfield calling for unilateral troops cuts in Europe. Instead, there is now broad congressional support behind the US efforts to strengthen NATO forces. The visceral antiwar feeling which tended to inhibit any attempts to strengthen the military has been significantly reduced - if not totally eliminated - by events in Europe and the Middle East in the late 1970s.

The Warsaw Pact force improvement program has coalesced informed opinion on both sides of the Atlantic in support of the strengthening of NATO. The appreciation of the Soviet threat seems even more widespread in light of Soviet adventurism in other parts of the world, notably the 1979 invasion of Afghanistan. In the minds of some it has raised the question as to whether the MBFR talks with their call for troop reductions should not now be terminated in view of the inability of the West to secure large-scale Eastern reductions and the present world situation. Furthermore, knowledgeable individuals on both sides implicitly recognize that MBFR did block a precipitious large-scale unilateral US withdrawal from Western Europe and hence was a success from this important standpoint. So perhaps, the argument goes, the breakdown of detente makes it a convenient time to bring a halt to the MBFR process.

The Soviet invasion of Afghanistan resulted in a number of retaliatory moves by the US Government. The Carter administration announced that as a result of the Soviet actions in Afghanistan the ratification of the SALT II treaty would be indefinitely postponed. It further announced that as for arms control negotiations which were currently in progress, such as MBFR, the US delegation will be instructed to simply sit and listen and not to offer any new initiatives. (9) This has led some to conclude that detente and hence its centerpiece, arms control, was dead as a vehicle for East/West cooperation.

Such a conclusion may prove to be premature and erroneous. In his State of the Union speech on 23 January 1980, President Carter reaffirmed commitment to nuclear arms control. (10) An indication of US determination to continue the arms control process was the 25 January 1980 meeting in NATO to hear the US position for the SALT III negotiations. (11)

Furthermore, one must keep in mind that MBFR is a multilateral negotiation. The participating West European nations have a vested interest in preserving detente and the ties with the East that were built up during the heyday of detente in the early 1970s. There has been a reluctance on the part of West Europeans to let the events in the Middle East and South Asia lead to a cutting of ties with the East. (12) Consequently, it would be surprising if the West Europeans would take any action to conclude the MBFR process unless the Soviet Union continued aggressive moves which more directly threatened West European vital interests. In effect, the MBFR process, despite the fact that no agreement has emerged since it began, has taken on a life of its own and has become established as the primary forum for discussions of the East/West military situation in Central Europe. At the start of the 20th round of negotiations on 31 January 1980, both sides made clear expressions of their desire to continue MBFR. (13)

However, the Soviets are dissatisfied with the current MBFR approach, especially the data problem, as evidenced by their desire to take MBFR credit for their unilateral withdrawals. The initially cool reception given the Western 1979 proposal no doubt dampened hopes in some Western quarters of any near-term progress. Furthermore, the Soviets have announced that under the present Western concept they will not participate in negotiations on reducing nuclear weapons in Europe - negotiations that were to be included in the SALT III process. (14) Yet there appears to be no desire on the part of the Soviets to return to a more confrontationary stance vis-a-vis Western

Europe. To be the first to walk away from MBFR would damage the Soviet image and objectives in Western Europe.

Thus, MBFR is entering a period of time in which no progress will receive official sanction in the West. Yet there is official evidence that both sides want to keep the process going. That being the case, what is the future of the MBFR process, assuming East/West relations return to the level that once again makes movement in MBFR attractive? For one thing, the negotiations will be faced with the same problems that were stalemating the negotiations before the Afghanistan crisis. With symmetrical reductions not being in the best interests of Western security and with asymmetrical Eastern reductions of the size needed to enhance Western security being unacceptable to the East, and with both exacerbated by the data problem, such a desire to rekindle the movement might prove to be an ideal time to redirect the negotiations toward a different approach, one that would have a higher probability of success yet still be militarily meaningful for the West.

It can only be guessed whether or not Soviet desire to continue the negotiation process would be maintained in the case of Western refusal to take symmetrical reductions. Of consideration also is the Brezhnev unilateral withdrawal offer which could be interpreted as a sign of impatience with the MBFR process, and a signal that Soviets consider negotiations on theater nuclear force to be of higher priority. Nevertheless, the Soviets do tend to place great importance on principles and process especially if the process enhances Soviet prestige in the context of a superpower relationship. MBFR clearly does this. Hence, it is a reasonable conclusion that if the Soviets were presented with a viable alternative to the current reductions approach, they would probably choose to continue the process.

Assuming that both sides wish to continue the MBFR process, the problem then becomes to develop an approach that would have a higher probability of success yet still be militarily meaningful for the West.

ATTEMPT A NEW APPROACH

One of the problems that has plagued past arms control initiatives is that they have been too one-sided in favor of the initiator. Negotiations must have a framework that contains sufficient common ground for both sides to see a probability of obtaining some worthwhile objectives.

Such is the problem with the current MBFR approach. For the East, there is still benefit in pursuing the present course to its conclusion, that is, symmetrical reductions leading to limitations. For the West, there is benefit only if the East takes large asymmetrical reductions - a rapidly diminishing prospect. Hence, if reductions took place, the East would achieve its basic goal of imposing limitations on the Bundeswehr and NATO, while the West would fail to obtain its basic objectives of enhancing Western security through the reduction of the threat of a

Warsaw Pact surprise attack. If the East is not going to agree to such reductions, then the West must seek an alternative approach which enhances Western security in ways more acceptable to the East.

There are several paths the negotiations could take. For example, one approach would be based on limiting and reducing specific weapon systems instead of manpower. However, the obstacles to this approach are formidable. The myriad weapon systems found in the conventional forces inventory, the fast pace of technology that can quickly make a specific weapon system obsolete, and more importantly, the very strong possibility that such an approach would hinder modernization and structural changes which both sides might wish to introduce in the future - all these factors make such an approach unattractive. Eastern appreciation of this is evidenced by the dramatic scaling down between their initial and their latest proposals of the spectrum of weapons they want reduced and limited.

On the other hand, there are additional approaches with greater promise than that of the above. For the sake of illustration the following discussion will address an approach containing several arms control concepts which have not been incorporated into MBFR but are worth considering under present circumstances. (15) It will be called here the "Force Realignment Approach."

This approach embodies four advantages over the present MBFR proposals. First, it addresses Western concerns about the Warsaw Pact threat and Eastern (mainly Soviet) fears about West German military strength, in ways which offer both sides incentives to pursue the negotiations. Second, it seeks to avoid the type of pitfalls which tend to lead to impasses due to specificity. Third, it is configured in such a way to implement in incremental fashion a series of arms control procedures aimed at building confidence and increasing stability in Central Europe. Finally, the approach uses a method of limitations on armed forces that greatly reduces other problems plaguing the current approach: how to compensate for future changes in armaments and force structure that alter the balance qualitatively without changing it quantitatively. As Christoph Bertram puts it, "When . . . quantitative definitions can no longer fully encapsulate the military mission that has to be curtailed, that mission itself must be made the primary focus of agreement." (16)

Today's ground forces are equipped to fight a mobile and nuclear war in a configuration which lends itself to moving quickly between the defense and the offense. Hence, to limit effectively the capability to perform a particular mission, a restructuring or realignment of the army's equipment and unit configuration would be required. In brief, the main elements necessary to fight in an offensive posture - tanks, infantry, and artillery - are also required for defensive actions; the difference in mission lies in the quantity of each element and their configurations. Therefore, in order to meaningfully restrict the capability of a ground force to conduct a surprise attack, its structure must be realigned so that it would be unfeasible to conduct such an operation as it was currently organized and equipped. By changing the focus of MBFR from one of quantitative reductions to one of

confidence-building through force realignment, the problems of counting rules, finite data counts, armament tradeoffs, and residual
limitations, which have created such difficulties in MBFR and which
currently threaten Western military stability, are no longer stumbling
blocks. For the West the force realignment approach is appealing in its
objective to reduce the possibility of a Warsaw Pact surprise attack.
For the East, such an approach would also be attractive because it
would restrict any offensive employment of NATO forces - most
importantly the Bundeswehr, which the Soviets fear could become, in
their words, "an instrument of German revanchism."

The following discussion of the possible components of such an
approach makes no attempt to persuade the reader that this approach is
the ultimate answer, nor to imply that needed technical analysis has
been done to determine the viability of all of its components. Rather,
its purpose is to provoke thought and consideration and to illustrate the
fact that there are alternatives to the current proposals within the
present MBFR framework.

UNDERTAKING FORCE REALIGNMENT

The prime objective of the force realignment approach is to restructure
the active duty forces immediately facing each other so that both sides
assume a defensive posture. It would then become necessary to resort
to highly visible troop movements and/or restructuring in order for a
potential aggressor to be able to mount a large-scale surprise attack,
thereby increasing the warning time to the other side in case of such an
attack. Such an approach would also contribute to the enhancement of
stability by reducing the capability of a large, poised Warsaw Pact
offensive force to intimidate the West European political/economic
process. The various elements of this approach would be instituted in a
building block process, which would increase confidence by moving from
more easily acceptable measures, through more demanding measures, to
the eventual goal of taking actual reductions. The time frame for the
process could be left relatively open-ended with the next step being
undertaken only after the preceding steps were functioning satis-
factorily.

The present Western associated measures proposal, with modification, could serve as the transition link between the current MBFR
approach and the force realignment approach. The first phase of the
latter approach would be to codify, that is to make mandatory in an
agreement, the confidence-building measures of the type voluntarily
agreed upon at CSCE and found in the Western MBFR proposal of 1979,
namely, prior notification of military maneuvers of division level and
above and the right to observe such maneuvers. But unlike the 1979
Western proposal, which would have these measures apply to all of
Europe, and unlike the rest of the current MBFR approach which is
restricted to the Benelux, FRG, GDR, Poland, and Czechoslovakia,

those codified measures would only be mandatory in a reduced arms control area astride the East/West border between West Germany and East Germany/Czechoslovakia.

Reducing the geographical span of the arms control area has several advantages, both military and political. From the military standpoint, a smaller area greatly enhances the capability to monitor an arms control agreement when compared to the current approach, whereby every active duty soldier must be accounted for in the GDR, Poland, and Czechoslovakia. Attempting to monitor maneuvers over all Europe, including the Western USSR, would be even more difficult. Another military advantage from the NATO standpoint is that the entire armies of the Benelux nations, and most importantly the Bundeswehr, would not fall under the agreement, thus mitigating Warsaw Pact meddling in future force improvement programs of these nations.

Reducing the area of arms control also has political advantages. It would accommodate as much as possible the West German sensitivity over making all of the two Germanies into a special arms control zone. It was largely for this reason that the Benelux nations were included in the current area of reductions along with Poland and Czechoslovakia. But expanding the arms control area for this reason has not erased German fear of becoming a special disarmament zone. Expanding it even further in the area of confidence-building measures while retaining the present area for reductions and limitations does not solve the special zone concerns of the FRG. Furthermore, the USSR has already indicated that it is not in favor of an expansion of the MBFR area especially to include western Russia even if it were just for confidence-building measures. Another advantage of a smaller area is that it would remove French forces stationed in the Western part of the Federal Republic and in Berlin from de facto inclusion in the MBFR reduction area, thus eliminating a source of continuing friction between France and the rest of NATO.

It is recognized that even only a partial inclusion of the two Germanies in an arms control area will not completely remove German concerns, but one must be realistic. Reaching a meaningful arms control agreement on ground forces that is not based on specific force structures and without geographically defined limits is impossible. Geographic limits are essential in order to bound and monitor the agreement. If there is to be arms control on the ground forces of Central Europe, then there must be geographical limits. The size of such an area certainly is flexible; the creation of one is mandatory. How large should the arms control area be? These tradeoffs are readily apparent: the deeper the area, the more the Warsaw Pact nations would have to realign their forces and the more the warning time for NATO is increased. However, it is also true that the deeper the area, the more the FRG that would officially fall under Warsaw Pact scrutiny and the more force realignment NATO would be required to undertake.

Conversely, the smaller the area of arms control, the less the force realignment required of the East and hence the potential increase in warning time is diminished proportionately. However, from the standpoint of German sovereignty the smaller the area the better, and also the less the East could meddle in NATO affairs. The size of the area acceptable to NATO would ideally be based on technical studies which would determine the optimum depth after all tradeoffs were considered; ultimately, of course, the size of the area must be negotiated with the East.

The delineation of such an area could be addressed by drawing boundaries on a map between easily identified geographical locations such as towns, rivers, and roads. Or, if both sides were willing to go to the opposite end of the spectrum, the area could be delineated and monitored by on-the-ground observers, fixed posts, and mobile inspection teams.

Once such an area had been established, and the confidence-building measures properly adhered to, the next phase could be negotiated. This would be the creation within the overall arms control area which the confidence-building measures encompass of a subarea directly along the border. Only certain types of military organizations would be permitted to operate or be stationed in it. Restrictions within the subarea would apply only to the military forces. Existing civilian living and economic patterns would not be disrupted or changed in any way. The types of forces permitted would be, for example, lightly armed border guards, mechanized (as opposed to armored) reconnaissance units, and motorized infantry equipped with portable antitank weapons. No units equipped with tanks, armored personnel carriers, artillery, armed helicopters, or other offensive type weapons would be permitted. Those units stationed and operating in the subarea would be identified by type of unit and location on a frequent periodic basis by an exchange of troop lists between the two sides.

Once the units in the subarea were realigned and reequipped to the satisfaction of both sides, a second subarea could then be established behind the first. Here, the required military structure would be one of defense. For example, combat units would be infantry divisions equipped with armored personnel carriers but not infantry fighting vehicles. The divisions would possess the artillery necessary to furnish adequate defensive fire support, some tanks for limited counterattack purposes, and the normal support troops. Units which are primarily offensive in nature - tank regiments or brigades, armored divisions, engineer bridging units, and the like - could not be stationed in this area. By withdrawing Warsaw Pact offensive units behind this second area, additional warning time would be gained by NATO. Placing NATO offensive forces to the rear could also be beneficial, for it could spur NATO to redeploy out of its present layer-cake cordon defense into one of echelon defense with armor heavy reserves that have the maneuverability to block and defeat Warsaw Pact armored thrusts.

Once the arms control area had been fully established and successfully operating over a period of time, the negotiators could conceivably agree on a further expansion of the arms control area or turn the talks to the subject of withdrawals and reduction of forces.

Verification would be much less complex for the West. Without having to monitor manpower ceilings in such a large geographic area, as the current MBFR approach would require, as well as the even greater task of monitoring division-size maneuvers all over Eastern Europe and Western Russia, the need for negotiated inspection measures diminishes considerably. With a greatly reduced area of East Europe to monitor and with the most important areas closest to the border, the need for redundant technical and negotiated inspection measures would also be reduced. Nevertheless, the placing of NATO or Warsaw Pact observers - or even neutral observers - in the area to carry out observations along the lines of the negotiated inspection measures called for in the 1979 Western proposal would certainly enhance monitoring and early warning. Of course, such an arrangement is intrusive and would be contingent on both sides finding it acceptable. Such National Technical Means (i.e., satellites) as well as tactical field army level intelligence-gathering organizations could be used for monitoring compliance. The monitoring tasks for Western systems would be greatly simplified over presently envisioned MBFR requirements - checking the armament zones for units of prohibited type and ensuring that units in the zones are in a defensive configuration. Verification, therefore, has in essence only to assure that the threshold has not been crossed from a defensive configuration to one of offensive capability.

BALANCING AIMS AND INTERESTS

In sum, an approach along the lines of force realignment offers alternatives that avoid most of the problems facing the West that now stymie the current MBFR approach. By setting modest goals within a progressive sequence, it builds confidence through an implementing time frame that does not create a destabilizing situation.

The force realignment approach is not without drawbacks. With forward defense (i.e., meeting the attack at the East/West border) so critical to NATO, especially and understandably so for the West Germans, setting restrictions on the composition of NATO units stationed close to the East/West border might weaken the capability of these units to conduct a successful forward defense. Furthermore, no matter what it is called, such a scheme would still not eliminate the creation within the two Germanies of a special arms control zone which, if handled improperly, could give the impression of partial demilitarization or disengagement. This could create less, not more, stability.

The major problem with force realignment is the actual depth of the area. West Germany is a narrow country. As an example, even a 100-kilometer zone would encompass roughly 40 percent of West German territory. In essence, such a geographical delineation creates a dilemma. Unless the area is made large enough so it would actually increase NATO's warning time of a Warsaw Pact surprise attack, then from a military security point of view, undertaking such an approach would be counterproductive. On the other hand, an area deep enough to increase NATO warning time may be so deep that it becomes detrimental to the concept of forward defense.

Despite these drawbacks, the force realignment approach does provide for consideration of an alternative to the current MBFR deadlock. Primarily by setting more modest goals, it would prevent potentially destabilizing reductions and limitations that threaten NATO under the current approach.

Should the West fail with what limited options are still available under the current approach to gain meaningful asymmetrical Eastern reductions, then serious consideration should be given to seeking East/West agreement to redirect the negotiations along a confidence-building and force realignment track. If both sides still see value in pursuing the goal of an arms control agreement for Central Europe, force realignment would seem to be an approach worth exploring.

As the years have shown, especially since 1973, there is no easy road or golden key to successful arms control in Europe. Lessening the criticality for such an arms control agreement is the fact that since World War II, the military situation in Central Europe has shown an impressive stability despite the existing asymmetries within the force structure. Hence, there has been a reluctance to tamper with it too much, especially if doing so meant surrendering some of one's national sovereignty (or hegemony in the Soviet case) and jeopardizing existing perceptions of what constitutes adequate security.

In this context, it is worth repeating the prophetic statement made by an anonymous State Department official in January 1972, concerning the results of studies which showed that any MBFR initiative that would be acceptable to the Soviets would jeopardize Western security: "It took us two years and God knows how much money to reach the common sense conclusion that stability in Europe can best be maintained by doing nothing." (17) ("Nothing" in this context meaning not to go forward with an MBFR proposal.)

Unless an arms control agreement can be found which by its provisions meaningfully enhances security in Central Europe, then it is better for the West to continue to take measures which can offset the current Warsaw Pact threat to the balance and thus maintain the stability that kept peace in Central Europe the last three decades.

There is much to be said for the thesis that in critical areas of the world like Central Europe, military stability rather than instability is created by the direct interface of the forces of the superpowers. Such military stability has accomplished what, when all is said and done, is the basic objective of any successful arms control agreement - preservation of peace.

Notes

CHAPTER 1

1. Joseph Schiebel, "Convergence or Confrontation," Intercollegiate Review 5 (1968-69): 109.

2. V.I. Lenin, Selected Works, vol. III (New York: International Publishers, 1943), p. 280.

3. Schiebel, "Convergence or Confrontation?" p. 109.

4. Ibid.

5. Walter Laquer, Russia and Germany, A Century of Conflict (Boston: Little, Brown and Co., 1954), p. 276.

6. James L. Richardson, Germany and the Atlantic Alliance. The Interaction of Strategy and Politics (Cambridge, Mass.: Harvard University Press, 1966), p. 114.

7. Laquer, Russia and Germany, p. 276.

8. Richardson, Germany and the Atlantic Alliance, p. 47.

9. Ibid. Such organizations included any which would be openly anti-Communist.

10. Laquer, Russia and Germany, pp. 227-228.

11. Thomas W. Wolfe, Soviet Power and Europe 1945-1970 (Baltimore and London: The Johns Hopkins University Press, 1970), p. 30.

12. Peter V. Curl, ed., Documents on American Foreign Relations, 1954 (New York: Harper and Brothers, 1955), pp. 107-124.

13. Eugene Hinterhoff, Disengagement (London: Atlantic Books, 1949), p. 175.

14. Ibid.

15. Ibid.

16. Wolfe, Soviet Power and Europe, p. 79.

17. Paul E. Zinner, ed., Documents on American Foreign Relations, 1955 (New York: Harper and Brothers, 1956), p. 199.

18. Ibid., p. 202.

19. Ibid., p. 203.

20. Ibid., p. 221.

21. Ibid., p. 248.

22. Ibid., p. 259.

23. Ibid., p. 260.

24. Richardson, Germany and the Atlantic Alliance, p. 36.

25. Ibid.

26. Elizabeth A. Parker, East European Arms Control and Disarmament Proposals (Arlington, Va.: Institute for Defense Analysis, 1969), p. 41.

27. Hinterhoff, Disengagement, p. 216. Coincidentally, the West would use the same argumentation some 12 years later in MBFR when the East proposed a freeze on force levels while negotiations were in progress.

28. US, Department of State, "Address by the Polish Foreign Minister (Rapacki) to the General Assembly, October 2, 1957," Documents on Disarmament, Volume II, 1957-1959 (Washington, DC: Government Printing Office, 1960), p. 890.

29. Ibid., p. 891.

30. Ibid.

31. Ibid., p. 946.

32. Ibid.

33. US, Department of State, "Note from the American Ambassador (Beam) to the Acting Polish Foreign Minister (Winiewicz), May 3, 1958," Documents on Disarmament, Volume II, 1957-1959, p. 1023.

34. Ibid.

35. US, Department of State, "News Conference Remarks by the Polish Foreign Minister (Rapacki) Regarding an Atom-Free Zone in Central Europe, November 4, 1958," Documents on Disarmament, Volume II, 1957-1959, pp. 1217-1219.

36. Wolfgang Kleiber, et al., Era of Negotiations (Lexington, Mass.: Lexington Books, 1973), p. 14ff. Kleiber quotes Hansjakob Stehle,

The Independent Satellite (New York: Praeger, 1956), in which Stehle reports that it took the Poles several months to convince the Soviets to accept the plan. Klaiber also cites a Der Spiegel article of 26 March 1958 which reported Soviet unhappiness with the Polish initiative.

37. US, Arms Control and Disarmament Agency, "Memorandum by the Polish Government on Freezing Nuclear and Thermonuclear Weapons in Central Europe, February 24, 1964," Documents on Disarmament, 1964 (Washington, DC: Government Printing Office, 1956), p. 54.

38. Richard Pipes, ed., Soviet Strategy in Europe (New York: Crane, Russak, 1976), p. 14.

39. Ibid., p. 18.

40. The Russians use their word "razryadka" instead of the word detente. "Razryadka" translates "relaxation."

41. K.M. Georgiyev, "Detente - The Formula and the Process," USA: Economics, Politics, Ideology 8 (July 1976): 5.

42. Ibid, p. 8.

43. US, Arms Control and Disarmament Agency, "Address by the Polish Foreign Minister (Rapacki) to the General Assembly, December 14, 1964," Documents on Disarmament, 1964 (Washington, DC: Government Printing Office, 1965), p. 524.

44. Lincoln P. Bloomfield, et al., Khrushchev and the Arms Race. Soviet Interests in Arms Control and Disarmament 1954-1964 (Cambridge, Mass.: The MIT Press, 1966), p. 275.

45. US, Department of State, "Communique of the Political Consultative Committee for the Warsaw Pact, January 20, 1965," Documents on Disarmament, 1965 (Washington, DC: Government Printing Office, 1966), pp. 6-7.

46. Ibid.

47. Ibid.

48. US, Arms Control and Disarmament Agency, "Declaration on European Security by the Political Consultative Committee of the Warsaw Pact States, July 6, 1966," Documents on Disarmament, 1966 (Washington, DC: Government Printing Office, 1967), p. 417.

49. Ibid., p. 410.

50. US, Arms Control and Disarmament Agency, "Statement on European Security by European Communist Parties, April 26, 1967," Documents on Disarmament, 1967 (Washington, DC: Government Printing Office, 1968), p. 201.

51. US, Congress, Senate, 90th Cong., 1st sess., 1967, Congressional Record 113: 967.

52. Ibid.

53. US, Congress, Senate, 89th Cong., 2d sess., 1966, <u>Congressional Record</u> 112: 17338.

54. Ibid.

55. US, Senate, 90th Cong., 1st sess., 1967, <u>Congressional Record</u> 113: 997.

56. Ibid.

CHAPTER 2

1. US, Arms Control and Disarmament Agency, "North Atlantic Council Communique, December 14, 1967," <u>Documents on Disarmament, 1967</u> (Washington, DC: Government Printing Office, 1968), pp. 676-677.

2. Ibid., p. 679.

3. Ibid., p. 681.

4. Ibid.

5. US, Arms Control and Disarmament Agency, "Communique and Declaration of the North Atlantic Council, June 25, 1968," <u>Documents on Disarmament, 1968</u> (Washington, DC: Government Printing Office, 1970), pp. 449-450.

6. Ibid.

7. S. Kovalev, "Sovereignty and the Internationalist Obligations of Socialist Countries," <u>Pravda</u>, 26 September 1968, p. 4.

8. US, Arms Control and Disarmament Agency, "Budapest Appeal by Warsaw Pact Nations to All European Countries, March 17, 1969," <u>Documents on Disarmament, 1969</u> (Washington, DC: Government Printing Office, 1970), p. 106.

9. Ibid., pp. 107-108.

10. US, Arms Control and Disarmament Agency, "Communique of the North Atlantic Council, April 11, 1969," <u>Documents on Disarmament, 1969</u> (Washington, DC: Government Printing Office, 1970), pp. 184-186.

11. US, Arms Control and Disarmament Agency, "Prague Declaration of the Warsaw Pact Foreign Ministers, October 31, 1969," <u>Documents on Disarmament, 1969</u> (Washington, DC: Government Printing Office, 1970), pp. 526-528.

12. Ibid.

13. Ibid.

14. US, Congress, Senate, 91st Cong., 1st sess., 1969, <u>Congressional Record</u> 115: 36147.

15. Ibid., p. 36419.

16. "Warsaw Pact Nations Communique," The Atlantic Community Quarterly 7 (Winter 1969-1970): 599-601.

17. "Communique and Declaration of the North Atlantic Council, December 5, 1969," Documents on Disarmament, 1969 (Washington, DC: Government Printing Office, 1970), pp. 623-628.

18. Ibid.

19. New York Times, 25 March 1970, p. 1.

20. US, Arms Control and Disarmament Agency, "Communique and Declaration of the North Atlantic Council, May 27, 1970," Documents on Disarmament, 1970 (Washington, DC: Government Printing Office, 1971), pp. 225-229.

21. Ibid., pp. 229-230.

22. US, Arms Control and Disarmament Agency, "Budapest Memorandum of Warsaw Pact Foreign Ministers on European Security, June 22, 1970," Documents on Disarmament, 1970 (Washington, DC: Government Printing Office, 1971), p. 246.

23. Ibid., p. 247.

24. US, Arms Control and Disarmament Agency, "Treaty Between the Soviet Union and the Federal Republic of Germany, August 12, 1970," Documents on Disarmament, 1970 (Washington, DC: Government Printing Office, 1971), pp. 403-404.

25. "The Polish-German Treaty," Atlantic Community Quarterly 9 (Spring 1971): 115-116.

26. "Documentation of the Warsaw Pact Summit Meeting of 2 December 1970," NATO Letter 19 (January-February 1971): 24-26.

27. US, Arms Control and Disarmament Agency, "North Atlantic Council Communique, December 4, 1970," Documents on Disarmament, 1970 (Washington, DC: Government Printing Office, 1971), p. 668.

28. Ibid., p. 671.

29. US, Department of Commerce, 24th Congress of the Communist Party of the Soviet Union, Stenographic Report (Part I) (Arlington, Va.: Joint Publications Research Service, 1971), pp. 48-49.

30. Ibid.

31. US, Arms Control and Disarmament Agency, "Address by CPSU General Brezhnev at Tbilisi (extract) May 14, 1971," Documents on Disarmament, 1971 (Washington, DC: Government Printing Office, 1972), p. 293.

32. US, Arms Control and Disarmament Agency, "Television-Radio Interview with Secretary of State Rogers: Mutual and Balanced Force Reductions in Europe (extract), May 16, 1971," Documents on Disarmament, 1971 (Washington, DC: Government Printing Office, 1972), p. 295.

33. US, Congress, Senate, 92d Cong., 1st sess., 1971, Congressional Record 117: 15949.

34. Ibid., p. 15947.

35. Ibid., p. 15952.

36. Ibid., p. 15957.

37. Ibid.

38. Ibid., p. 15958.

39. Editorial, New York Times, 19 May 1971, quoted in US, Congress, Senate, 92d Cong., 1st sess., 1971, Congressional Record 117: 15952.

40. US, Congress, Senate, 92d Cong., 1st sess., 1971, Congressional Record 117: 15952.

41. Ibid., p. 15959.

42. "Luncheon for Canadian PM Trudeau," Daily Report Soviet Union, Foreign Broadcast Information Service, 24 May 1971, p. 6.

43. Such an approach was in keeping with the Soviet tactic of once accepting a Western proposal, and then initiating a highly visible propaganda campaign depicting the idea as one of Soviet origin.

44. US, Arms Control and Disarmament Agency, "Communique of the North Atlantic Council, June 4, 1971," Documents on Disarmament, 1971 (Washington, DC: Government Printing Office, 1972), pp. 307-311.

45. "Preelection Speech, 11 June 1971," Daily Report Soviet Union, Foreign Broadcast Information Service, 14 June 1971, p. J-11.

46. Roger Hill, "MBFR Prelude: Explorations Before Negotiations," NATO Review, July-August 1972, pp. 3-4.

47. US, Department of State, Department of State Bulletin, 3 January 1972, p. 105.

48. US, Arms Control and Disarmament Agency, "Communique of the North Atlantic Council, December 10, 1971," Documents on Disarmament, 1971 (Washington, DC: Government Printing Office, 1972), pp. 858-859.

49. US, Arms Control and Disarmament Agency, "Prague Declaration on Peace, Security, and Cooperation in Europe, January 26, 1972," Documents on Disarmament, 1972 (Washington, DC: Government Printing Office, 1973), p. 6.

50. Ibid.

51. US, Arms Control and Disarmament Agency, "Joint American Soviet Communique, May 29, 1972," Documents on Disarmament, 1972 (Washington, DC: Government Printing Office, 1973), p. 245.

52. US, Arms Control and Disarmament Agency, "Communique of the North Atlantic Council, May 31, 1972," Documents on Disarmament, 1972 (Washington, DC: Government Printing Office, 1973), p. 250.

53. US, Arms Control and Disarmament Agency, "125th Annual ACDA Report, January 31, 1973," Documents on Disarmament, 1972 (Washington, DC: Government Printing Office, 1973), p. 880.

54. New York Times, 17 November 1972.

55. Pravda, 21 December 1972, p. 1.

56. Washington Post, 12 January 1973, p. 1.

57. Ibid.

58. "Soviet-French Communique," Daily Report Soviet Union, Foreign Broadcast Information Service, 12 January 1973, p. F-10.

59. New York Times, 19 January 1973.

60. "USSR Ready to Begin MBFR Talks on 31 January," Daily Report Soviet Union, Foreign Broadcast Information Service, 19 January 1973, p. H-3.

CHAPTER 3

1. "Bulgarian Commentor Views CSCE, MBFR as Separate Issues," Daily Report Eastern Europe, Foreign Broadcast Information Service, 22 January 1973, p. A-1.

2. "Moscow Proposal on MBFR Talks Is Step Forward," Daily Report Eastern Europe, Foreign Broadcast Information Service, 22 January 1973, p. I-2.

3. "Tanjug Notes Romanian Views on MBFR Talks," Daily Report Eastern Europe, Foreign Broadcast Information Service, 1 February 1973, p. A-13.

4. "Preparation Talks for MBFR Conference Opens in Vienna," Daily Report Eastern Europe, Foreign Broadcast Information Service, 1 February 1973, p. I-3.

5. "Soviet Papers Optimistic on Atmosphere of Vienna Talks," Daily Report Soviet Union, Foreign Broadcast Information Service, 2 February 1973, p. I-2.

6. "Yugoslavia's Sundic Criticizes Bloc Nature of MBFR," Daily

Report Eastern Europe, Foreign Broadcast Information Service, 1 February 1973, pp. A-13-A-14.

7. "Soviet Philosophy on Timeliness of MBFR," Daily Report Soviet Union, Foreign Broadcast Information Service, 30 January 1973, p. R-1.

8. Hedrick Smith, "Soviets Seen Stalling on Troop Cuts to Break Link to Security Talks," New York Times, 6 April 1973, p. 10.

9. Ibid.

10. International Institute for Strategic Studies, The Military Balance 1977-1978 (London: IISS, 1977), pp. 9 and 14.

11. Drew Middleton, "US Reports Soviet Buildup," New York Times, 6 April 1973, p. 10.

12. Ibid.

13. Hedrick Smith, "Soviets Seen Stalling," p. 10.

14. "Magyar Hirlip Comments on MBFR," Daily Report Eastern Europe, Foreign Broadcast Information Service, 1 November 1973, p. I-2.

15. "Zycie Warszawy Assesses Course of Vienna Consultations," Daily Report Eastern Europe, Foreign Broadcast Information Service, 16 February 1973, p. A-3. A special participant actively takes part in the negotiations but unlike the direct participant, neither its territory nor forces are subject to reductions or limitations.

16. "NATO Stance Delaying MBFR Talks," Daily Report Eastern Europe, Foreign Broadcast Information Service, 9 March 1973, p. A-1.

17. Don Cook, "Talks on Europe Troop Cuts Slip Into 1st Gear," Los Angeles Times, 17 May 1973, p. 18.

18. Gene Oishi, "Hungary's Role in Troop Talks Reduced" Baltimore Sun, 15 May 1973, p. 2.

19. "Zycie Warszawy Warns That Problems Remain at Vienna Talks," Daily Report Eastern Europe, Foreign Broadcast Information Service, 11 May 1973, p. A-3.

20. US, Arms Control and Disarmament Agency, "Record of Plenary Meeting of Preparatory Consultations on Central Europe: Rules of Procedure and Participation, 14 May 1973," Documents on Disarmament, 1973 (Washington, DC: Government Printing Office, 1975), p. 253.

21. Ibid., p. 254.

22. Ibid.

23. Ibid.

24. Ibid.

25. Oishi, "Hungary's Role," p. 2.

26. US, Arms Control and Disarmament Agency, "Record of Plenary Meeting of Preparatory Consultations," p. 254.

27. "Tanjug Discussed NATO, US Attitude Toward MBFR Talks," Daily Report Eastern Europe, Foreign Broadcast Information Service, 7 February 1973, p. A-10.

28. "Nepzabadzag Sees Many Difficulties Facing Vienna Talks," Daily Report Eastern Europe, 6 February 1973, p. A-5.

29. Eric Bourne, "East West Find Basis for Troopcut Talks," Christian Science Monitor, 2 July 1973, p. 1.

30. US, Arms Control and Disarmament Agency, "Final Communique on Preparatory Consultations Relating to Mutual Reduction of Forces and Armaments in Central Europe, 28 June 1973," Documents on Disarmament, 1973 (Washington, DC: Government Printing Office, 1975), p. 363.

31. Weekly Compilation of Presidential Documents (Washington, DC: Government Printing Office, 2 July 1973), p. 844.

32. "States which will take the necessary decisions" means the direct participants.

33. US, Arms Control and Disarmament Agency, "Final Communique," pp. 363-364.

34. "Statement by Deputy Secretary of State Rush to the House Committee on Foreign Affairs, 10 July 1973," Department of State Bulletin, 6 August 1973, pp. 213-214.

35. Marilyn Berger, "Mansfield Repeats Call for 50% Cut in US Troops Abroad," Washington Post, 26 July 1973, p. 7.

36. US, Congress, House, 93d Cong., 1st sess., 1973, Congressional Record 119: H6950.

37. Ibid., p. H6951.

38. Ibid., p. H6952.

39. Ibid., p. H6956.

40. Ibid., p. H6959.

41. Ibid.

42. Ibid., p. H6968.

43. Ibid., p. H6971.

44. US, Congress, Senate, 93d Cong., 1st sess., 1973, Congressional Record 119: S17627.

45. Ibid.

46. Ibid.

47. US, Congress, Senate, 93d Cong., 1st sess., 1973, Congressional Record 119: 15949.

48. US, Arms Control and Disarmament Agency, "Message from President Nixon to the Congress (extract), 10 September 1973," Documents on Disarmament, 1973 (Washington, DC: Government Printing Office, 1973), p. 634.

49. US, Congress, Senate, 93d Cong., 1st sess., 1973, Congressional Record 119: S17621.

50. Ibid.

51. Ibid., p. S17625.

52. Ibid., p. S17627.

53. Ibid.

54. Ibid., No. 24, p. 31522.

55. Ibid., No. 142, p. S17636.

56. Ibid., p. S17649.

57. Ibid., p. S17651.

58. John W. Finney, "Senate Votes, Then Voids 40% Cut in Troops Abroad," New York Times, 27 September 1973, p. 1.

59. US, Congress, Senate, 93d Cong., 1st sess., 1973, Congressional Record 119: S17696.

60. Spencer Rich, "US Troop Cut Wins Then Loses in Senate," Washington Post, 27 September 1973, p. 1.

61. US, Congress, Senate, 93d Cong., 1st sess., 1973, Congressional Record 119: S17954.

62. Ibid., p. S17962.

63. Albert Sehlstedt, "Foreign Troop Cut Voted," Baltimore Sun, 28 September 1973, p. 1.

CHAPTER 4

1. Don Cook, "Parley Opens on East-West Troop Cuts," Los Angeles Times 31 October 1973, p. 9.

2. Craig R. Whitney, "Formal Talks on Troop Reductions in Europe Open in Vienna," New York Times, 31 October 1973, p. 12.

3. Cook, "Parley Opens," p. 9. In March 1974 the talks were moved to more sumptuous surroundings in the famous Hofberg Palace in the heart of Vienna.

4. Ibid.

5. Ibid.

6. Michael Parks, "Mutual Force Cut: An Open Question," <u>Baltimore Sun</u>, 11 November 1973, p. 1.

7. Don Cook, "US Proposes Big Forces Cut for Central Europe Ground Forces," <u>Los Angeles Times</u>, 1 November 1973, p. 21.

8. US, Arms Control and Disarmament Agency, "Speech by General Secretary Brezhnev to World Conference on Peace Forces, 23 October 1973 (excerpt)," <u>Selected Background Documents Relating to Mutual and Balanced Force Reductions</u>, Part II, Disarmament Document Series DDS Ref. #619, 23 November 1973.

9. <u>Weekly Compilation of Presidential Documents</u> (Washington, DC: Government Printing Office, 8 October 1973), p. 1211.

10. US, Arms Control and Disarmament Agency, "Statement by the United States Representative (Resor) on the Negotiations on Mutual Reduction of Forces and Armaments in Central Europe, October 31, 1973," <u>Documents on Disarmament, 1973</u> (Washington, DC: Government Printing Office, 1974), p. 718.

11. Ibid.

12. Ibid., p. 721.

13. Ibid.

14. Ibid., p. 722.

15. Whitney, "Formal Talks on Troop Reductions," p. 12.

16. John Goshko, "Equal Force Levels Pressed by US," <u>Washington Post</u>, 1 November 1973, p. 18.

17. V.V. Viktorov and A.V. Stoleshnikov, "The Vienna Talks After Two and a Half Years," <u>USA: Economics, Politics, Ideology</u> 4 (June 1976): 25-35.

18. Gene Oishi, "Soviet Asks Troop Cuts in 1975," <u>Baltimore Sun</u>, 16 November 1973, p. 4.

19. Ibid.

20. Richard Homan, "Soviets Leak Troop Cut Plan," <u>Washington Post</u>, 18 November 1973, p. 16.

21. Reuters, "Soviet Push for Troop Cuts Over 3-Year Span," <u>Chicago Tribune</u>, 20 November 1973, p. 7-3.

22. Ibid.

23. Ibid.

24. "After One Month of Negotiation," <u>Pravda</u> (Moscow), 2 December 1973, p. 5L.

25. Reuters, "NATO Proposes Troop Cut," <u>Baltimore Sun</u>, 23 November 1973, p. 1.

26. Gene Oishi, "US, Russia Wide Apart on Troop-Reduction Plan," Baltimore Sun, 4 December 1973, p. 5.

27. "After One Month of Negotiation," Pravda, p. 5L.

28. Vladimir Komlev, "US-NATO Proposal Seeks Unilateral Advantages," Moscow Radio, 5 December 1973, as reported in Foreign Broadcast Information Service, 6 December 1973, p. BBI.

29. K. Borisov, "Vienna: Two Positions," Novoye Vremya 50 (14 December 1973): 4-5.

30. Ibid.

31. For an excellent discussion of the problems of determining the balance, see US, Congress, Congressional Budget Office, Assessing the NATO/Warsaw Pact Military Balance, by James Blaker and Andrew Hamilton, December 1977. For a very lucid analysis of the balance, see Robert Lucas Fischer, Defending the Central Front: The Balance of Forces, Adelphi Paper 127 (London: IISS, 1976).

32. NATO Information Service, "NATO's Long Term Defense Program," NATO Review 26 (June 1978): 3-15.

33. John Erickson, Soviet Military Power (London: Royal United Services Institute for Defense Studies, 1971), p. 103.

34. Stanley Sloan, Prospects for the Vienna Force Reduction Talks (Washington, DC: Congressional Research Office, 30 June 1978), p. 13.

35. Viktorov and Stoleshnikov, "Vienna Talks," p. 6.

36. "Speech by General Secretary Brezhnev to the World Conference on Peace Forces, 23 October 1973 (excerpt)."

37. The Chinese have been quite worried about MBFR. They fear a withdrawal of Soviet manpower in Europe would result in a subsequent buildup on the Sino-Soviet border. As a result they have ironically become one of NATO's strongest supporters.

38. "Zeri I. Popullit Comments on Hypocrisy of MBFR Talks," Foreign Broadcast Information Service, Eastern Europe Daily Report, November 1973, p. A-1.

CHAPTER 5

1. The reader should keep in mind that both the 1973 and 1976 Eastern proposals have been replaced by the 1978 Eastern proposal. But because the latter contains many of the aspects of the former two, a detailed discussion of them is necessary in order to understand Soviet tactics and objectives in MBFR.

2. V.V. Viktorov and A.V. Stoleshnikov, "The Vienna Talks After Two and a Half Years," USA: Economics, Politics, Ideology 4 (June 1976): 11.

3. Ibid.

4. The Western participants tabled six figures of data when they presented their proposal on 22 November 1973, in order to support their contention that asymmetrical reductions were necessary. The West claimed there were 925,000 Warsaw Pact active duty ground personnel, of which 460,000 were Soviet. On the NATO side were 777,000 active duty ground personnel, of which 193,000 were US. Department of Defense "What's Behind the Mutual and Balanced Force Reduction Talks," Commanders Digest, 16 (14 November 1974): 6.

5. Where data are required that have not been made public, the data published by the International Institute for Strategic Studies are used.

6. The Soviets did not clarify the figure on which the Stage II (5%) and Stage III (10%) reduction would be based. If the percentages in Stages II and III are based on the residuals of Stages I and II, respectively, instead of the pre-Stage I figure, the differences resulting are of such small magnitude as to have no significant impact on the methodology or conclusions reached in this study.

7. Since France refused to take part in the talks, NATO has made a commitment to the East that French forces would be considered to be under the common collective ceiling, and that direct participants would take the necessary reductions to compensate for the lack of French reductions under the Western proposal. No demands are specifically made on France in the Eastern proposals. However, Eastern statements clearly imply they expect French forces in the FRG to fall under the common ceiling. There are approximately 60,000 French troops stationed in the FRG. Atlantic News, 16 June 1978, p. 1.

8. Assuming the East had tabled its 1976 data in 1973 of 987,000, the magnitude of the Eastern reduction would have been less than if using the Western estimate, as follows:

1973	Stage I	Stage II (5%)	Stage III (10%)	Total
Using West Estimates	20,000	56,250	112,500	188,750
Using 1976 Pact Data	20,000	49,350	98,700	168,000

The East would have taken 21,000 less reductions if Eastern data rather than Western estimates were to have been used.

9. The Military Balance 1977-78, p. 110. If totaled, the figures presented on this page will not equal those on the preceding page because IISS data totals very slightly from official Western totals.

10. K. Borisov, "Vienna: Two Positions," Novoye Vremya 50 (14 December 1973): 4-5.

11. Michael Getler, "Cuts in Bonn Army Called Soviet Goals," The Washington Post, 22 January 1976, p. 21. This goal will be discussed in more detail later.

12. Sidney Weiland, "Soviet Bloc Presents New MBFR Proposals," Reuters, 19 February 1976.

13. Ibid.

14. The impact of the Western nuclear proposal on the MBFR negotiations will be discussed in Chapter 6.

15. Proclaimed at the 24th Party Congress. See Chapter 2 above.

16. Foreign Broadcast Information Service, Daily Report Soviet Union, 24 February 1976, p. AA-1.

17. New Initiative Shows the Way," Neues Deutschland, 21-22 February 1976, p. 6.

18. Warsaw PAP, "Vienna: New Contributions of Socialist Countries," Radio Broadcast, 2114 GMT, 23 February 1976, FBIS Eastern Europe, 24 February 1976, p. BB-1.

19. George Possaner, "Eastern Information Offensive on Ground Forces Reduction," Die Presse, 28-29 February 1976, p. 1.

20. "New Initiative Shows the Way," Neues Deutschland, p. 7.

21. Andrzej Rayzacher, "Vienna Negotiations - Socialists' Studies Constructive Initiative - Speech by Poland's Representative," Trybuna Ludu, 5 March 1976, pp. 1-2.

22. D. Goos, "Moscow Wants Pie in the Sky," Die Welt, 22 May 1976, p. 1.

23. The West had made no specific demands for withdrawals of Soviet nuclear forces. However, the Western demand for a withdrawal of a Soviet tank army implicitly required the withdrawal of FROG and SCUD battlefield surface-to-surface missile launchers assigned to that Army. Under the 1979 Western proposal FROG launchers, as organic elements of Soviet divisions, would probably be withdrawn.

24. This calculation is based on the revised NATO figure tabled in Vienna in the summer of 1976 which showed that the NATO ground figure has increased from 777,000 to 791,000 for a total ground-air figure of 984,000. See Stanley Sloan, Prospects for Vienna Force Reduction Talks (Washington, DC: Congressional Research Office, 30 June 1978), p. 13.

25. Stanley Sloan, Prospects for the Vienna Force Reduction Talks (Washington, DC: Congressional Research Office, 1978), p. 13.

26. Andrezev Szarecki, "Green Light in Vienna," Slowo Powzechne (Warsaw), 12 March 1976, p. 2.

27. Dr. Ingo Oeser, "Who is Promoting and Who is Obstructing Progress in Vienna?" Horizont 18 (1976): 33-34.

28. The Military Balance, p. 110.

29. D. Goos, "Moscow Wants Pie in the Sky."

30. John Erickson, Soviet Military Power (London: Royal United Services Institute for Defense Studies, 1971), p. 75.

31. The inclusion in the 1976 proposal of the other armaments, specifically nuclear capable aircraft, tactical surface-to-surface missile launchers, and warheads will be discussed in Chapter 6.

32. "Warsaw Pact Offers Troop Cut - or Does It?" Christian Science Monitor, 13 June 1978, p. 3.

33. "Soviet Offers Plan for Reducing Forces in Central Europe," New York Times, 13 June 1978, p. 1.

35. Ibid.

36. Gerhard Bornemann, "Now It's Up to the NATO States to Make the Next Move in Vienna," Horizont 29 (1978): 19.

37. This is consistent with the three-division withdrawal offer; the strength of a Soviet tank division is considered to be about 10,000 men.

38. George Possaner, "Movement Behind Tactical Walls: Summer Thinking Pause for Force Reduction," Die Presse, 18 July 1978, p. 3.

39. Pravda, 9 June 1978, p. 1.

40. Pravda, 27 June 1978, p. 4.

41. Sloan, Prospects for Vienna Talks, p. 13.

42. This is the unofficial figure used in the 1977/78 Military Balance. The West tabled a figure of 460,000 for the Soviets in 1973 to help support their contention there was asymmetry in Central Europe. Since that time, the Soviets have been undergoing a vigorous force improvement program which would make the 475,000 seem a more valid number, hence its use here.

43. See Chapter 7 for an analysis of the Eastern limitation proposals.

44. Die Zeit, 20 October 1978, p. 7.

45. Based on the 428,000 deduced as the Soviet strength.

46. While the East had informally agreed to a US/Soviet first phase in 1975, it was not until the 1978 proposal that the East dropped insistence that air force personnel make up part of the withdrawal.

47. The East accepted the concept in principle, but the scope of the Soviet withdrawal is not as great as the West had demanded. Under the Western proposal of December 1979 equipment reductions have been deferred to Phase II.

48. The official NATO position is that it cannot take reductions greater than 10 percent. This was based on NATO reducing from its 1973 strength of 777,000 to a 700,000 common ceiling. But with the tabling of the revised NATO estimate of 771,000 in 1976, NATO was then required to reduce 91,000 to reach the 700,000 common ceiling, a reduction of 11 percent. It should be remembered that 60,000 of the 791,000 consists of French forces not subject to reductions, for which NATO must compensate.

49. Za Rubeshom, 15 June 1978, p. 17.

50. Tass (Moscow), 6 October 1979.

51. Baltimore Sun, 12 October 1979, p. 4.

52. Washington Post, 22 October 1979, p. A-3.

53. Zycie Warszawy (Warsaw), 8 October 1979, p. 6.

54. Tass (Moscow), 6 October 1979.

55. Tass (Moscow), 22 November 1979.

56. Selskaya Zhizn (Moscow), 24 November 1979, p. 3.

57. Washington Post, 6 December 1979, p. A-21. Moscow reported a withdrawal of 1,000 personnel.

58. Military Balance, 1977-1978, p. 9.

59. See Chapter 4.

60. Brateslava Pravda, 15 June 1978, p. 9.

61. Frankfurter Rundschau, 25 October 1978, p. 10.

62. Brateslava Pravda, 15 June 1978.

63. Ibid.

64. Bonn, Press Service of the FDP, 4 November 1979, p. 4.

65. Frankfurter Rundschau, 16 November 1979, p. 11.

66. New York Times, 15 December 1979, p. A-6.

67. Elements of the new Western proposal were taken from articles in The New York Times, 14 December 1979, p. A-3. Bonn, General Anzeiger, 8 November 1979, pp. 1-2.

68. New York Times, 15 December 1979, p. A-6.

69. Frankfurter Rundschau, 16 November 1979, pp. 10-11.

70. To be discussed in Chapter 6.

71. <u>FBIS</u>, Eastern Europe, 26 December 1979, p. BB-5.

72. <u>FBIS</u>, Eastern Europe, 26 December 1979, p. BB-2.

73. <u>Tass</u> (Moscow), 20 December 1979.

74. <u>Tass</u> (Moscow), 20 December 1979.

75. Strengths of West European direct participants and Canada were taken from <u>The Military Balance 1977-78</u>. Because the total strength for these countries was 1,000 greater than the official total, the Netherlands strength was arbitrarily reduced by 1,000 to 74,000 in order to fit the analysis.

76. <u>The Military Balance 1977-78</u>, pp. 13-14. The <u>Military Balance</u> did not include homeland, surface-to-air missile units of Poland and Czechoslovakia in these figures. The East has attacked Western counting rules for including them in Western estimates (see Chapter 7). This may account for the 27,000 discrepancy between the <u>Military Balance</u> estimate and the official Western estimate. Thus, this table, while it gives a truer picture of the impact of the Western proposals on pure ground forces, will not be additive to the 487,000 figure.

77. US, Department of Defense, "What's Behind the Mutual and Balanced Force Reduction Talks," <u>Commanders Digest</u>, p. 2.

78. <u>Frankfurter Rundschau</u>, 16 November 1979, p. 11.

79. <u>Bratislava Pravda</u>, 7 December 1979, p. 7.

80. Ibid.

81. Bonn, <u>Press Service of the FDP</u>, 4 November 1979, p. 4.

82. <u>Cologne Deutschlandfunk</u>, 16 September 1979, FBIS Western Europe, 19 September 1979, p. C-1.

CHAPTER 6

1. Walter Slocombe, <u>The Political Implications of Strategic Parity</u>, Adelphi Papers No. 77 (London: IISS, 1971), p. 5.

2. James R. Schlesinger, <u>The Theater Nuclear Force Posture in Europe: A Report to the US Congress in Compliance with Public Law 93-365</u> (Washington, DC: Department of Defense, 1 April 1975), p. 8.

3. Federal Republic of Germany, Minister of Defense, <u>White Paper 1975-76, The Security of the Federal Republic of Germany and the Development of the Federal Armed Forces</u> (Bonn: 20 January 1976), p. 20.

4. Alexander M. Haig, "New Soviet Nuclear Threat to West Europe," San Diego Union, 10 September 1978.

5. R. Meller, "European New Generation of Combat Aircraft, Part 1: The Increasing Threat," International Defense Review 8 (April 1975): 146. This does not mean that every Soviet aircraft has been assigned the mission of carrying a nuclear weapon. In fact, only about one-third are so designated.

6. General David Jones, Chairman, Joint Chiefs of Staff, United States Military Posture for FY 1980 (Washington, DC: Government Printing Office, 1979), p. iv.

7. Jeffrey Record, US Nuclear Weapons in Europe (Washington, DC: The Brookings Instition, 1977), p. 111.

8. Helmut Schmidt, Defense or Retaliation (New York: Praeger, 1962), p. 103.

9. Wynfred Joshua, Nuclear Weapons and the Atlantic Alliance, (New York: National Strategy Information Center, 1973), p. 32.

10. Frankfurter Allegemeine, 14 February 1976, p. 4.

11. New York Times, 5 September 1975, p. 6.

12. Washington Post, 18 September 1975, p. 23.

13. Frankfurter Allegemeine, 14 February 1976, p.4.

14. Harold Brown, Secretary of Defense, Department of Defense Annual Report, Fiscal Year 1979 (Washington, DC: Department of Defense, 2 February 1978), p. 130.

15. International Institute for Strategic Studies, The Military Balance, 1977-78 (London: The International Institute for Strategic Studies, 1977), p. 24.

16. "Polish Delegate's Vienna Press Conference," Trybuna Ludu (Warsaw), 31 January-1 February 1976, pp. 1-2.

17. Die Welt (Bonn), 13 January 1976, p. 2.

18. Frankfurter Allegemeine, 14 February 1976, p. 4.

19. Die Welt (Bonn), 22 May 1976, p. 1.

20. Ibid.

21. Peter Borgart, "The Air Attack Potential of the Warsaw Pact," International Defense Review 9 (April 1976): 194-195.

22. Jane's All the World's Aircraft, 1978-1979 (New York: Watts, Inc., 1978), p. 345.

23. Die Welt (Bonn), 22 May 1976, p. 1.

24. Christopher Donnelly, et al., Soviet Ground and Rocket Forces (London: Salamander Books, 1976), p. 58.

25. Haig, "New Soviet Nuclear Threat."

26. The Military Balance 1977-1978, p. 10.

27. Ibid., p. 24.

28. R. Meller, "European New Generation of Combat Aircraft," p. 146.

29. Total Soviet withdrawal based on their 8 June 1978 proposal.

30. For example, see: Jeffrey Record, "US Tactical Nuclear Weapons in Europe: 7,000 Warheads in Search of a Rationale," Arms Control Today, April 1974; Colin S. Gray, "Deterrence and Defense in Europe: Revising NATO's Theater Nuclear Posture," Strategic Review, Spring 1975; Manhard Worner, "NATO Defense and Tactical Nuclear Weapons," Strategic Review, Fall 1977; US, Congressional Budget Office, Planning US General Purpose Forces: The Theater Nuclear Forces, (Washington, DC: Government Printing Office, 1977).

31. Washington Post, 15 December 1979, p. A-6.

32. Washington Post, 13 December 1979, p. A-1.

33. Ibid.

34. Washington Post, 25 October 1979, p. A-3.

35. Helmut Schmidt, "Germany in the Era of Negotiation," Foreign Affairs, October 1970, p. 42.

36. Manfred Worner, "NATO Defenses and Tactical Nuclear Weapons," Strategic Review, Fall 1977, p. 12.

37. Die Welt (Bonn), 28 August 1978, p. 6.

38. Washington Star, 11 January 1980, p. A-5.

39. Pravda, 25 October 1979, pp. 4-5.

40. Atlantic News, 16 June 1978, p. 1.

41. Trybuna Ludu (Warsaw), 31 January 1976, pp. 1-2.

42. Kenneth Hunt, "Deterrence" NATO Review 1 (Brussels: NATO Information Service, 1974): 10-11.

43. Actually 11 percent based on the revised 1976 Western strength of 791,000 active duty ground force personnel.

44. The Military Balance, 1977-1978, pp. 80-81.

45. The Financial Times (London), 19 November 1979, p. 18.

46. Handelsblad (Rotterdam), 8 November 1979, p. 2.

47. Frankfurter Rundschau, 16 November 1979, p. 11.

48. Ibid.

49. Der Spiegel, 29 January 1979, p. 39.

50. The Military Balance, 1977-1978, p. 81.

51. Westdeutscher Rundfunk (Cologne), 23 April 1979; Daily Report Western Europe, Foreign Broadcast Information Service, 26 April 1979, p. C-3.

52. The Observer (London), 18 November 1979, p. 7.

CHAPTER 7

1. Lech Niekroez, "Roads to Detente - Fair Play in the Viennese Manner," Zycie Warszawy, Warsaw, 28 January 1976, p. 5.

2. FRG White Paper 1975/76, The Security of the FRG and the Development of the Federal Armed Forces, p. 109.

3. Perevoshchikov and Polyanov, "Before the Eighth Round in the Hofburg," Izvestia, 25 January 1976, p. 2.

4. Ryszard Dreck, "Socialist States' Proposals - New Impulse for Vienna Negotiations," Trybuna Ludu, Warsaw, 8 March 1976, p. 9.

5. Dusair Rovensky, "After the Eighth Round in Vienna," Rude Pravo, Prague, 20 April 1976, p. 6.

6. Peter Vajda, "The Reduction of Armed Forces and Armaments: Prospects in Vienna," Nepszabadsag, Budapest, 11 February 1976, p. 4.

7. "NATO - Thinning the Ranks," Newsweek, European Edition, 1 November 1976, p. 19.

8. Die Presse, Vienna, 5 July 1976, p. 1. It should be noted that the increase in Bundeswehr combat brigades came from organizational restructuring of existing active units rather than an actual add-on of additional soldiers. See FRG White Paper 1975/76, p. 109.

9. Cologne Domestic Service, 7 November 1978, Foreign Broadcast Information Service, Western Europe, 8 November 1978, p. J-2.

10. Lother Ruehl, "The Negotiations on Force Reductions in Central Europe," NATO Review 5 (October 1976): 23.

11. Frankfurter Allegemeine, 14 January 1976, p. 3.

12. Ibid.

13. Michael Getler, "Cuts in Bonn Army Called Soviet Goals," Washington Post, 22 January 1976, p. 21.

14. Eric Bourne, "Europe Troop Cut Talks Expected to Go Slowly," Christian Science Monitor, 27 January 1976, p. 9.

15. "At the Heurige," Der Spiegel, 1 March 1976, pp. 32-33.

16. Ibid.

17. Dr. Ingo Oeser, "Who is Promoting," p. 4.

18. Ibid.

19. Denmark is not a direct participant and hence its forces are not subject to reduction.

20. Yury Maksinov, "MBFR Talks Impeded by Attitudes of US, UK, FRG," Tass, 28 July 1976.

21. Ibid.

22. Yurig Sibirtsev, "The Stance of the Federal Republic of Germany," Daily Report Soviet Union, FBIS, 7 November 1978, p. BB-1.

23. Rabotnichesko Delo, 4 November 1978, p. 5.

24. Atlantic News, 28 June 1978, p. 1.

25. Horizont 28 (1979), p. 4.

26. Ibid.

27. Contributing to this, of course, was the Mansfield push for reductions in manpower. Since MBFR was initially a counter to Mansfield, it was almost mandatory to construct a proposal that would show results in manpower.

28. This may have been motivated by the fact that the nuclear-capable Nike Hercules surface-to-air system is in the West German air force. Also, in the case of Poland and Czechoslovakia, the national air defense forces are considered a separate third service.

29. London Times, 19 December 1974, p. 14.

30. A Western spokesman also referred to their rules as "uniform counting rules," uniform meaning that all personnel assigned to the army, regardless of their functional mission, were counted as army.

31. New York Times, 11 June 1976, p. 8. The West also tabled updated figures at the same time.

32. Pravda, 23 July 1976, p. 5.

33. Pravda, 27 June 1978, p. 1.

34. Includes 60,000 French troops stationed in West Germany.

35. Izvestya, 27 July 1976, p. 1.

36. Stanley R. Sloan, Prospects for the Vienna Force Reduction Talks (Washington, DC: Library of Congress Congressional Research Service, June 30, 1978), p. 13.

37. The ground force disparity.

38. Bratislava Pravda, 23 October 1978, p. 4.

39. Weiner Zeitung, 14 December 1978, p. 3.

40. Moscow Tass, 25 November 1978, FBIS Soviet Union Daily Report, 28 November 1978.

41. Stanley Sloan, p. 16.

42. Bratislava Pravda, 25 November 1978, p. 6.

43. Ibid.

44. Stanley Sloan, pp. 16-17. It is indeed difficult for one who is knowledgeable on the size of the Eastern forces to understand how the East could man two times the number of divisions and tanks and three times the number of aircraft with the same number of personnel the West uses to man it forces.

45. East German Horizont 45 (1978): 5. V. Komlev in a later article in Novoye Vremya, No. 33, 11 August 1978, again hit on the point the Warsaw Pact uses active duty servicemen to perform duties for which the West uses civilians. According to Die Zeit, 20 October 1978, p. 7, the Poles have also been arguing that a considerable part of the Polish army is more of a paramilitary labor force than it is an army.

46. Komlev, 11 August 1978, p. 8.

47. For a view of Soviet writings on this subject, see Dr. Keith A. Dunn, "Soviet Perceptions of NATO," Parameters, September 1978.

48. Military Balance, 1977-78, p. 22.

49. Horizont 46 (1978): 5. The East, however, has not seriously pressed for French participation since 1973. Such participation is extremely doubtful given the current French attitude toward MBFR.

50. Federal Republic of Germany White Paper 1975/76. The Security of the FRG and the Development of the Federal Armed Forces, January 20, 1976, p. 113.

51. Suddeutsche Zeitung, 17 August 1978, p. 4.

52. The Soviets have claimed that the elementary basis of the talks is mutual trust and that the West should trust that the Eastern figures are correct. Novoye Vremya, 22 December 1978, p. 9.

53. Der Spiegel, 19 June 1978, p. 109.

54. Suddeutsche Zeitung, 6 July 1979, p. 4.

55. Cologne Deutschlandfunk Network, 16 September 1979. FBIS Western Europe, 19 September 1979, p. C-1.

56. New York Times, 14 December 1979, p. A-3.

57. Atlantic Constitution, 9 November 1979, p. A-23.

58. Der Spiegel, 19 June 1978, p. 109. It was also reported that Western MBFR observers believe they can help the Soviets correct the data considered too low by NATO without Moscow losing face.

59. Baltimore Sun, 20 June 1980, p. 20.

CHAPTER 8

1. For a description of how agreement was reached on the official title of the negotiations, see pp. 40-41.

2. Department of Defense, "What's Behind the Mutual and Balanced Force Reduction Talks," Commanders Digest, p. 2.

3. Ibid., pp. 116-117.

4. Dmitriy Ardamatskiy, "Dear Lasse Budtz," Copenhagen Aktuelt, 12 June 1976, p. 6.

5. Roman Drobny, "NATO's Attempt at One-Sided Supremacy; 25th Party Congress on the Vienna Negotiations on Reduction of Armed Forces," Prague Tribuna 12, 17 March 1976): 16.

6. US, Arms Control and Disarmament Agency, Verification, Publication No. 85, Washington, DC, March 1976, p. 114.

7. Ibid.

8. In arms control terminology, monitoring (observing and reporting the situation) is an intelligence function and verification (determining if there has been a violation of treaty provisions) is a political function.

9. US, Arms Control and Disarmament Agency, "Statement by the Soviet Foreign Minister (Molotov) at the Geneva Meeting of Foreign Ministers, 10 November 1955," Documents on Disarmament 1945-1954, pp. 540-541.

10. US, Arms Control and Disarmament Agency, "Statement by the United States Representative (Lodge) to the First Committee of the General Assembly, 9 December 1955," Documents on Disarmament 1945-1959, p. 577.

11. Annex 15, United Nations Document DC/SCI/26/R2, 10 May 1955, p. 15.

12. United Nations General Assembly, Report of the Conference of Experts for the Study of Possible Measures Which Might Be Helpful in Preventing Surprise Attack and for the Propagation of a Report Thereon to Governments UN Document A/40785/4145), 5 January 1959.

13. Bruce M. Russett and Carolyn C. Cooper, Arms Control in Europe: Proposals and Political Constraints (Denver, Colo.: University of Denver, 1967), p. 81.

14. US, Arms Control and Disarmament Agency, "An Illustrative Outline of a Possible System for Observation and Inspection of

Ground Forces," Documents on Disarmament 1945-1959, Vol. II (5 December 1958): 1290.

15. US, Arms Control and Disarmament Agency, "Soviet Bloc Proposal at the Geneva Surprise Attack Conference: The Tasks and Functions of a Ground Control Post and Aerial Inspection," Documents on Disarmament 1945-1959, Vol. II (August 1960): 1298-1299.

16. Ibid., p. 1301.

17. Ibid., pp. 1301-1302.

18. Ibid., pp. 1298-1299.

19. Bernhard C. Beckhoefer, Postwar Negotiations for Arms Control (Washington, DC: The Brookings Institution, 1961), p. 464.

20. Ibid., p. 487.

21. James E. Dougherty, Zonal Arms Control, pp. 513-514. It is interesting to note that the Soviets find such a system of mobile inspection to be unacceptable because they have been participating in such a system since 1946. The British, French, and United States maintain liaison missions which have the right to travel and inspect Soviet forces in East Germany, albeit they are heavily restricted. The Soviets, in return, have the same privilege of traveling through West Germany and observing British, French, and US forces.

22. US, Arms Control and Disarmament Agency, Verification, p. 10.

23. Der Spiegel, 1 March 1976, pp. 32-33.

24. New York Times, 14 December 1979, p. A-3.

25. Ibid; New York Times, 15 August 1979, p. A-9; and Baltimore Sun, 3 January 1980, p. 19.

26. US, Department of Defense, "What's Behind the Mutual and Balanced Force Reduction Talks," pp. 5-6.

27. US, Arms Control and Disarmament Agency, "Final Act of Conference on Security and Cooperation in Europe: Document on Confidence Building Measures and Certain Aspects of Security and Disarmament," Documents on Disarmament, 1975, pp. 304-307.

28. Ibid.

29. Moscow Tass, 30 November 1978, FBIS, Daily Report, Soviet Union, 1 December 1978, p. BB-1.

30. New York Times, 1 December 1978, p. 5.

31. Moscow Pravda, 27 June 1978, p. 4.

32. V. Komlev, "What is Hampering the Vienna Debate," Novoye Vremya 43 (20 October 1978), p. 5. While it is true there has been no massive increase in Soviet strength in Central Europe since

Czechoslovakia, it is hard to accept, given the overwhelming evidence to the contrary, that the Soviets quantitatively increased the size of its forces in Central Europe since 1968.

33. Wall Street Journal, 29 September 1978, p. 13.

34. Moscow Tass, 6 October 1979.

35. Les Aspin, "Surprise Attack," NATO Review, August 1977, pp. 6-13.

36. Ibid., p. 12.

37. Sam Nunn, "Force Reduction Negotiations: A New Focus Needed," The Baltimore Sun, 19 December 1977, p. 15.

38. New York Times, 26 May 1978, p. 3.

39. Moscow Tass, 5 December 1979.

40. New York Times, 15 August 1979, p. A-9, and 14 December 1979, p. A-3.

41. Cologne Westdeutscher Rundfunk, 14 December 1979, FBIS, Western Europe, 17 December 1979, p. J-1.

42. Moscow Tass, 31 January 1980.

43. Frankfurter Allegemeine, 28 September 1979, p. 4.

44. Cologne Westdeutscher Rundfunk, 14 December 1979, FBIS, Western Europe, 17 December 1979, p. J-1.

45. Ibid.

46. New York Times, 14 December 1979, p. A-3.

47. James Dougherty, Zonal Arms Control, pp. 478-479.

48. Washington Star, 2 December 1978, p. A-10.

49. US, Arms Control and Disarmament Agency, "Tripartite Proposal of the Geneva Meeting of Foreign Ministers. Reunification of Germany and Security," Documents on Disarmament 1945-1958, Vol. I (27 October 1955): 531-532.

50. Ibid.

51. Ibid.

52. Helmut Schmidt, Defense or Retaliation: A German View, translated by Edward Thomas (New York: Praeger, 1962), pp. 131-158.

53. Ibid., p. 152.

54. Ibid., p. 160.

55. "Arms Policy and Stability in Europe," Working Papers Presented to the Fourth Annual Conference of the IISS, 29 June-2 July 1962, as

quoted in James E. Dougherty, "Zonal Arms Limitations in Europe," Orbis, Fall 1963, p. 447.

56. US, Arms Control and Disarmament Agency, "Tripartite Proposal of the Geneva Meeting of Foreign Ministers: Reunification of Germany and Security, October 27, 1955," Documents on Disarmament, 1945-1959, Vol. I: 531-532.

57. Ibid.

58. Christoph Bertram, "The Future of Arms Control: Part II, Arms Control and Technological Change: Elements of a New Approach. Adelphi Papers 146 (London: International Institute of Strategic Studies, 1978): 20.

59. Frederick S. Wyle, "European Security: Beating the Numbers Game," Foreign Policy, Spring 1976, pp. 52-54.

60. Baltimore Sun, 19 December 1977, op. cit.

61. J.I. Coffey, "New Approaches to Arms Reduction in Europe," Adelphi Papers 105 (London: IISS, 1974): 21.

62. Steven Canby argues that the best stabilizing measure is a robust military balance. He argues that NATO must set its own force structure in order before agreeing to any MBFR reductions. See Steven Canby, "Mutual Force Reductions: A Military Perspective," International Security, Winter 1978, p. 125.

CHAPTER 9

1. New York Times, 26 May 1978, p. 3.

2. The preponderance of Soviet conventional forces in Central Europe in some respects is the conventional equivalent of the Soviet intercontinental ballistic missile preponderance that is the heart of the Soviet strategic power projection. The lack of Soviet receptiveness to significantly reducing these missiles in SALT is analogous to the Eastern refusal to take 3:1 conventional restrictions in Central Europe.

3. London Times, 19 December 1974, p. 14.

4. Ironically, such a perception would not be in the Soviets' best interest either, from the standpoint of power projection. For the policy of intimidating the West Europeans to work, a threat must be apparent.

5. Even with current threat projections, such a tactic was used by the left wing of the majority SPD faction in the Bundestag. By claiming that Soviet forces are not offensive in nature, they argued against the modernization of NATO's nuclear systems in the fall of 1979.

6. Army Times, 12 March 1979, p. 34.

7. New York Times, 31 January 1972, p. 10. The conclusion was based on the judgment that NATO active duty strength is marginal and that symmetrical reductions would only weaken NATO while Warsaw Pact strength would retain its present force ratio vis-a-vis the West.

8. For example, see John Yochelson, "MBFR: The Search for an American Approach," Orbis, Spring 1973, pp. 155-175; Christoph Bertram, "Mutual Force Reductions in Europe, the Political Aspects," Adelphi Papers, No. 84 (London: The International Institute for Strategic Studies, 1972): 31-33.

9. Washington Star, 11 January 1980, p. A-5.

10. Washington Post, 24 January 1980, p. A-1.

11. Washington Star, 26 January 1980, p. A-5.

12. Washington Post, 26 January 1980, p. A-15.

13. Washington Post, 1 February 1980, p. A-13.

14. New York Times, 6 January 1980, p. 17.

15. Besides ideas of the author, discussion here draws on J.I. Coffey, New Approaches to Arms Reduction in Europe, Adelphi Papers No. 105 (London: IISS, 1974); Frederick S. Wyle, "European Security: Beating the Numbers Game," Foreign Policy, Spring 1973; Christoph Bertram, The Future of Arms Control: Part II, Arms Control and Technological Change: Elements of a New Approach, Adelphi Papers No. 146 (London: IISS, 1978).

16. Christoph Bertram, The Future of Arms Control: Part II, p. 19.

17. New York Times, 31 January 1972, p. 10.

Bibliography

OFFICIAL DOCUMENTS

Federal Republic of Germany. Ministry of Defense. White Paper 1975-76, The Security of the Federal Republic of Germany and the Development of the Federal Armed Forces. Bonn: Press and Information Office of the Government of the Federal Republic of Germany, 1976.

Jones, David, General, Chairman of the Joint Chiefs of Staff. United States Military Posture for FY 1980. Washington, DC: Government Printing Office, 1979.

Schlesinger, James R. The Theater Nuclear Force Posture in Europe: A Report to the US Congress in Compliance With Public Law 93-365. Washington, DC: Department of Defense, April 1975.

United Nations. General Assembly. Report of the Conference of Experts for the Study of Possible Measures Which Might Be Helpful in Preventing Surprise Attack and for the Propagation of a Report Thereon to Governments, UN Document A/40785/4145, 5 January 1959.

_____. United Nations Document DC/SC1/26/Rev. 2, 10 May 1955.

US. Arms Control and Disarmament Agency. Documents on Disarmament, 1964-1973, 1975. Washington, DC: Government Printing Office, 1965-1973, 1975.

_____. Selected Background Documents Relating to Mutual and Balanced Force Reductions, pt. II. Disarmament Document Series DDS Ref. #617, 23 November 1973.

_____. Verification. Publication No. 85. Washington, DC, 19 March 1976.

US. Congress. Congressional Budget Office. Assessing the NATO/War-saw Pact Military Balance. Washington, DC: Government Printing Office, 1977.

_____. Congressional Record, 89th Cong., 2d sess., vol. 112, pt. 13. Washington, DC: Government Printing Office, 1966.

_____. Congressional Record, 90th Cong., 1st sess., vol. 113, pt. 1. Washington, DC: Government Printing Office, 1967.

_____. Congressional Record, 91stCong., 1st sess., vol. 115, pt. 27. Washington, DC: Government Printing Office, 1969.

_____. Congressional Record, 92d Cong., 1st sess., vol. 117, pt. 12. Washington, DC: Government Printing Office, 1971.

_____. Congressional Record, 93rd Cong., 1st sess., vol. 119, pt. 123. Washington, DC: Government Printing Office, 1973.

_____. Congressional Record, 93rd Cong., 1st sess., vol. 119, no. 141. Washington, DC: Government Printing Office, 1973.

_____. Congressional Record, 93rd Cong., 1st sess., vol. 119, no. 142. Washington, DC: Government Printing Office, 1973.

_____. Congressional Record, 93rd Cong. 1st sess., vol. 119, no. 143. Washington, DC: Government Printing Office, 1973.

_____. Planning US General Purpose Forces: The Theater Nuclear Forces. Washington, DC: Government Printing Office, 1977.

_____. House. Committee on Armed Services. Status of the MBFR Negotiations.

US. Department of Commerce. 24th Congress of the Communist Party of the Soviet Union. Stenographic Report, pt. 1. Arlington, Va.: Joint Publications Research Service, 1971.

US. Department of Defense. Department of Defense Annual Report, Fiscal Year 1979, by Secretary of Defense Harold Brown. Washington, DC: Department of Defense, 1978.

_____. "What's Behind the Mutual and Balanced Force Reduction Talks," Commanders Digest 16:10 (14 November 1974).

U.S. Department of State. Conference on Security and Cooperation in Europe.

Final Act. Department of State Publication 8826, August 1975.

_____. Department of State Bulletin, 3 January 1972. Washington, DC: Government Printing Office, 1972.

_____. Documents on Disarmament, vol. 2, 1957-1959. Washington, DC: Government Printing Office, 1960.

_____. "Statement by Deputy Secretary Rush to the Committee on Foreign Affairs, July 10, 1973." Department of State Bulletin, 6

August 1973. Washington, DC: Government Printing Office, 1973.

US. Library of Congress. Congressional Research Service. Prospects for the Vienna Force Reduction Talks, by Stanley Sloan. Washington, DC: Library of Congress, 1978.

Weekly Compilation of Presidential Documents. Washington, DC: Government Printing Office, 2 July and 8 October 1973.

BOOKS

Beckhoefer, Benhard C. Postwar Negotiations for Arms Control. Washington, DC: The Brookings Institution, 1961.

Bloomfield, Lincoln P.; Clemens, Walter C., Jr.; and Griffiths, Franklin. Khrushchev and the Arms Race. Soviet Interests in Arms Control and Disarmament 1954-1964. Cambridge, Mass.: The MIT Press, 1966.

Coffey, Joseph I. Arms Control and European Security: A Guide to East-West Negotiations. New York: Praeger, 1977.

Curl, Peter V. ed. Documents on American Foreign Relations, 1954. New York: Harper and Brothers, 1955.

Donnelly, Christopher. Soviet Ground and Rocket Forces. London: Salamander Books, 1976.

Erickson, John. Soviet Military Power. London: Royal United Services Institute for Defense Studies, 1971.

Hahn, Walter F. Between Westpolitik and Ostpolitik: Changing West German Security Views. London: Sage, 1975.

Hinterhoff, Eugene. Disengagement. London: Atlantic Books, 1959.

International Institute for Strategic Studies. The Military Balance 1977-1978. London: The International Institute for Strategic Studies, 1977.

Jane's All The World's Aircraft 1978/79. New York: Watts Inc., 1978.

Joshua, Wynfred. Nuclear Weapons and the Atlantic Alliance. New York: National Strategy Information Center, 1973.

Kleiber, Wolfgang, et al. Era of Negotiations. Lexington, Mass.: Lexington Books, 1973.

Laquer, Walter. Russia and Germany, A Century of Conflict. Boston: Little, Brown and Co., 1954.

Lenin, V.I. Selected Works. New York: International Publishers, 1943.

Lukacs, John. The Last European War, September 1939/December 1941. Garden City, N.Y.: Doubleday, 1976.

Parker, Elizabeth A. East European Arms Control and Disarmament Proposals. Arlington, Va: Institute for Defense Analysis, 1969.

Pendergast, William B. Mutual and Balanced Force Reduction. Issues and Prospects. Washington, DC: American Enterprise Institute for Public Policy Research, 1978.

Pipes, Richard, ed. Soviet Strategy in Europe. New York: Crane, Russak, 1976.

Record, Jeffrey. US Nuclear Weapons in Europe. Washington, DC: Brookings Institution, 1977.

Richardson, James L. Germany and the Atlantic Alliance. The Interaction of Strategy and Politics. Cambridge, Mass.: Harvard University Press, 1966.

Russett, Bruce M., and Cooper, Carolyn C. Arms Control in Europe: Proposals and Political Constraints. Denver, Colo.: University of Denver, 1967.

Schmidt, Helmut. Defense or Retaliation: A German View. Translated by Edward Thomas. New York: Praeger, 1962.

Wolfe, Thomas W. Soviet Power and Europe, 1945-1970. Baltimore and London: The Johns Hopkins Press, 1970.

Zinner, Paul E., ed. Documents on American Foreign Relations, 1955. New York: Harper and Brothers, 1956.

ARTICLES

"At the Heurige." Der Spiegel, 1 March 1976.

Aspin, Les. "Surprise Attack." NATO Review, August 1977.

Bertram, Christoph. "The Future of Arms Control: Part II, Arms Control and Technological Change: Elements of a New Approach." Adelphi Papers No. 146. London: International Institute for Strategic Studies, 1978.

_____. "Mutual Force Reductions in Europe: The Political Aspect." Adelphi Papers No. 84. London: International Institute of Strategic Studies, 1978.

Borgart, Peter. "The Air Attack Potential of the Warsaw Pact." International Defense Review 9:2 (April 1976).

Borisov, K. "Vienna: Two Positions." Novoye Vremya 50.

Burt, Richard. "Implications for Arms Control," New Conventional Weapons and East West Security, Part II. Adelphi Papers No. 145. London: International Institute for Strategic Studies, 1978.

"New Weapons Technologies. Debates and Directions." Adelphi Papers No. 126. London: International Institute for Strategic Studies, 1976.

Carter, Barry. "What Next in Arms Control." Orbis, Spring 1973.

Canby, Steven. "Mutual Force Reductions: A Military Perspective." International Security, Winter 1973.

Coffey, J.I. "New Approaches to Arms Reduction in Europe." Adelphi Papers No. 105. London: International Institute for Strategic Studies, 1974.

Dougherty, James E. "The Soviet Union and Arms Control." Orbis, Spring 1973.

_____. "Zonal Arms Limitations in Europe." Orbis, Fall 1963.

"Documentation of the Warsaw Pact Summit Meeting of 2 December 1970." NATO Letter 19:1-2 (January-February 1971).

Dunn, Keith A. "Soviet Perceptions of NATO." Parameters VIII:3 (September 1978).

Fischer, Robert, Lucas. "Defending the Central Front. The Balance of Forces." Adelphi Papers No. 127. London: International Institute for Strategic Studies, 1976.

Georgiyev, K.M. "Detente - The Formula and the Process." U.S.A.: Economics, Politics, Ideology 8 (July 1976).

Gratzl, J. "Some Thoughts on the New Soviet Main Battle Tank." International Defense Review 9:1 (February 1976).

Gray, Colin, S. "Deterrence and Defence in Europe: Revising NATO's Theater Nuclear Posture." Strategic Review, Spring 1975.

Hill, Roger. "MBFR Prelude: Explorations Before Negotiations." NATO Review, July/August 1972.

Holst, Johan, and Melander, Karen. "European Security and Confidence Building Measures." Survival, July/August 1977.

Horhanger, Dr. Axel. "The MBFR Talks - Problems and Prospects." International Defense Review 9:2 (April 1976).

Hunt, Kenneth. "Deterrence." NATO Review I. Brussels: NATO Information Service, 1974.

Kamler, V. "What's Hampering the Vienna Debate." Novoye Vremya 43 (20 October 1978).

Karber, Phillip A. "The Soviet Anti-Tank Debate." Survival XVIII:3 (May/June 1976).

Meller, R. "Europe's New Generation of Combat Aircraft. Part I: The Increasing Threat." International Defense Review 8:2 (April 1975).

NATO Information Service. "NATO's Long Term Defence Program." NATO Review 26:3 (June 1978).

"NATO - Thinning the Ranks." Newsweek. Europe edition, November 1, 1976.

Oeser, Ingo. "Who is Promoting and Who is Obstructing Progress in Vienna?" Horizont 18 (1976).

"The Polish-German Treaty," Atlantic Community Quarterly 9:1 (Spring 1971).

Record, Jeffrey. "MBFR. Little Progress But Disquieting Trends." Strategic Review, Summer 1978.

_____. "US. Tactical Nuclear Weapons in Europe: 7000 Warheads in Search of a Rationale," Arms Control Today, April 1974.

Ruehl, Lother. "The Negotiations on Force Reductions in Central Europe." NATO Review 5 (October 1976).

Schiebel, Joseph. "Convergence or Confrontation?" Intercollegiate Review 5:2 (1968-69).

Schmidt, Helmut. "Germany in the Era of Negotiation." Foreign Affairs, October 1970.

Viktorov, V.V., and Stoleshnikov, A.V. "The Vienna Talks After Two and a Half Years." U.S.A.: Economics, Politics, Ideology 4 (June 1976).

Wagner, Hans. "The Buildup of the Red Army." Quick Magazine 5 (22-28 January 1975).

"Warsaw Pact Nations Communique." The Atlantic Community Quarterly 7:4 (Winter 1969-1970).

Worner, Manfred. "NATO's Defenses and Tactical Nuclear Weapons." Strategic Review, Fall 1977.

Wyle, Frederick S. "European Security Beating the Numbers Game." Foreign Policy, Spring 1973.

Yochelson, John. "MBFR: The Search for an American Approach." Orbis, Spring 1973.

NEWSPAPERS

Foreign Broadcast Information Service. Daily Report Eastern Europe. Springfield, Va: US Department of Commerce, 1972-1980.

Foreign Broadcast Information Service. Daily Report Western Europe. Springfield, Va.: US Department of Commerce, 1972-1980.

Foreign Broadcast Information Service. Daily Report Soviet Union. Springfield, Va: US Department of Commerce, 1972-1980.

Atlantic Union

Army Times

Baltimore Sun
Chicago Tribune
Christian Science Monitor
Die Presse
Die Welt
Frankfurter Allegemeine
Izvestiya
London Times
Los Angeles Times
New York Times
Pravda
San Diego Union
Suddeutsche Zeitung
Washington Post
Washington Star
Weiner Zeitung

NEWS SERVICES

Associated Press
Foreign Broadcast Information Service
Reuters
Tass
United Press

Index

About the Author

JOHN G. KELIHER, PhD, is a Colonel in the U.S. Army. Drawing on over four years experience in MBFR to include extensive service on the U.S. MBFR Delegation in Vienna, Austria, Colonel Keliher wrote this book while a Senior Research Fellow and a Professor at the National Defense University, Washington, D.C. where he taught Soviet military strategy. Prior to joining the National Defense University, Colonel Keliher was a specialist on the Soviet military with the Department of Defense SALT Task Force. He is presently a Fellow at the Center for International Affairs, Harvard University.